Items should be returned on or before the last date
shown below. Items not already requested by other
borrowers may be renewed in person, in writing or by
telephone. To renew, please quote the number on the
barcode label. To renew on line a PIN is required.
This can be requested at your local library.
Renew online @ **www.dublincitypubliclibraries.ie**
Fines charged for overdue items will include postage
incurred in recovery. Damage to or loss of items will be
charged to the borrower.

Leabharlanna Poiblí Chathair Bhaile Átha Cliath
Dublin City Public Libraries

Dublin City
Baile Átha Cliath

Brainse Rátheanaigh
Raheny Branch
Tel: 8315521

Date Due	Date Due	Date Due

Reimagining Ireland

Edited by Dr Eamon Maher
Institute of Technology, Tallaght

PETER LANG

Oxford • Bern • Berlin • Bruxelles • Frankfurt am Main • New York • Wien

Eamon Maher (ed.)

The Reimagining Ireland Reader

Examining Our Past, Shaping Our Future

PETER LANG

Oxford • Bern • Berlin • Bruxelles • Frankfurt am Main • New York • Wien

Bibliographic information published by Die Deutsche Nationalbibliothek.
Die Deutsche Nationalbibliothek lists this publication in the Deutsche
Nationalbibliografie; detailed bibliographic data is available on the Internet at
http://dnb.d-nb.de.

A catalogue record for this book is available from the British Library.

Library of Congress Control Number: 2017957169

ISSN 1662-9094
ISBN 978-1-78707-739-3 (print) • ISBN 978-1-78707-740-9 (ePDF)
ISBN 978-1-78707-741-6 (ePub) • ISBN 978-1-78707-742-3 (mobi)

Cover image: *To Distant Shores* © Paul Butler.

Cover design by Peter Lang Ltd.

© Peter Lang AG 2018

Published by Peter Lang Ltd, International Academic Publishers,
52 St Giles, Oxford, OX1 3LU, United Kingdom
oxford@peterlang.com, www.peterlang.com

Eamon Maher has asserted his right under the Copyright, Designs and
Patents Act, 1988, to be identified as Editor of this Work.

This publication has been peer reviewed.

Printed in Germany

Contents

vi

Note on the Cover Artist

Paul Butler is a photographer living in Farnaght, Co. Leitrim. For the last sixteen years he has been recording this unique landscape, which was also the home place of the writer John McGahern. He has hosted exhibitions and contributed imagery and articles to various publications with specific emphasis on visualising McGahern's landscapes and rituals. This work is now part of a Research Masters.

To view more images from this project please visit: <http://www.paulbutler.me>.

Preface

The editor of the series *Reimagining Ireland* is to be congratulated not only on the remarkable success of the venture but moreover on what, as an intellectual project, it has meant for Irish studies as a whole. This selection of essays stands as a testimony to the vitality of Irish thinking and thinking about Ireland over the past few decades, a period that has seen a flourishing of diverse and multiple projects unprecedented since the all too often maligned Revival. A glance at the contents page reveals what Irish matter has yielded to new approaches, from postcolonialism to feminist and queer theory, from political economy to media theory. Some of the yield has to do with adjusting one's sense of Ireland's contribution to familiar areas of culture globally as well as 'on the island'. That Ireland made a contribution to international modernism beyond what its small and supposedly provincial population would have seemed likely to sustain is well known. That Ireland also generated so much of the New Woman fiction of the early twentieth century or that Northern Ireland, despite its homophobic official cultures, would give rise nonetheless to a rich literature of queerness are critical openings onto the actual diversity of Irish cultures that is reflected throughout the essays in this volume. This achievement is further evidence, if such is still needed, not only of the ways in which new material gives rise to new theoretical approaches but also of those in which the angle of a given theory brings to light materials formerly overlooked or neglected. To reimagine Ireland is at one and the same time to bring forward what was always already there but occluded by the official narratives in play at any moment.

To say that this makes of *Reimagining Ireland* a profoundly postcolonial project is not to foreground postcolonial theory at the expense of other no less crucial modes of thought. It is to suggest that the work of reimagining Ireland involves opening up once more the trajectories and survival of modes of thinking and living that had been occluded for all too long both by the narrow nationalism that came to dominate in the wake of the civil war and by the no less narrow historiography that has seen its project as one of demythologisation of the Irish past. If the former captured the energies of the Irish revolution for a conservative state in the South and for a reactionary settler colony in the North, the latter found itself projecting its own myths onto those phenomena in Irish culture that it found recalcitrant to a single-minded modernising and state-building project inevitably associated with British colonial institutions. If, then, it is possible to compare the work of *Reimagining Ireland* to that of the Revival, it is because that work has, along with many related projects, helped us to see the great diversity and continuing appositeness of the ferment of thinking that characterised the early years of the last century. Far from mere narrow nationalism, it involved its own reimagination of Ireland's possibilities, from the suffrage and syndicalist labour movements to environmental concerns that seem all too prescient now.

That reimagination of the Revival over the past couple of decades, evidenced in several of the essays reprinted here, recognises as a constant thread in Irish cultural history its capacity to think the alternative and in particular, to live modernity differently. Historicism – to borrow Walter Benjamin's ever-apt phrasing – is wedded to a view of modernisation as a single track of 'progress and development' and considers alternative imaginations as lagging behind in premodernity, subjected to myth rather than agents of rationality. To reimagine Ireland is to release into the present the diverse possibilities that various narratives of progress and their institutions have blocked and occluded. If the Revival undertook such a task in the face of British colonial hegemony and its self-assured common sense, reimagining Ireland now takes place in face of a no less hegemonic and single-minded devotion of our complacent and complicit elites to the belief that there are no alternatives: for them, it is self-evident that the neoliberal dispensation of global capitalism is the baleful future that awaits every province of the planet, environmental catastrophe and savage inequality notwithstanding.

More is at stake, then, in a volume like this than simply the provision of new materials for Irish studies, important as that task remains. It has often enough been remarked that Ireland had a great capacity to supply the works that others would theorise: it is our lot to create, so disposed – as Matthew Arnold long ago argued – by our very incapacity for modernity.

It is for others to reflect. Nothing more surely relegates Ireland to the colonial periphery than this assumption: as Husserl once claimed, it is Europe's capacity for theory – for self-reflection or *Selbstbesinnung* – that makes it the unique avant-garde of humanity. That assertion places Ireland, along with every other colonial culture, outside the European core of which it is the ragged western edge. It has been the work of the last decades, however, and the work of *Reimagining Ireland* as a series, to theorise Ireland from our own location. To do so is to displace the dogmas of modernity and to rethink the constitutive place of Ireland and other colonised cultures in the formation of and not as mere objects of modernity. But it is no less to imagine athwart the direction in which hitherto modernisation has directed us, towards catastrophe and mounting injustice, and to seek again in the experience of our recalcitrant cultures the possibility of living otherwise. In this respect, *Reimagining Ireland* has proven a profoundly ethical as well as an invaluable scholarly project.

—David Lloyd, Distinguished Professor of English
at the University of California, Riverside

Introduction: Examining Our Past and Shaping Our Future

It is hard to believe that it is ten years since *Reimagining Ireland* started inviting book proposals in an attempt to map the important and rapidly evolving field of Irish studies. Our objective was to make the series as inter-disciplinary and multidisciplinary as possible in order to underline the fact that there is no one way to approach issues of identity, culture, history, literature and politics.

Certain books have had the capacity to change the way people perceive Irish studies. To name but a few, Terence Brown's *Ireland: A Social and Cultural History 1922–2002* (1981), Joe Cleary's *Outrageous Fortune: Capital and Culture in Modern Ireland* (2007), Diarmaid Ferriter's *The Transformation of Ireland 1900–2000* (2004), Louise Fuller's *Irish Catholicism since 1950: The Undoing of a Culture* (2002), Luke Gibbons' *Transformations in Irish Culture* (1996), Declan Kiberd's *Inventing Ireland* (1996), Joe Lee's *The Modernisation of Irish Society 1848–1918* (1973) and David Lloyd's *Ireland after History* (1999) all fall into this category. These are works that have left an indelible mark. They can be challenged, certainly, but never ignored by those coming in their wake. They stand the test of time and are cited over and over again by scholars and general readers alike. Like canonical figures in literature, they are touchstones to which one returns again and again in search of illumination and understanding.

The initial idea behind *Reimagining Ireland* was to produce a series that might emulate and expand upon what individual monographs such as the ones just mentioned have achieved. A series is, of course, substantially different from a single-authored book because of its scope and its capacity to supply a repository whereby important issues and emerging developments can be analysed through several different lenses. When one considers some of the seismic events that have occurred in Ireland during the past few decades – peace in Northern Ireland; the massive decline of the heretofore dominant Catholic Church in the wake of the clerical abuse scandals; the huge prosperity and brutal austerity that characterised the rise and fall of the Celtic Tiger; the death of four of Ireland's most iconic twentieth-century writers, John McGahern, Seamus Heaney, Brian Friel and William Trevor – it becomes clear that there is a need like never before for an outlet where such developments can be parsed and analysed in an objective and scholarly manner.

With eighty-five volumes in print, the breadth of topics covered and the number of scholars who have contributed to *Reimagining Ireland* are most impressive. It therefore seemed like the right time to put together a Reader which will give people a flavour of the areas explored in the first fifty volumes. Following a chronological order, the book begins with an essay by Luke Gibbons, tracing the roots of modernity from the middle decades of the nineteenth century, and concludes with Michael Cronin's discussion of time and place in global Ireland. Between these bookends, there are essays on poetry, drama, literary criticism, photography, advertising, visual culture, modernity, immigration and feminism – a rich panoply of subjects. We do not deem it necessary to summarise the chapters here, as the relevance and significance of what is covered should be clear from the list of titles.

This is a collection to whet the appetite of anyone with a scholarly or personal interest in the forces that have shaped Ireland's evolution. It also underlines the fact that Irish studies is in rude good health, thanks to the highly talented array of scholars currently working in the field.

Our sincere thanks go to all the contributors, many of whom have substantially reworked their original essays. All have been models of efficiency and courtesy. The ease with which we were able to compile the Reader is a tribute to their professionalism and dedication. We would also like to acknowledge all those who have contributed, as authors and editors, to making *Reimagining Ireland* such a resounding success. Without your talent and energy, there would be no series in the first instance, let alone one that will soon reach the milestone of 100 volumes in print.

Finally, our deep gratitude to Professor David Lloyd for agreeing to write such a wonderful Foreword in spite of the huge demands on his time.

— Eamon Maher and Christabel Scaife, General Editor and
Commissioning Editor for *Reimagining Ireland*

LUKE GIBBONS

1   Roots of Modernity: Primitivism and Primitive Accumulation in Nineteenth-Century Ireland

> It is not a potato-fed face that will ever lead the way in arts, arms or commerce.[1]
>
> — RICHARD COBDEN

Travelling immediately after the Famine on one of the first transatlantic steamships to sail from Galway, the *Indian Empire*, a journalist noted a passenger with an unusual piece of luggage:

> Near the capstan we observed lying on the deck a box filled with Irish earth and in it were planted three shamrocks. We had the curiosity to enquire whose property it was and was told by the owner, a woman from Longford, that she was going out with her daughter to join her people who had sent for her, and in sweet and pathetic accents added 'It was all I had to bring.'[2]

Still rooted in the soil, the poor woman was bringing her locality with her on the crossing to modernity. The fact that transatlantic steamships were already leaving Galway suggests, moreover, that for all the remoteness of the western seaboard, modernity had already come to the romantic periphery of Ireland. As Kerby Miller has noted, Western peasants often knew more about Boston or New York than about Dublin, Cork, or even their

---

1   Quoted in 'Alfred Marshall; Principles of Economics', *Edinburgh Review* 173 (1891), reprinted in *Alfred Marshall: Critical Responses*, vol. 1, ed. Peter Groenewegen (London: Routledge, 1998), 7.

2   Quoted in Tim Collins, *Transatlantic Triumph and Heroic Failure; the Story of the Galway Line* (Cork: Collins Press, 2002), 45.

own counties: 'when Horace Plunkett asked a girl from County Galway why she refused to join relatives on a farm thirty miles distant and instead preferred emigrating to New York City, she replied, in so many words, "because it is nearer".[3]

The image of a migrant travelling with a piece of home ground has a resonance in Irish culture, if only because it calls to mind Count Dracula carrying his coffin of soil on the boat to England. Landscape already was of a restless disposition in Bram Stoker's work, most notably his novel *The Snake's Pass* (1890), set on the Atlantic coast of Ireland, which features a moving bog that eludes the attempts of Ordnance Survey cartographers to map its shifting contours. Though located in the fastnesses of the west, the landscape reveals its own international ties when, having slipped its moorings, the bog uncovers a treasure chest of bullion left behind by the invading French republican force during the 1798 rebellion. For the most part, however, the emigrant Irish brought little with them on the emigrant boat other than the habits and political allegiances – including republicanism – that clung to them like their native soil. As Frederick Engels noted of the chronic poverty of the Irish in mid-nineteenth-century Manchester, in the midst of the industrial heartlands of Britain:

> The Milesian deposits all garbage and filth before his house here, as he was accustomed to do at home, and so accumulates the pools and dirt-heaps which disfigure the working people's quarters and disfigure the air. He builds a pig-sty against the house wall as he did at home, and if he is prevented from doing this, he lets the pig sleep in the room with himself ... The Irish man loves his pig as the Arab his horse.

Living in squalor 'which places him but little above the savage', Engels notes that it is with 'such a competitor the English working man has to struggle, with a competitor upon the lowest place possible in a civilized country'.[4]

---

3   Kerby A. Miller, *Emigrants and Exiles: Ireland and the Irish Exodus to North America* (New York: Oxford University Press, 1985), 425.

4   Friedrich Engels, *The Condition of the Working Class in England* [1845] (London: Panther, 1969), 124–5.

It is for this reason that ethnographic descriptions in nineteenth-century Irish and Scottish fiction invariably return to scenes of filth – of potatoes, dirt, and disorder – having given the mandatory tour of the more picturesque aspects of the Celtic periphery.[5] As Ian Duncan observes, this ethnographic turn was responsible for the transformation of the 'national tale' or regional genre into the *historical* novel, if by that is understood the consigning of regional or national difference to history, internal cultural dislocations that have outlived their time.[6] By its very association with dirt and waste matter, Celtic 'otherness' was destined to become the refuse of history. Ethnographic details furnished local colour and evidence of national character but in so doing were only marking time before the discrepancies were swept – or flushed – away by the logic of improvement, both aesthetic and political. As Jonathan Swift noted in the early eighteenth century:

> A man that walks through the Edinburgh streets in a morning ... is as careful as he can to watch diligently and spy out the filth in his way; not that he is curious to observe the colour and complexion of the ordure, or take its dimensions, much less to be paddling in or tasting it; but only with a design to come out as cleanly as he may.[7]

As with filth, the point of noting quaint customs or vernacular culture was not to celebrate but to avoid them, to identify the obstacles that stood in the way of progress and development. Not least of the paradoxes here was that while presenting themselves as anachronistic, such features called for meticulous observation, thus furnishing 'the reality effect' of fiction that linked accounts of romantic outposts to travel writing or early forays into anthropology. The tension here was akin, as Ernest Baker pointed out, to the strain between narrative and spectacle, the tendency of ethnographic

---

5   For a useful discussion, under the headings of 'The Pig', 'The Manure Pile', 'Rags, Rags, Everywhere Rags', and 'The Potato', see William H. A. Williams, *Tourism, Landscape, and the Irish Character* (Madison: University of Wisconsin press, 2008), Ch. 5.

6   See Ian Duncan, *Scott's Shadow: The Novel in Romantic Edinburgh* (Princeton, NJ: Princeton University Press, 2007), Ch. 3.

7   Swift, *A Tale of a Tub* [1704], quoted in Peter Stallybrass and Allon White, *The Politics and Poetics of Transgression* (London: Methuen, 1986), 109.

asides and accumulations of local detail to clog the progression of the narrative towards its eventual civilising dénouement:

> [Irish fiction] relied far too much on the odd charm of national idiosyncrasies, of manner and customs strange and quaint to the English. They are illustrators rather than disinterested artists. Often the story is forgotten while the writer expiates, like a showman, on the motley garb, the strange habits, the picturesque idioms, and the curious superstitions, so different from the ordinary population of a novel ... The scene painting overshadows the play.[8]

Primitivism and 'Primitive Accumulation'

> The Englishman, who is still somewhat civilized, needs more than the Irishman who goes in rags, eats potatoes, and sleeps in a pig-sty.
> — FREDERICK ENGELS, *Condition of the English Working Class*

It is no coincidence that the pig, the potato, and the compulsory dungheap outside the cabin door became the prime suspects of a perceived retarded development and sub-human, primitive existence among the Irish. As Peter Stallybrass and Allon White describe it, 'a clean ideal sphere of judgment was being constructed and defined in terms of a low and dirty periphery, a notional and literal "outside" which guaranteed a coherence and privilege to the "inside".[9] Just as 'thick description' acted as a drag on narrative, the coarse materiality of a subsistence diet, of *homo appetitus* as against *homo economicus* in Catherine Gallagher's terms, also impeded the progress of political economy not only in the Irish countryside but also

8   Ernest Baker, *The History of the English Novel*, vol. vii (London: H. F. and G. Witherby, 1936), 19.
9   Stallybrass and White, *The Politics and Poetics of Transgression*, 109.

in English cities.[10] Taking issue with E. P. Thompson's argument that the rise of market relations and commodities in food-stuffs signaled the end of the 'moral economy', Gallagher argues that the demand for bread in times of acute shortage – as in the food riots of 1794–5 – was characterised by a repudiation of the potato as a means of preventing starvation. Recourse to the potato would, in effect, have meant relapsing into a primitive state, a factor which leads Gallagher to conclude that the demand for bread was motivated not just by obvious material needs but also by *cultural* factors: a determination on the part of the working class not to fall below certain standards of Englishness. As David Lloyd shows, the inscription of cultural and racial factors on supposedly 'pure' economic laws relating to the minimum wages and the cost of labour-power was apparent from the outset in the writings of Adam Smith, Thomas Malthus, and J. R. McCulloch, McCulloch drawing explicitly on Smith's assertion that 'the natural or necessary rate of wages' is 'whatever the custom of the country renders it indecent for creditable people, even of the lowest order, to be without'.[11] By the 1790s, it would seem, the potato had been rendered 'indecent for creditable people, even of the lowest order'. Notwithstanding its nutritional properties, travel writers such as Sir John Carr contended that it could not supply the dietary – or perhaps moral – fibre necessary to invigorate the industrial working class:

> I am ready to acknowledge the nutritious quality of the potatoe, and that it may be sufficient for the purposes of mere existence of an Irish rustic, who having little to do, does little; but an enlightened and experienced medical friend of mine assured me, that it could not supply the frame with its necessary support under the pressure of violent exercise. A workman in an iron foundry would not be able to endure the fatigue of his duty for three hours altogether, if he had not food other than potatoes.[12]

10   Catherine Gallagher, 'The Potato in the Materialist Imagination', in Catherine Gallagher and Stephen Greenblatt, *Practicing New Historicism* (Chicago: University of Chicago Press, 2000), 131. Though the essays in the book are collaborative efforts, Gallagher claims primary authorship of this chapter.

11   David Lloyd, 'The Political Economy of the Potato', *Nineteenth-Century Contexts*, 29.2–3 (June/September 2007), 322. Lloyd is quoting from J. R. McCulloch's *Principles of Political Economy* [1849], 411.

12   John Carr, *The Stranger in Ireland* (London: Richard Phillips, 1806), 154–5.

The old moral economy may have been breaking down but it was not superseded by pure economic categories such as 'class': rather, it was also built on a new moral consensus around Englishness and empire in which the industrial working class, for all its lowly status at home, could view itself as a labour aristocracy in relation to the condition of even the highest echelons – be they chiefs or potentates – of more primitive societies.[13] Thus, as Gallagher points out, 'When English people refused to eat potato stews because they were swill – not human food – and resisted even the moderate proposal that they should add potatoes to their home-baked bread', this was on account of their claim to membership of a new moral (or imperial) economy at the apex of the civilising process.[14] Expounding the views of William Cobbett, Gallagher notes that a reversion to the potato was tantamount to falling out of the realm of culture itself into an animal, swinish level of existence:

> Since they are outside of the 'radiating complexities' of the bread market, the Irish that Cobbett depicts have no point of entry into a shared community or moral economy. Indeed, in Ireland, because of the potato, there is no community. For Cobbett, potato eating marks the border, not simply between going hungry and being satisfied, but between sharing in *civilization's* nourishment and being deprived of it.[15]

13   From John Locke to Adam Smith, the observation that the lower orders in a market economy possessed a superior lifestyle to the chief of an African or Native American tribe was constantly adduced to argue for the moral superiority of capitalism to other social systems.

14   Gallagher, 'The Potato in the Materialist Imagination', 125. Friedrich Engels, for one, contested this, suggesting that rather than starve, the English labouring poor would descend to the level of the pig. But even this was still couched is terms of the descent of man, the filth reducing 'the Englishman's level of civilization, down to the Irishman's level' (*Condition of the Working Class*, 109).

15   Gallagher, 'The Potato in the Materialist Imagination', 126. That it was an Irishman, Edmund Burke (himself associated in caricatures with potatoes and primitive Irishness) who appeared to apply the epithet 'swinish' to the English multitude, was not the least of its offensive ironies: in fact, Burke referred to '*a* swinish multitude' (*Reflections on the Revolution in France* [1790], ed. Conor Cruise O'Brien [Harmondsworth: Penguin, 1969], 173).

The potato, in other words, marks the boundary not just between Irish and English culture but culture itself and a brutish state of nature.[16]

The elements of primitivism in these economic debates fail to acknowledge one of the key insights into modernity under colonialism, as identified by Rosa Luxemburg: that capital accumulation not only thrives on so-called 'pre-capitalist' formations but *actively reproduces* them to keep its own territorial power in place. 'If this system is to last any length of time', writes David Harvey, 'the non-capitalist territories must be kept (forcibly if necessary) in a non-capitalist state'.[17] Lineages of capitalism have little difficulty accounting for the original violent phase of 'primitive accumulation' in which the emergent forces of the new capitalist order penetrated and expropriated feudal/peasant economies in order to establish a new civic realm of formally free wage-labour and market relations. Luxemburg's achievement was to re-align this allegedly transient phase from a temporal to a present-day *spatial* axis, contending that expropriation of the 'other' is intrinsic to advanced capitalism – except it is located in the colonial periphery rather than the past.[18] While formally free wage-labour and related standards of living are the preserve of advanced core nations, capitalism operates as a *world system* in the search for cheaper labour, raw materials, land, and new markets – an 'endeavour', according to Luxemburg,

---

16   In Archbishop Richard Whately's *Introductory Lectures on Political Economy* [1831], it was only by means of the mental aptitudes generated by political economy – forethought, hard work, providentialism, self-improvement – that man was separated from the brute or savage (Lloyd, 'Political Economy of the Potato', 325).

17   David Harvey, *The New Imperialism* (Oxford: Oxford University Press, 2003), 138, 140.

18   Rosa Luxemburg, *The Accumulation of Capital* [1913], trans. Agnes Schwartzchild (London: Routledge, 2003), 350: 'At the time of primitive accumulation, i.e., at the end of the Middle Ages, when the history of capitalism began, and right into the nineteenth century, dispossessing the peasants of England and on the Continent was the most striking weapon in the large scale transformation of means of production and labour power into capital. Yet capital in power performs the same task even to-day, and on an even more important scale – by modern colonial policy.'

that 'leads to the most peculiar combinations between the modern wage system and primitive authority in the colonial countries'.[19]

Just as, therefore, an interior of decorum and cleanliness is defined against an exterior realm of dirt and disorder, in Stallybrass and White's formulation above, so also 'the idea that capitalism must perpetually have something "outside of itself" in order to stabilize itself is [also] worthy of scrutiny'.[20] Close scrutiny of 'inside' and 'outside' is required if only because, as a world system, the outside of capitalism – whether modes of production or social formations – is already contained within it: 'Nothing in this sense', Dipesh Chakrabarty writes, 'is inherently "precapitalist." Precapitalist could only be a designation used from the perspective of capital'.[21] Hence, as Luxemburg pointed out, the slave trade and plantation slavery, for example, were not formally capitalist but were integrated into industrial capitalism and, indeed, were a function of its rapid development in certain key phases of accumulation.[22] By the same token, though the rhetoric of political economy was one of demonising the potato as a primitive root, in reality, the consolidation of landlordism as a 'colonial garrison' in late eighteenth and early nineteenth-century Ireland could not have taken place without it – in effect, the subsistence economy of the potato subsidising the commercialisation of the cash-crops that were

19   Luxemburg, *The Accumulation of Capital*, 343–4. As Andrea Nye summarises Luxemburg's position: 'If communism is not possible in one country, neither is capitalism' (Andrea Nye, *Philosophia: The Thought of Rosa Luxemburg, Simone Weil, and Hannah Arendt* [New York: Routledge, 1994], 37.

20   Harvey, *The New Imperialism*, 140.

21   Dipesh Chakrabarty, 'The Two Histories of Capital', in *Provincializing Europe: Postcolonial Thought and Historical Difference* (New Delhi: Oxford University Press, 2001), 271.

22   As Immanuel Wallerstein elaborates: 'The relations of production that define a system are the relations of production of the whole system, and the system at this point in time is the European world economy. Free labour is indeed a defining feature of capitalism, but not free labour throughout the productive enterprises. Free labour is the form of labour control used for skilled work in the core countries whereas coerced labour is used for less skilled work in peripheral areas. The combination thereof is the essence of capitalism.' Immanuel Wallerstein, *The Modern World System*, I (New York: Academic Press, 1974), 127.

exported to the industrial heartlands.[23] At no point in her account does Gallagher explore the possibility that the subsistence economy was located – or, perhaps more accurately, dislocated – *within* modernity, and facilitated the spread of the market at a number of variegated uneven levels. The potato was not merely a subsistence foodstuff: it was also a rotation crop, rendering ground arable for production of cash crops such as the exported grain that formed the staple of the industrial working-class diet in Britain. As Kevin O'Neill describes this process: 'The potato filled an almost magical combination of needs ... It brought rough land into tillage, provided a major part of the farm's vegetable food, served as the major form of animal fodder, and acted as a restorative root crop which replenished land exhausted by successive cereal [cash] crops.'[24]

The primitive tuber was thus structurally integrated into capitalist market relations; indeed, it provided the material base without which the market and civility could not operate in Ireland.[25] Of course, wages were not the norm for the toilers in the fields; rather, they paid rent to gain access to their meagre subsistence plots, rent generated by the 'surplus' of cash crops produced for the market. Even more obviously, labour was not formally free under landlordism, for with a subsistence holding at their doorstop – perceived by native occupiers to be their own confiscated land – there was

23 As Luxemburg noted: 'How much capitalist accumulation depends upon means of production which are not produced by capitalist methods is shown for example by the cotton crisis in England during the American War of Secession [i.e., the Civil War], when the cultivation of the plantations came to a standstill ... We need only recall that imports of corn raised by peasants – i.e., not produced by capitalist methods – played a vital part in the feeding of industrial labour ... for a further illustration of the close ties between non-capitalist strata and the material elements necessary for the accumulation of capital.' *The Accumulation of Capital*, 337.

24 Kevin O'Neill, *Family and Farm in Pre-Famine Ireland: the Parish of Killeshandra* (Madison: University of Wisconsin Press, 1984), 86.

25 As noted by Gallagher, the most influential exponents of such views were Adam Smith and Arthur Young, who saw no incompatibility between the potato and the market, and recommended the nutritional properties of the potato for the English working poor. Such benign views were to change, as we have noted, by the 1790s. For a wide-ranging critical discussion the relation of the potato to political economy, see Lloyd, 'The Political Economy of the Potato.'

no reason labourers should expend additional toil to produce a surplus for the landlord, or allow subsistence itself to be dictated by the market, except under political constraints of coercion and confiscation. Though some scholars, following the lead of Michael Davitt, have spoken of 'feudalism' in relation to the landlord system, there was no shared culture or aristocratic hegemony to link alien owner and native occupier in a system of mutual, hierarchical relations. Rather, as O'Neill observes, the system was one of coercive 'primitive accumulation'[26] within agrarian capitalism with the proviso that this was not a temporary, initial brutal stage but, as the litany of insurrection acts throughout the century indicated, central to the entire duration of colonial modernity.

With the smashing of the Gaelic political order in the seventeenth century, the kind of resistance offered by old regimes to agrarian capitalism in Europe was pushed from elite strata to the margins of Irish life, emerging in the subaltern form of agrarian insurgency and secret societies. For this reason, Kevin O'Neill notes, 'The Irish peasant [was placed] in a situation unique among the peasantry of Europe. [The] system of property rights, modeled on the English system, did not recognize any form of limitation on land usage ... There were no recognized community rights, no commons, and no village decisions regarding land distribution, crop choice or crop rotation.'[27] Rentier capitalism thus enjoyed a free run, legally and politically, in colonial Ireland, its success marred only by the refractory indigenous population, mediated by layers of middlemen and acquisitive farmers it had to rely on to do its bidding. As O'Neill goes on to explain, a number of factors – the export of capital, the lack of draft animals, the tardiness of agricultural 'improvement' – ensured that increased production of grain for the market could only be secured through more intensive exploitation, and a numerical expansion of this recalcitrant labour-force. As noted above, it was in this sense that the process of sub-letting land for conacre and subsistence holdings facilitated, rather than retarded, the penetration of the market into the countryside:

26   O'Neill, *Family and Farm in Pre-Famine Ireland*, 22.
27   O'Neill, *Family and Farm in Pre-Famine Ireland*, 34.

The potato was the perfect mate for corn under these conditions because it sustained the high population densities needed for corn tillage to survive in an undercapitalized system. Thus, contact between intensive agricultural production for a capitalist market (i.e., grain production) and a predominantly subsistence crop (the potato) substantially altered all sectors of the agricultural economy.[28]

For the purposes of the landlord system, therefore, subsistence and commerce were not in competition with each other, representing different 'stages' of production: 'Pure subsistence activity can accompany sophisticated commercial economy.'[29] As Kevin Whelan has shown, it was largely by means of the potato and its related rundale agricultural system, based on sub-division in small nucleated village settlements ('clacháns'), that hitherto waste lands west of the Shannon or in boggy or mountainous regions were reclaimed for economic expansion:

> On the mid-nineteenth century Down Survey maps, settlement limits were at c.500 feet; by 1840, they had climbed to 800 feet – an important consideration in a country of fragmented uplands like Ireland ... The west of Ireland was a zone of settlement discontinuity, not of continuity. It was not an archaic but a very modern society, whose very existence was underpinned by a relatively novel development – the extensive infiltration of the ecological interloper – the potato.[30]

Contrary to the conventional nostrums of political economy, the potato, the pig in the parlour, and the perennial manure heap were not impediments to progress but were rather, in more than one sense, the very fertilising agents of progress.[31] The cruel irony, however, was that while land

---

28 O'Neill, *Family and Farm in Pre-Famine Ireland*, 22.
29 O'Neill, *Family and Farm in Pre-Famine Ireland*, 21.
30 Kevin Whelan, 'Pre- and Post-Famine Landscape Change', in *The Great Irish Famine* (Cork: Mercier Press, 1995), 24.
31 This uneasy co-existence was perhaps the basis of the misplaced perception that 'reciprocal' relations existed between landlord and tenant in pre-Famine Ireland. A society based on Penal Laws, on systematic political and cultural discrimination, and under the constant threat of rebellion, whether Jacobite or Jacobin, could hardly be described as possessing the common culture that sustains a moral economy. Though integrated into a 'common' agrarian capitalism, profound social, cultural, and political cleavages eliminated any semblance of consensus to colonial rule.

was converted from waste to a source of wealth, the producers on the land, the real source of wealth, were swept away themselves by the most efficient means of human waste-disposal, the Great Famine.

The Politics of the Potato

> The English ... [have] found it more economical to reduce all working people to the lowest possible wages on which they can subsist ... She [has] found it more economical to feed the Irish with potatoes, and clothe them in rags; and now every packet brings legions of Irish who working for less than the English, drive them from every employment. What is the fruit of this immense accumulation of wealth?
>
> —J. C. SISMONDI [1847], cited in Rosa Luxemburg,
> *The Accumulation of Capital*

By the mid-century, and particularly in the wake of the catastrophe of the Great Famine, the fissures and indeed seismic fault-lines began to show in the colonial mode of primitive accumulation in Ireland. At one level, this can be attributed to the increasing rhetoric of free trade and 'unencumbered' market relations, the logic of opening up the countryside to unfettered capitalist forces, as David Harvey observes, signalling the beginning of the end of the 'territorial' logic that secured the privileged position of the colonial elites. Writing of India in terms that could equally apply to Ireland, Harvey notes:

> From this standpoint, colonial repressions of the sort that undoubtedly occurred in the late nineteenth century have to be interpreted as self-defeating, a case of territorial logic inhibiting the capitalist logic. Fear of emulation led Britain, for example, to prevent India from developing a vigourous capitalist dynamic and thereby frustrated the possibilities of spatio-temporal fixes [autonomous sites of accumulation] in that region.[32]

32   Harvey, *The New Imperialism*, 140.

It is in this light that some commentators are disposed to attribute the irreconcilable conflicts that opened up in the second half of the nineteenth century to the erosion of a putative 'moral economy' that existed in pre-Famine Ireland, the harsh logic of class and economic relations sweeping away the deference towards Ascendancy territorial rule. As noted above, however, the Irish countryside was devoid of any such moral economy: there was no shortage of hierarchy and aristocratic hauteur, but it was bound up with domination and state power rather than feudal codes of honour and mutual obligation. In this respect, the intensification of conflict in the later nineteenth century owed less to unmediated class relations than to the fissiparous residues of the pre-Famine economy, the relative autonomy of subsistence producers from direct dependence on their masters. As Charles Trevelyan, Assistant Secretary to the Treasury and presiding figure over government policy during the Famine, lamented, it was precisely the potato economy that encouraged habits of independence, preventing the reliance on the employer for subsistence that comes from wage-labour: 'The relation of employer and employed, which knit together the framework of society, and establish a mutual dependence and good will, have no existence in the potato system. The Irish small holder lives in a state of isolation, the type of which is to found in the islands of the South Sea, rather than in the great civilized communities of the ancient world.'[33] Trevelyan's point here is not that the potato impedes entry into modernity but that it blocks the route under British rule, the royal road of empire. The lack of 'mutual dependence' is based not on access to subsistence alone (for this was mediated by conacre, rack-renting, and so on) but on the belief of rural occupiers that the land is theirs, thus vitiating any shared moral economy or investment in 'the mighty principles of civil society which have formed the greatness of England'.[34] In this sense, it is not wage-labour that promotes progress but the opposite, the refusal of the periphery to recreate its path to modernity

33 Charles Trevelyan, *The Irish Crisis* [1848], p. 231, cited in Gordon Bigelow, *Fiction, Famine, and the Rise of Economics in Victorian Britain and Ireland* (Cambridge: Cambridge University Press, 2003), 123.

34 Shafto Adair's verdict on the potato economy, as recorded in *The Winter of 1846–7 in Antrim* (London, 1847), quoted in Bigelow, *Fiction, Famine, and the Rise of Economics*, 124.

in the image of the centre: 'The forces of progress' in the periphery, writes
Samir Amin, 'are not those aligned with the requirements of capitalist
accumulation but those struggling against it'.[35]

Not least of the ironies here is that the compatibility of the potato
with 'improvement' had already been championed by Adam Smith and
Arthur Young in the late eighteenth century, before its demotion on the
culinary scale by Thomas Malthus, Sir John Carr, William Cobbett, and
others. The new animus against the potato was motivated by the fear that
it operated not simply as a subsistence crop but usurped the role of money
in ushering in modernity: 'the potato has become the labour coin of the
agricultural community', wrote Jasper Rogers: 'It is ... a bona fide representative of gold, unjustly permitted to usurp its place.' As Gordon Bigelow
has shown, the problem with the potato as a circulating medium lay not just
in its association with filth and physical refuse but with *social* waste, values
related to kinship, social solidarity, and communal obligations that were
considered obsolete, or were being relegated to nostalgia, under the new
economic order. The link between the potato and a peripheral modernity
based on different social priorities 'suggests that in Ireland one finds not
the absence of a social system, nor the vacant exterior of Britain's economic
atmosphere, but rather a system unique unto itself, one that operated *within
English money*, but with a money system all its own'.[36] Commerce and the
circulation of money had extended to the outer fastnesses of Ireland, but
the harsh values of economic rationality had not followed suit: as Thomas
Boylan and Tadhg Foley have shown, it was precisely because of the strong
adherence to alternative conceptions of justice and social attachment that
the subjectivity of the peasantry was targeted for 'improvement'. To this
end, the full energies of the new National School system were addressed
under the direction of Archbishop Richard Whately of Dublin, his mass-
produced school text *Easy Lessons in Money Matters* becoming the new
catechism of political economy across the British Empire.

That the Irish peasantry had a lot to learn about egoism, selfishness,
and the hard work ethic (but not necessarily drudgery and hard menial

---

35   Samir Amin, *Unlinking: Towards a Polycentric World* (London: Zed Books, 1990),
      103.
36   Bigelow, *Fiction, Famine, and the Rise of Economics*, 129–30.

labour) is abundantly clear in the fiction and travel accounts of the period, which draw attention repeatedly to the willingness to share, whether in the conditions of dire poverty or everyday contact with the market. In Sydney Owenson's *The Wild Irish Girl*, the author moves from the fictive world of the text to a memory of her own, recounting in a lengthy footnote an encounter with *Irish* civility accompanied by potatoes in a mud cabin in the west of Ireland:

> Yet even in these miserable huts you will seldom find the spirit of urbanity absent – the genius of hospitality never. I remember meeting with an instance of both, that made a deep impression on my heart; in the autumn of 1804, in the course of a morning ramble with a charming Englishwoman, in the county of Sligo, I stopped to rest myself in a cabin, while she proceeded to pay a visit to the respectable family of the O'H.s, of Nymph's Field: when I entered I found it occupied by an old woman and her three granddaughters; two of the young women were employed scutching flax, the other in some domestic employment. I was instantly hailed with the most cordial welcome; the hearth was cleared, the old woman's seat forced on me, *eggs and potatoes roasted, and an apology for the deficiency of bread politely made*, while the manners of my hostesses betrayed a courtesy that almost amounted to adulation. They had all laid by their work on my entrance, and when I requested I might not interrupt their avocations, one of them replied 'I hope we know better – we can work any day, but we cannot any day have such a body as you under our roof.' Surely this was not the manners of a cabin but a court.[37]

The compliments to the author aside, what is of note here is the association of the rude tuber with preparations of flax for the market, 'politeness', 'courtesy', and 'manners' – the accomplishments of modernity.[38] Though often depicted as a Robinson Crusoe crop, a stand-alone foodstuff that cut the self-subsistent producer off from social intercourse, in fact the potato became the signature for sharing and hospitality – not just with kith and kin but also with the civic world of strangers. In an account of a visit to a cabin in 1822 similar to that of Owenson's, Thomas Reid recounted how

37 'Sydney Owenson [Lady Morgan], *The Wild Irish Girl: A National Tale* [1806] (London: Pickering & Chatto, 2000), 20; emphasis added.

38 For the relations between flax production and the use of the potato as a rotation crop, see Eric L. Almquist, 'Pre-Famine Ireland and the Theory of European Proto-Industrialization: Evidence for the 1841 Census', *Journal of Economic History* 39.3 (September 1979), 699–718.

he politely declined the offer of buttermilk in lieu of the customary whis-
key but then felt obliged to accept a potato, which turned out to be only
partially cooked: 'We always have the praties hard', explained the man of
the house: 'they stick to our ribs, then we can fast longer that way.' The
half-raw 'Lumper' potato was cooked by the rural poor in such a way as
to leave 'the bone', the hard-core, intact, which took longer to digest and
thus allowed for longer fasting between meals. By contrast, better potatoes
were reserved for visitors (even if not always cooked sufficiently, as in Reid's
case): 'Let us not be blinded', noted Reid's contemporary Leith Ritchie,
'to the real hardship of his [the peasant's] lot, by the stories of sentimental
tourists, who talk of the amiable hospitality of the cottagers in presenting
them, from their pot, with a beautiful *mealy* potato!'[39]

To associate the potato with civil society is, in effect, to reclaim it for
an alternative project of modernity, and in this lay the true source of the
visceral opposition to the crop. In Thomas Moore's *Memoir of Captain
Rock* (1824), the voice of the (mythical) leader of the most notorious insurgent agrarian movement is simulated but presented as the very model of a
modern gentleman (albeit with a few strange nervous tics in his comport-
ment). As the insurgent leader himself states, alluding in passing to the
modernity of the potato in the Irish countryside:

> Accordingly, in that potatoe-tithed region have I always fixed my head-quarters
> of Rebellion; and if, by good luck, the encroaching spirit of the Church, which,
> *modern as the introduction of the potatoe is*, has contrived thus effectually to 'mark
> it for her own', – should succeed in extending this tithe into other provinces,
> the parsons and I shall, at length, like Jove and Caesar, divide the empire of the
> whole island between us.[40]

Hence, the Captain notes ruefully, 'the odious taxes, by which a starving
peasantry' and 'the pig-stye of the poor Catholic [are] made tributary to

---

39   Thomas Reid, *Travels in Ireland in the Year 1822* (London, 1823); Leitch Ritchie,
      Ireland, Picturesque and Romantic (London, 1837), quoted in Williams, *Tourism,
      Landscape and the Irish Character*, 98–9.
40   [Thomas Moore], *Memoirs of Captain Rock* [1824], ed. Emer Nolan (Dublin: Field
      Day, 2008), 154. Further references to this edition will be cited in the text.

the ornamental spire of the Protestant, and wretches, who are all but starving themselves, are taxed to provide the church with sacramental bread and wine' (144) – a process, he might have added, in which the potato economy was also integral to the grain that supplied the English market place with bread. The humble root crop, indeed, provides food for thought, its deficiencies in diet allowing ample room for memory and imagination, particularly as they bear upon the wretched history of Ireland:

> I was indeed indebted for my first glimmering knowledge of the history and antiquities of Ireland, to those evening conversaziones round our small turf fire, where, after a frugal repast upon that imaginative dish, 'Potatoes and Point', my father used to talk of the traditions of other times – of the first coming of the Saxon strangers among us – of the wars that have been ever since waged between them and the *real* Irish, who, by a blessed miracle, though exterminated under every succeeding Lord-Lieutenant, are still as good as new, and ready to be exterminated again.[41]

It was a small step from such history lessons to construing the potato as the root of revolution, the rotation crop for the soil in which the tree of liberty was to be planted. Though Dr William Drennan, one of the founders of the United Irishmen, was invoked by Cobbett for his view that the potato was 'the lazy root' and the 'root of all misery',[42] in fact it was Drennan who, not without a wry sense of humour, alluded to its seditious culinary potential. Discussing that type of sectarian Protestant who opposed reform by 'conjuring up the horrid images of civil war, massacres, pestilence, and famine, to scare our women and our boys', Drennan recounted that the eating habits of such zealots often confounded their principles.

> I remember I once took the liberty of expressing my surprise to a gentleman of this class during the time of dinner, that he would admit such things as potatoes to his

---

41   In Moore's political satire, 'Potatoes and Point' denotes the ironic symbolic properties of the potato: 'When there is but a small portion of salt left, the potatoe, instead of being dipped into it by the guests, is merely, as a sort of indulgence to the fancy, pointed at it', 126.

42   Cited in *Cobbett in Ireland: A Warning to England*, ed. Denis Knight (London: Lawrence and Wishart, 1984), 118.

table, which were known to support the lowest dregs of the people, and were indeed neither more nor less than *a republican root*.[43]

From such sketches of the expanded cultural field of the potato, it is clear that it was not its subsistence function *per se* that posed a challenge to the territorial and economic logic of colonialism. Potato allotments were, in fact, envisioned as way of keeping wages down in Britain, in keeping with Cobbett's fears of its corrosive effects on working-class standards of living, but this relegated the potato to a mere garden crop, in isolation from a whole way of life. In Ireland, by contrast, it was at the centre of an entire cultural eco-system that, by its very recalcitrance, as Charles Trevelyan remarked, stood in the way of empire. As Sir William Wilde noted in the immediate aftermath of the famine, while other nations may have adapted to the upheavals that swept Europe in 1848: 'Not so the Irishman; all his habits and modes of life, his very nature, position, and standing on the social scale of creation, will and must be altered by the loss of the potato':

> If ever there was a nation that clung to the soil, earned patriotism by the very ground they walked on, it is (or we may now write was) the Irish peasantry ... Not many years ago, we stood upon the custom-house quays of Dublin, watching a large emigrant ship, bound for St John's, getting under weigh. The wind and the tide were favourable; the captain was impatient, and the names of the passengers having been called over, it was found that one was missing, a stout labourer from Kilkenny ... the last plank was about to be hauled on board when the missing passenger rushed breathless through the crowd towards the ship, carrying in his hands a green sod, about as a large as that used to 'estate' a lark, which he had just cut from one of the neighbouring fields. 'Well', said he, as he gained the deck amidst the shouts of his friends, 'with the blessing of God, I'll have this over me in the new country'.[44]

43   [Dr William Drennan], *Letters of Orellana, An Irish Helot* (Dublin: J. Chambers and T. Heery, 1785), 43–4.

44   W. R. Wilde, *Irish Popular Superstitions* [1852] (Shannon: Irish University Press, 1972), 19–20.

CATHERINE MAIGNANT

2   Reimagining Ireland through Early Twentieth-Century French Eyes

In May 1913, two French ladies in their thirties, Marguerite Mespoulet and Madeleine Mignon, sailed to Ireland, carrying sophisticated photographic equipment. The mission that had been entrusted to them by banker and philanthropist Albert Kahn was to take pictures of the fast-disappearing Irish traditional lifestyles for his *Archive of the Planet*, a visual record of world cultures on the verge of disintegration in a changing world. A few weeks later, they returned to Paris with seventy-three autochromes, the first ever colour photographs of that type to have been taken in Ireland. Several exhibitions, press articles and two documentaries, one produced by the BBC and the other by RTE, have brought the Albert Kahn collection to the attention of the Irish public. As a result, the story of the two young non-professional photographers' Irish expedition is now well known in Ireland. Reviewers of all kinds have lavished unanimous praise on the artistic qualities of the photographs, and the collection as a whole has received unqualified critical acclaim.

Yet on closer examination, the image of Ireland that was conveyed in France as a result of the photography expedition bears little resemblance to the original. Even if one takes into account Albert Kahn's specific agenda, it can be argued that the photographers primarily took pictures that corresponded to the image of Ireland they had formed in France. The remarkably interesting notebook which complements the photographs also documents the way educated middle-class French women reacted to the Irish realities they chose to investigate. This chapter will seek to analyse the nature and origin of the clichés which shaped their perceptions of Ireland and were used as a filter through which the country and its people were reinvented for the French public. The recent success of this collection in Ireland itself will also be analysed as part of the re-mythification process which has arguably characterised late modern reimaginings of Ireland. When Albert Kahn launched his ambitious project, he sought to develop the knowledge of foreign habits and customs with a view to fostering world peace. Contemporary Ireland's perception of the French photographs of 1913 naturally bears witness to a radically different understanding of their value. It is also indicative of the way late modern Irish society is now viewing its past and the world of a hundred years ago, which, according to Grace Neville is 'so gone, so distant, so unimaginably past'.[1] Writing about 'Time and Place in Global Ireland', Michael Cronin reminds his readers that 'it is something of a philosophical and sociological truism (which does not make it any the less true) that our identity is defined through others'.[2] It is tempting to suggest that the 1913 French autochromes have contributed – however modestly – to the reinvention of this lost past for the benefit of new generations.

Discovery and the Process of Distanciation from the Past

The Albert Kahn collection of photographs was first exhibited in Ireland on the initiative of the French Embassy and the Alliance Française, in 1981. Why then, and not before, can only be guessed at. Whatever the reason, it is significant that the event should have been organised at a time when the Arts Council had become aware of the necessity both to adapt its policy to the new European context and to promote the democratisation of culture.[3]

---

1   Roy Esmonde and Grace Neville, RTÉ Documentary *Not Fade Away*, 2004, final words.
2   Michael Cronin, 'Inside Out: Time and Place in Global Ireland', in Eamon Maher (ed.), *Cultural Perspectives on Globalisation and Ireland* (Oxford, Bern, Berlin, Frankfurt am Main, New York, Wien: Peter Lang, 2009), 17.
3   Alexandra Slaby, *L'Etat et la culture en Irlande* (Caen and Mont Saint Aignan: Publications des universités de Rouen et du Havre, Presses universitaires de Caen, 2010), 133–4.

The exhibition was successively shown in Dublin, Galway and Cork and it attracted the attention of the national and local press. The *Irish Independent* recommended it on grounds that it was worth reading 'the intelligent, sympathetic and occasionally heartfelt comments appended by *Messieurs*[4] Mespoulet and Mignon'.[5] *The Irish Times*, *The Irish Press* and *The Connacht Sentinel*[6] were equally enthusiastic and equally blind to the fact that the photographers were women and not men. That the photographers should have been females did not dawn on the journalists of patriarchal Ireland. As a result, not only did they fail to comment on this most unusual pair, but the feminine if not feminist dimension of the collection and commentaries were lost on them. All articles offered a non-committal analysis of the aesthetic and documentary interest of the photographs. Unlike the French ladies, however, the last two newspapers over-emphasised the political context of the expedition and suggested that the social effects of the Great Famine were still visible in the country in 1913. This clearly was not a central preoccupation of the travellers, even though they were obviously aware both of the Famine, and of the nationalist agenda.

None of the articles however questioned the unexpected itinerary chosen by the two women, or the fact that more than half of the collection was made up of photos of monuments and archaeological sites, which went against the spirit of the Archive of the Planet project. Quoting Mespoulet's notebook,[7] *The Irish Press* journalist simply noted that they 'appreciated the beauty of Ireland with its many places of historical and religious interest, and were charmed by the people "who (...) possessed such a lively and ardent imagination which enabled them to create the most beautiful legends in Europe"'. By contrast, it is quite striking that *The Irish Times*

---

4   My emphasis.

5   Exhibition at the Alliance Française, Kildare Street, Dublin. Untitled article, *Irish Independent*, 12 February 1981, 6; Fergus Pyle, 'French Eyes on Ireland in 1913', *The Irish Times*, 11 February 1981, 8.

6   Exhibition at UCG Art Gallery. 'Nation in Focus', *Irish Press*, 3 July 1981, 9; 'The Claddagh 70 years ago', *The Connacht Sentinel*, 14 July 1981, 5.

7   It seems that Marguerite Mespoulet was the author of the travel diary. She also took the photographs. Madeleine Mignon was probably no more than her assistant.

and *Irish Independent* hardly mentioned these photographs at all. Yet, as will be shown at a later stage in this chapter, it is meaningful that the two young graduates should have devoted so much of their energy tracking the remains of Ireland's distant past.

After the initial travelling exhibition in 1981, the collection was again taken to Ireland on two occasions, to Drogheda in 1984, and to Dublin and Galway in 2007 and 2008. Only in 1989, did one commentator realise that Marguerite Mespoulet and Madeleine Mignon were females, in an *Irish Times* article about the publication in France of *Irlande 1913*, the first edition of the travel diary and photographs. Interestingly, the journalist added that the collection had 'never been seen in Ireland',[8] an indication of the limited impact of the 1981 event. As early as 1984 however, Judi Doherty had emphasised how little her contemporaries shared with their forebears as immortalised by the French visitors of 1913: 'Perhaps what is so remarkable about the photographs is how much the people have changed and how little everything else has', she wrote. She went on to list what had survived and what had not and concluded: 'the one thing the people of today do have in common with the people of the past is the weather which was bemoaned frequently by the photographers.'[9] Such an approach was to set the agenda for later comments, which systematically dissociated 1913 from the time of writing. Irish receptions of the collection may therefore arguably be understood as one symptom of the process of distanciation which has characterised Ireland's reconsiderations of its history since the 1980s and beyond.

The evolution of Irish attitudes towards photographic archives is significant in this respect. In her 1989 article, Lorna Siggins pointed to Ireland's indifference towards its own collections and marvelled at the French commitment to popularising Albert Kahn's work. In so doing, she endorsed George Morrison's comment on 'the awareness of the humanities to be found in French culture and the pitiable inadequacy and irresponsibility of our Irish attitudes to our photographic heritage, whether

---

8   Lorna Siggins, 'Portraits from a Lost Landscape', *The Irish Times*, 22 July 1989, 21.
9   Judi Doherty, 'Rare Photographs on Exhibition', *The Irish Times*, 27 April 1984, 7.

still or motion picture'.[10] One can only note that if the documentary-maker rescued from oblivion old photographs and newsreels chronicling Ireland's fight for independence[11] in 1959 and 1961, using photograph collections to document people's traditional lifestyles was not yet on the agenda in the early 1980s.

Archives became openly central to the reconstruction of history as a result of the revolution in history writing initiated by T. W. Moody and R. D. Edwards. Scholarly history of the kind they promoted was to be a bulwark against myth. Their followers continued in their step to such an extent that it allowed Ronan Fanning to interpret the 'continuous compulsion to confront myth and mythology' as a major 'characteristic of modern Irish historiography'.[12] The archive-based revision of history was initially made complex by the fact that official records remained closed for a very long time and were then only gradually opened until the National Archive Act was passed 1986. The opening of archives is always a highly symbolical turning point since it somehow induces the passage from an age of faith to an age of evidence. However, one may discuss the nature and meaning of the historical truth which archives can reveal. Ricoeur suggests that history writing primarily results from questions and hypotheses that documents merely confirm. Archives are traces that historians manipulate and articulate into a meaningful presentation of past events,[13] hence allegations that the revisionist debate in Ireland may just as well be a 'state of the art' as 'an ideological project', to quote M. A. G. O'Tuathaigh's assertion.[14] In all cases, archival work leads to distanciation.

---

10   Siggins, 'Portraits from a Lost Landscape.'
11   *Mise Éire*, 1959; *Saoirse*, 1961. In order to make these two documentaries about the Irish struggle for freedom, George Morrison edited old photographs and original newsreels.
12   Ronan Fanning, '"The Great Enchantment": Uses and Abuses of Modern Irish History' [1988], in Ciaran Brady (ed.), *Interpreting Irish History* (Dublin: Irish Academic Press, 1994), 146.
13   Paul Ricoeur, *La mémoire, l'histoire, l'oubli* (Paris: Seuil, 2000), 209–26.
14   M. A. G. O'Tuathaigh, 'Irish Historical "Revisionism": State of the Art or Ideological Project', in Ciaran Brady (ed.), *Interpreting Irish History*, 306.

As archives, photographs are in no way different from written documents and they may just as well be interpreted to serve the purpose of their analysts. First of all, as Bourdieu convincingly argues, it would be naïve to imagine that a photograph is an objective and realistic representation of life since it results from a process of selection. It is also based on the respect of conventions and ultimately proceeds from its author's flawed perception of reality.[15] Besides, the viewer himself is never neutral and his understanding of photographic archives is connected with the world view of his day. This must be borne in mind when one examines the reception in Ireland of photographic collections, whether native or foreign. In the follow-up to the creation of the National Archives, Irish photograph collections were collated and made accessible to the public. As a consequence, when Gerard Moran reviewed a new exhibition of the Kahn collection at the recently created National Photographic Archive in 2007, he was aware of the now well-known work of Irish photographers of the turn of the twentieth century and he recalled their contribution before proceeding to his flattering presentation of the French collection. He compares the nature of the French and Irish missions as well as the merits of the collections, which he examines with complete critical detachment – distance again.[16] Within two decades, Ireland's perception of its past had considerably evolved. The nationalist press of 1981 still seemed to take historical continuity for granted. By 2007, memories of 1913 had faded away and Ireland was ready to confront a period of its history which felt distant to the point of being foreign. In 1989, native collections of photographs were neglected. By 2007, a brand new building in trendy renovated Temple Bar was devoted to the 630,000 photographs of the National Library collection.[17] Commenting on the planned creation of the National Photographic Archive in 1996, Michael D. Higgins, then Minister for Arts, Culture and the Gaeltacht, emphasised the fact that it would lead to 'greater public awareness of these valuable

15   Pierre Bourdieu, *Unartmoyen– Essai sur les usages sociaux de la photographie* (Paris: Editions de minuit, 1965), 108–13.
16   Gerard Moran, 'Before the Storm', *Irish Arts Review* (Winter 2007), 102.
17   The National Photographic Archive (Meeting House Square, Dublin) opened in 1998.

collections of the National Library of Ireland, many of which [had] been unseen to date'.[18] The cultural policy of the Irish government in the 1990s no doubt contributed to raising Irish people's interest in their heritage. But the institutionalisation of culture itself was the result of changes which were ultimately to induce a new approach to the Albert Kahn collection of photographs. The revision of Irish history, but also European integration, globalisation, economic success and the growing importance of the media altered Ireland's understanding of its own past beyond recognition.

The Assertion of Contemporary Identities and the Re-mythification of the Past

From the 1990s and throughout the Celtic Tiger era, Ireland underwent seismic changes. Its distinctiveness was eroded by the internationalisation process and the constant exposure to new models of behaviour. Little now remains of Irish identity as it was understood in the early years of the twentieth century. This particularly applies to Irish rural society, a central emblem of traditional Ireland as the French travellers understood it. In their eyes, the essence of the Ireland of yore could only be captured in the countryside. That is why, if we except Galway, they tended not to linger in cities and took no photographs of Dublin. The view that was most prevalent in French publications of the early twentieth century was that the most picturesque rural area was Connemara and that the essential characteristic of rural society in the west of the island was its extreme poverty. The photographs of Marguerite Mespoulet simply echoed those stereotypes. As she had predicted, this type of rural society is now long gone. Poverty in rural Ireland still exists, but its nature has radically changed. In *Poverty in Rural Ireland*, published in 1996, John Jackson and Trutz Haase argue that

18   Dáil Éireann – Volume 473 – 19 December 1996 – Written answers – National Photographic Archive <http://debates.oireachtas.ie/dail/1996/12/19/00097.asp> accessed 27 February 2012.

rural and urban Ireland are no longer fundamentally distinct societies.[19] As for poverty, it has changed in the context of the affluent society of the turn of the twenty-first century. There is also an international dimension to Irish rural poverty, which is 'a spatial and social manifestation of the uneven process of global capitalist development'.[20] According to the editors of the volume, 'both rural and urban are [now] subject to broad national and international developmental processes'.[21] Situations are so different that allegations of historical continuity are hardly credible. Yet, if people have no option but to see the past of their nation with new eyes, distance has a positive effect on self-esteem.

David Lynch, writing about the commemoration of the Great Famine by Celtic Tiger Ireland, noted that 'affluence meant more when measured against the heartbreak and deprivation Ireland had once endured'.[22] He also quoted Terence Brown's humorous comment that 'The country had become rich enough to face how poor it had been.'[23] We may suggest that the same remarks apply to recent attitudes towards poverty as depicted in the Kahn photographs. In *Not Fade Away*, Grace Neville says that what strikes her most in the series of photographs is the poverty of the people. All commentators similarly underline the dismal poverty portrayed in the collection. And yet comparatively few of the photographs, ten at most, document destitution in the West of Ireland. Besides, whether or not Marguerite Mespoulet's view was inspired by the myth of the noble savage as is suggested in the documentary, her view of extreme poverty was difficult to decipher. Indeed, on the one hand, she emotionally reacted to it as any middle-class Parisian would, but on the other hand she introduced a positive note. Just like Marie-Anne de Bovet, another French woman who visited Ireland in 1889, she comments that however apparently poor

19   Chris Curtin, Trutz Haase and Hilary Tovey (eds), *Poverty in Ireland: A Political Economy in Perspective* (Dublin: Oak Tree Press, 1996), 77.
20   Curtin, Haase and Tovey, *Poverty in Ireland*, 8.
21   Curtin, Haase and Tovey, *Poverty in Ireland*, 8.
22   David Lynch, *When the Luck of the Irish Ran Out* (New York: Palgrave Macmillan, 2010), 112.
23   Lynch, *When the Luck of the Irish Ran Out*, 112.

they may have been, these people looked happy and lived in relative comfort.[24] Yet experience of contemporary life makes such understanding of comfort difficult to grasp. In his blog, a Dublin visitor to the exhibition thus comments on the autochrome of the girl in the red shawl (Figure 2.1): 'On closer inspection of the photograph, the life of hardship does show ... her hands and fingers are toughened and nails are grimy from hard manual work and indeed the same could be said of her bare feet. Her teeth look yellowy and in need of modern care.'[25] Marguerite Mespoulet underlined the filth in her diary but said no more. In this commentary, the superiority of today's Ireland comes through, even though empathy prevails, as it did in the French travellers' words.

But there is more to say. The world depicted appears uncannily other; the girl has 'rotten teeth',[26] she lived a hundred years ago and yet there is something about her that strikes the viewer as different. Talking about the girl in the red shawl, Grace Neville says that 'you have to almost pinch yourself before you realize that this was a young girl, it's not a painting, it's not artificial and it wasn't somehow touched up afterwards'.[27] Temporal, social and emotional distance paradoxically does not lead to complete estrangement as might be expected. Perhaps colours have something to do with it. The early twentieth century in colour does look like real life. A certain Clare, who posted a comment on the exhibition writes that she was 'bowled over by [...] the "right-here" vividness of the autochromes'.[28] As for John of Dublin, he notes: 'When we think of the rural Irish people in the early 1900s the images we have are invariably in black and white. To see the faces and garments of the local people in full colour gives a whole

---

24   Beausoleil, *Irlande 1913* (Paris: Presses artistiques/Conseil des Hauts de Seine, 1989), 18; Marie-Anne de Bovet, in *Irlande 1889 – Trois mois en Irlande*, ed. Denis Ar Gwendal and Art Hughes (Releg-Kerhuon: Editions An Here, 1997), 262.

25   <http://earthanduniverse.blogspot.com/2007/11/1913-rural-irelandstunning-colour.html> accessed 28 February 2012.

26   'Archives of the Planet', *Temple Bar Magazine*, January 2008 <http://object-lesson.blogspot.com/2008/02/archives-of-planet.html> accessed 28 February 2012.

27   RTÉ documentary *Not Fade Away*.

28   <http://earthanduniverse.blogspot.com/2007/11/1913-rural-irelandstunning-colour.html>

Figure 2.1: Girl in the Red Shawl (Beausoleil, *Ireland 1913*, 25).

new dimension.'[29] Colour photographs were already known in Ireland at the time, but what makes this collection exceptional is the technical quality of the shots and the mesmerising freshness of colours. Colours somehow bring the past back to life.

The technical achievement needs to be underlined for other reasons. Fidelma Mullane, the guest curator of the 2007 exhibition at Galway city museum declared in a 1989 interview that technical innovation 'profoundly influenced the direction of the project'.[30] It can also be understood as a symbol of what the photographers represented. The two French women actually embodied modernity. Even though they were not professional photographers, they were able to operate complex equipment. They also essentially travelled by train, the modern means of conveyance par excellence, and they needed the support of no man. Mespoulet and Mignon formed the only all-female team of Albert Kahn's photographers and today's commentators underline 'the female perspective (...) in the photographing of women'[31] and the 'proto-feminist'[32] nature of the French graduates' approach. They were educated,[33] had an urban background and in the end shared much with present-day commentators. Fidelma Mullane, who is a geographer, insists that they embodied academic innovation as well since they were disciples of Jean Brunhes, one of the founding fathers of 'human geography'. Their approach to their subject is familiar to us in many ways, as it is 'based on the idea of milieu and genres de vie' or on 'the interaction between people and environment'[34] which has become common since then. Consequently it is easy to identify with the French photographers. Great admiration is generally expressed for

29   <http://earthanduniverse.blogspot.com/2007/11/1913-rural-irelandstunning-colour.html>
30   Siggins, 'Portraits from a Lost Landscape', 21.
31   Moran, 'Before the Storm', 104.
32   'Archives of the Planet', *Temple Bar Magazine*.
33   They were laureates of the *agrégation*, a highly selective and prestigious competitive exam which qualifies young people to teach. Very few women took this exam in the early years of the twentieth century. M. Mespoulet and M. Mignon can therefore be considered to have been members of the French intellectual elite.
34   'Peaceful Pictures on the Eve of War', *The Irish Times*, 19 June 2007.

these pioneers, particularly in *Not Fade Away*, the RTÉ documentary. We may therefore suggest that the extraordinary modernity of the project and its realisation have something to do with the popularity of the collection today.

We may add that the image that the French travellers gave of Ireland is radically different from that bequeathed by the nationalist ideology. True, what they depict is, broadly speaking, rural Ireland, but they took strikingly few photographs of rural life outside villages. Village activity in rural communities is portrayed, but little else. Besides, their representation of pastoral life is in no way idealised. We may add that, even though an *Irish Times* article of November 2007 notes that 'They capture a people described by Yeats as adding "prayer to shivering prayer",[35] Catholicism is totally absent from the picture. Yet priests and religious ceremonies were a common feature of contemporary press photographs and postcards. Coming from secularised France, the photographer may have obliterated that central aspect of rural life in Ireland. As for nationalist activity, it is only mentioned in passing in the travel diary. Albert Kahn was not interested in establishing a visual record of political events. Documenting changes as such, or the causes of change, was precisely what he did not want. The two women had another mission and they adopted a different perspective. 1913 was an eventful year, but only the notebook alludes to home rule and the hope of people.

The photographs themselves only document everyday life. *Temple Bar Magazine* comments that 'at a time when so many figurative images are imbued with colonial surveillance or a nationalistic recalcitrance, these are just pictures of people being themselves'.[36] As for the girl in the red shawl, she is not 'a nationalist image of Mná na hÉireann, or some guardian of Ireland's virtue'.[37] This may well be part of her appeal to contemporary Ireland, which has rejected the ideals of nationalist times. 'Revisionists

35   'Autochrome Photos of Irish Life in 1913 go on Display', *The Irish Times*, 15 November 2007, 3.
36   'Archives of the Planet', *Temple Bar Magazine*.
37   'Archives of the Planet', *Temple Bar Magazine*.

attributed much of what ailed Ireland to its stagnant blend of Catholicism and nationalism.'[38]

Albert Kahn's Irish collection hides Catholic nationalist Ireland from view and suggests the existence of another more acceptable nation, whose daughters looked like 'any teenage girl'[39] or 'Leaving Cert student'[40] of the early twenty-first century. The *Temple Bar Magazine* also notes that she behaves as someone who dresses up for tourists,[41] which makes sense for the well-travelled younger generations. 'The shockingly modern technology'[42] of the autochrome makes the people in the photographs look so very much alive today that a new form of continuity can be imagined. 'We really are not so far separated from this type of Ireland and seeing colour photographs of the early 1900s brings this to mind even more', blogger John concludes.[43] In the midst of the present transmission crisis, the girl in the red shawl can even be reclaimed as a respectable ancestor. Her identity is disclosed in John's blog: her name was Mian Kelly, she was approximately fifteen in 1913 and she died in 1975. What's more, she is recognised by one of the anonymous commenters as his/her grandmother. 'Wow, Anon', John exclaims, 'that's really interesting!'[44] That the girl should have a name and that she should be somebody's grandmother suddenly makes her more real and connects her with present-day Ireland. She becomes a new, more positive, face of what the past might have been.

Contemporary Ireland has debunked the founding myths of the nation and new identities have emerged. New myths tinged with nostalgia have appeared in the process. In the RTE documentary, the collection

38   Lynch, *When the Luck of the Irish Ran Out*, 113.
39   'Archives of the Planet', *Temple Bar Magazine*.
40   <http://earthanduniverse.blogspot.com/2007/11/1913-rural-irelandstunning-colour. html>
41   'Archives of the Planet', *Temple Bar Magazine*.
42   'Archives of the Planet', *Temple Bar Magazine*.
43   <http://earthanduniverse.blogspot.com/2007/11/1913-rural-irelandstunning-colour. html>
44   'Anon' is short for 'anonymous'; <http://earthanduniverse.blogspot.com/2007/ 11/1913-rural-irelandstunning-colour.html>.

of photographs is said to reflect 'a sense of urgency and nostalgia'. *Not Fade Away* itself appears much more nostalgic than the photographs or accompanying notes ever were. As for the admirers of Mian Kelly, we may argue that they use the photograph as the medium through which a new implicit mythical speech takes shape. According to Roland Barthes's analysis, any object may thus become the prey to the mythification process for a while, after which it is replaced by others.[45] Since 'a myth is a speech defined by its intention',[46] this object is then integrated in an ideological system of interpretation of reality. In an age of hybridised cultures and global reinventions of the local, it is therefore significant that the photographer should have been a foreigner.

Talking of 'the imaginary "Real" Ireland of the post-Hinde 1980s postcards', Kieran Keohane and Carmen Kuhling write that 'the Real Ireland of the postcard is the Lacanian "Real": the void in the symbolic order of modern Ireland, into which the lover projects his own fantasy and through pursuing the fantasy of the Real, succeeds only in destroying the imagined thing he thought he loved'.[47] Without suggesting such a harsh appreciation of the success of the Albert Kahn Irish collection, we may all the same express doubts as to its legitimacy. Barthes says that myth is distorted into meaning;[48] Irish attitudes towards Marguerite Mespoulet's photographs are an apt illustration of this remark. From a French perspective, the two young graduates do not fully deserve the praise they have received in Ireland. Whether or not Albert Kahn found that the photographs fell short of his expectations is unknown. But evidence allows us to argue that the travellers' understanding of Ireland was more limited than is reported in Ireland, and that it was dictated by the prejudices of their day and age.

45   Roland Barthes, *Mythologies* (Paris: Seuil, 1957), 194.
46   (My translation) ['Le mythe est une parole définie par son intention']. Barthes, *Mythologies*, 209.
47   Kieran Keohane and Carmen Kuhling, *Collision Cultures – Transformations in Everyday Life in Ireland* (Dublin: The Liffey Press, 2004), 177–8.
48   Barthes, *Mythologies*, 207.

Ireland through French Eyes

In 1913, the Irish situation was well known in France, as is evidenced by the regular publication of newspaper articles and books of all kinds. The political context and the expectation of changes certainly stand at the origin of the mission Marguerite Mespoulet and Madeleine Mignon were commissioned to engage in. The previous year, Albert Kahn had organised an expedition to Bosnia Herzegovina, torn apart by the Balkan Wars; the debate over Home Rule and the transformations which might ensue were sufficient justification to motivate the trip to Ireland. French historians were particularly interested in the Irish nationalist struggle and several books on the question had been published in the recent past, in particular *L'Irlande contemporaine et la question irlandaise* [*Contemporary Ireland and the Irish Question*] by Dubois (1907) and *L'Irlande et le Home Rule* [*Ireland and Home Rule*] by Maisonnier and Carpentier (1912). Since the early 1900s, the popular press had also regularly published articles on the question, some of them written by Irish nationalists, including Maud Gonne, who resided in Paris. The opinions expressed by these publications were generally supportive of Irish nationalism and they contributed to popularising the view that Celtic Ireland had for too long been suppressed under the cruel yoke of England, which was largely responsible for the rampant poverty. In the same way, the traditional friendship between France and Ireland was placed to the fore even though new friendly relations with England invited circumspection. Maisonnier and Lecarpentier thus rejoice at the prospect of Home Rule, which will reconcile France's 'old friends, the Irish, and the English, her new but loyal friends'.[49]

The views expressed by Marguerite Mespoulet in her travel diaries echo these positions. How much she knew of the detailed situation is impossible to establish, but her commentaries suggest that she was in fact aware of what was taking place in the country. She mentions the impatience with

---

49 (My translation) ['ses vieux amis, les Irlandais, et les Anglais, ses amis nouveaux mais fidèles']. Louis Maisonnier and Georges Lecarpentier, *L'Irlande et le Home Rule* (Paris: Librairie des sciences sociales et politiques, 1912), 308.

which the people are expecting the enforcement of 'the famous Home Rule',[50] but she remains non-committal: 'Whatever the results of the new law, it will at least have given a moment of happiness to millions of men.'[51] In the same way, as stated above, the two French women mirror the commonly accepted view relating to the extraordinary poverty and filth that one encountered in the West of Ireland. Black and white photographs of the kind she took had been published in the French press in recent years. Concerning this particular point, if the notebook doesn't allow the reader to know how much she had read about the contemporary history of the island, we may legitimately suspect she was aware of Marie-Anne de Bovet's illustrated travel diary. It had initially been published in a newspaper, *Le tour du monde* [*Round the World*], in 1889, and then in book form two years later. A new edition of this work was published in Paris in 1908. Its readers cannot fail to be struck by the parallels between the two accounts of the West of Ireland. Marie-Anne de Bovet warmly recommends Claddagh which she presents as justifying the trip to Galway on the grounds that it is a preserve of traditional ways which have disappeared elsewhere. She also lists the scenes and characters she found particularly appealing in the West of Ireland, which are also exactly those Marguerite Mespoulet chose as subjects for her photographs: the fish market, boys in skirts, women wearing traditional costumes,[52] men smoking pipes. The similarities between the commentaries are also quite striking. In some cases the exact same words are used. Anyone wondering why the Parisians rushed to Claddagh immediately on arriving in Ireland for a short trip might find a convincing answer here.

The two ladies might also have been aware of photographs or postcards which had been taken in the Claddagh. As early as the first years of the twentieth century coloured postcards of the Claddagh produced in

50   (My translation) ['Le célèbre Home Rule']. Beausoleil, *Irlande 1913*, 70.
51   (My translation) ['Quels que soient les résultats de la nouvelle loi, elle aura au moins donné un instant de bonheur à plusieurs millions d'hommes']. Beausoleil, *Irlande 1913*, 70.
52   The traditional clothes which had been worn in 1889 had been abandoned by 1913, but the French women managed to procure the last surviving costume, had three different women wear it and took five photographs as a whole.

Germany were sold in Dublin. Anne de Bovet notes in her diary that children had little respect for the sketches that her companion was drawing because photographers were frequent visitors to the village. No wonder then that Marguerite Mespoulet had no difficulty convincing villagers to pose for her, however shy[53] they may have been. The children of 1889 already made blasé commentaries among themselves: 'They're French (...), they are visiting the country and they are portraying people, boats and houses.'[54] The 1913 visitors did nothing else: they piled cliché upon cliché. Besides, despite all their kindness and empathy, they were not immune from condescension. The author of the *Temple Bar Magazine* article writes that there is no sign of 'the typical Victorian or Edwardian attitude that these people who are happy to be poor and too simple-minded not to be'. It is difficult to agree with this interpretation after reading what Mespoulet (and Bovet) say about their living 'quite happily – that is to say in relative comfort'.[55] It is also debatable that she is slightly condescending when she comments on how she cheated the shy women into posing and keeping quiet by telling stories and jokes.[56]

Marguerite Mespoulet did not treat the people she met as her equals. She behaved as a charitable outsider who felt for the natives she had come to study. After all she, the embodiment of modernity, was looking for vestiges of a crumbling world that was very far removed from her experience of reality. She was undoubtedly moved by the people she met, but her situation, the nature of her mission and her background all restricted the possibility of sincere warmth. She adopted the detached scientific approach of a professional photographer to try and 'use space to capture time',[57] as if a freeze-frame could freeze time and confer eternity on the instant the

---

53   Both Bovet and Mespoulet use the adjective *farouche* in French.

54   (My translation) ['Ce sont des Français, (...) ils visitent le pays et tirent le portrait des gens, des bateaux, des maisons']. De Bovet, *Irlande 1889 – Trois mois en Irlande*, 259.

55   (My translation) ['Assez heureusement – c'est à dire dans une aisance relative']. Beausoleil, *Irlande 1913*, 18.

56   Beausoleil, *Irlande 1913*, 32.

57   (My translation) ['piéger le temps par l'espace']. Régis Debray, *Vie et mort de l'image* (Paris: Gallimard, 1992), 40.

photographs were taken, as Régis Debray argues.[58] Detachment is also
palpable when she comments on the racial characteristics of her subjects.
In 1840, Gustave de Beaumont had warned against the dangers of such an
approach,[59] but by the beginning of the twentieth century, applying the
phrenological system to nations had become the norm. In 1911, a book
entitled *Les races du monde* [*The Races of the World*] was published in Paris.
It was illustrated by photographs which were supposed to document the
physical characteristics distinguishing the various races. This work postu-
lated the superiority of the white race but introduced subtle distinctions
between varieties of whiteness. The Irish race is illustrated by the postcard
of a spinner, reproduced in black and white from one of the Zürich pho-
tochromes shot in 1890. The appended commentary describes the Irish as
enthusiastic, endowed with 'vivid imagination' and 'quickness of mind',
but totally devoid of patience and determination.[60]

Marguerite Mespoulet's remarks tended to confirm this analysis. She
particularly stressed the imaginative side of this 'race of dreamy artists',[61] who
tended to talk like poets[62] but underlined the impatience of the Claddagh
women.[63] She went as far as to introduce a subtle hierarchy between people
originating from different parts of the country: she found people from the
Midlands less quick and friendly than their Connemara counterparts.[64] The
notebook also records physical distinctions between different racial types.
She commented on the matt complexion and dark eyes of a woman whom
she saw as obviously descended from 'Spanish settlers'[65] and she contrasted
her appearance with that of blond-haired and fair-skinned true Irish Celts.

58   Debray, *Vie et mort de l'image*, 54.
59   Gustave de Beaumont, *L'Irlande sociale, politique et religieuse*, Godeleine Carpentier
      (ed.) (Lille: CERIUL [1840] 1990), 356 & ff.
60   (My translation) ['imagination vive'], ['promptitude d'esprit']. *Les races humaines*
      (Paris: Hachette, 1911), 174.
61   (My translation) ['une race d'artistes rêveurs']. Beausoleil, *Irlande 1913*, 88.
62   Beausoleil, *Irlande 1913*, 60.
63   Beausoleil, *Irlande 1913*, 34.
64   Beausoleil, *Irlande 1913*, 126.
65   (My translation) ['colons espagnols']. Beausoleil, *Irlande 1913*, 20.

Figure 2.2: *La vie illustrée*, 28 November 1902.

She also compared the features of a long-faced, purple-eyed young man, the very type of 'men of the Celtic race,'[66] with those of men from lower Brittany. In so doing, the French ladies contributed to the work that had been assigned by Alophe to photographers as early as 1861. In his book entitled *Le passé, le présent et l'avenir de la photographie* [*The Past, Present and Future of Photography*], he encouraged photographers 'to portray the different types of the human race, including all anatomic varieties of the body, in all parts of the world.'[67] In his estimation, such was the mission assigned to all photographers, whose social function was to conquer the visible world and connect the local with the global by 'drawing up a new inventory of the real in the shape of (...) archives.'[68] Albert Kahn's project and his Irish project, must no doubt be understood with that ideal in mind. The French ladies, who were looking for remnants of the eternal Celtic culture, strangely make no reference whatsoever to the Literary Renaissance or even the Gaelic language. Even though English presence is not in any way part of the picture, the language that was spoken is clearly English, even in Connemara, but they seem to pay no attention to this paradox. Yet, they were aware of contemporary realities – they mentioned emigration, the temperance movement and the work of the Congested District Board. They seem in fact to have approached the question from a different angle. They were interested in the genius, which they believed characterised the very *nature* of the Gaelic race, rather than in its modern *cultural* expression. They hungered for magic Ireland, where 'gods of the earth, the sea and the wind, where the spirits and the fairies still fared with the Saints of early Christian Ireland.'[69] Anyone familiar with early Irish literature will note how

66   (My translation) ['les hommes de la race celte']. Beausoleil, *Irlande 1913*, 44.
67   (My translation) ['représenter tous les types de la race humaine, avec toutes les variétés de l'anatomie du corps sous les diverses latitudes']. Quoted by André Rouillé, *La photographie* (Paris: Gallimard, 2005), 122.
68   (My translation) ['en dressant unnouvel inventaire duréel sous forme (...) d'archives']. Rouillé, *La photographie*, 120.
69   (My translation) ['où les dieux de la terre, de la mer et du vent, où les esprits et les fées sont encore en la compagnie des Saints de la première époque chrétienne']. Beausoleil, *Ireland 1913*, 88.

little Marguerite Mespoulet knew of Celtic Ireland. Yet Celtic studies were fashionable in France at the time: D'Arbois de Jubainville had published his *Cours de littérature celtique* [*Lessons in Celtic Literature*] in 1908, Dom Louis Gougaud, his *Les chrétientés celtiques* [*Celtic Christianity*] in 1911, and the periodical *Revue celtique* [*Celtic Review*] was in its hey-day. Marguerite Mespoulet, who had an excellent command of the English language, could also have read recently published Irish material. Did she? It is unlikely.

The two women spent a lot of their time rushing from monument to monastic site, but the commentaries confirm how superficial their knowledge of Celtic and early Christian Ireland really was. It is striking in this respect to note that they were unable to distinguish between major sites such as Glendalough, Clonmacnoise, Monasterboice, and minor ones. For instance, they took great pains to travel as far as Roscam, which neither their driver nor local people could locate. Given that they only spent a couple of weeks in Ireland, the choice of that destination is puzzling for all but the readers of Murray's guidebook, whose latest edition by Cooke had been published in 1912.[70] The two photographs of Roscam show the round tower and holed stones that the guidebook describes. Pairing Murray's handbook and the travel diary is rewarding. Not only does the book recommend a visit to Roscam near Oranmore, but he also suggests the itineraries followed by the French graduates. Once in Athlone, it is advised to take the boat up Lough Ree and then visit Clonmacnoise, which can be reached by road.[71] On the way, Murray notes that the visitor will be able to see turf-cots.[72] M. Mespoulet took pictures of Lough Ree, Clonmacnoise, and a turf cot. In a similar way, the expedition to Drogheda, via Navan, Newgrange, the Boyne and Monasterboice exactly corresponds to itinerary 3 of the guidebook.[73] All in all, the Albert Kahn collection of archaeological sites illus-

---

70   The 1906 edition is accessible on the site of the Open Library. John Cooke, *Murray's Handbook for Travellers in Ireland* (London: E. Stanford, [1866] 7th edn 1906) <http://openlibrary.org/books/OL24591180M/Handbook_for_travellers_in_Ireland>, 245. Accessed 2 March 2012.

71   Cooke, *Handbook for Travellers in Ireland*, 227–8.

72   Cooke, *Handbook for Travellers in Ireland*, 231.

73   Cooke, *Handbook for Travellers in Ireland*, 52.

trates what John Cooke presents as the three types of interesting vestiges: those of pagan Ireland, early Christian ruins and Anglo-Irish architecture.[74] The political views expressed by John Cooke, who had an MA from Trinity College and wrote for English publisher Murray, could also have confirmed the French travellers' non-committal positions. Finally, Mespoulet goes as far as to borrow Cooke's quote from a *Journey to Connaught* by Thomas Molyneux,[75] of which she gives a very free translation.[76] As a full forty-two out of seventy-three autochromes depict monuments, one may wonder how Albert Kahn's missionaries reconciled their inclination for tourism and their scientific mission.

The young ladies had clearly formed a very romantic view of Ireland before they ever visited the country. They took for granted historical continuity between Celtic times and the twentieth century and they were convinced that Celtic genius was an eternal trait of the race. They were also fascinated by the ruins which had appealed to all nineteenth-century French visitors to Ireland. The two works by Joseph Prévost, respectively published in 1845 and 1846, were already full of ruins.[77] In 1913, Marguerite Mespoulet and Madeleine Mignon perpetuated a long tradition. Just as Marie-Anne de Bovet, they also loved graveyards, which they described in lyrical terms. Graves feature on fourteen photographs and churchyards were the places where the travellers seemed to find the true spirit of Ireland:

> This melancholy country expresses itself mainly in its graveyards where ruins collapse over graves; where nettles and weeds grow between closely spaced graves, those of the sixth century and those of the present century; where death has no companion but the changing sky and the running wind; yet where great softness prevails.[78]

---

74   Cooke, *Handbook for Travellers in Ireland*, 39.
75   Cooke, *Handbook for Travellers in Ireland*, 246.
76   Beausoleil, *Irlande 1913*, 54.
77   Joseph Prévost, *L'Irlande au XIXe siècle* (1845) and *Un tour d'Irlande* (1846). *L'Irlande au XIXe siècle* can be accessed at <http://gallica.bnf.fr/ark:12148/bpt6k5664678c. r=joseph+prevost.langFR> accessed 4 March 2012. *Un tour d'Irlande* (Boston: Adamant Media Corporation, Elibron Classics, [1846] 2001).
78   (My translation) ['Ce pays de mélancolie parle surtout dans ses cimetières où des ruines s'écroulent sur des tombes, où entre les tombes serrées, celles du sixième siècle

All this was far removed from the ambition of Jean Brunhes and Albert Kahn. Less than one third of the autochromes corresponded to the recommended model. The spinners, the fringe maker, the jaunting car driver, the fishermen, the curraghs, the turf cutter, the fishmongers, the cattle fair, the Claddagh houses – which were to be destroyed in 1937 – all fell into that category. These photographs do succeed in capturing the dignity and humanity of their subjects. But the French visitors' propensity to follow tourist tracks and their love of stereotypes are a disappointment.

All in all, the collection falls short of perfection: the mission was not fulfilled as it might have been and the Ireland that is portrayed does not correspond to the reality of the time. It is a photographic creation which looks real. Rouillé writes that 'an infinite series of invisible but operating images always come between the real and the picture, and they produce a new visual order'.[79] In the case of the Albert Kahn Irish collection, the effect of all distortions is a 'derealised'[80] French early twentieth-century view of Ireland. In those days, this perception supported a conformist world view, which documentary photograph – presented as an instrument of truth – aimed at legitimising and perpetuating. Raymond Boudon, quoting Husserl, reminds his readers that 'the intentionalities (...) which guide the eyes form a priori categories of perception'.[81] The photographs that were taken in Ireland for the Archive of the Planet are an illustration of this process, just as much as they confirm that 'words teach the eye'.[82]

---

et celles de notre siècle, poussent drues les orties et les mauvaises herbes, où la mort n'a de compagnons que le ciel mouvant et le vent qui court, où pourtant plane une grande douceur']. Beausoleil, *Irlande 1913*, 130.

79 (My translation) ['Entre le réel et l'image s'interpose toujours une série infinie d'autres images invisibles mais opérantes qui se constituent en ordre visuel']. Rouillé, *La photographie*, 17.

80 Bourdieu talks about photographs derealising ['déréalisant'] their subjects. Bourdieu, *Un art moyen – Essai sur les usages sociaux de la photographie*, 295.

81 (My translation) ['Les intentionnalités (...) qui dirigent le regard constituent des catégories a priori de la perception']. Raymond Boudon, *L'idéologie ou l'origine des idées reçues* (Paris: Fayard, 1986), 106.

82 (My translation) ['Le regard s'éduque par les mots']. Debray, *Vie et mort de l'image*, 69.

The collection's contemporary Irish career bears witness to another form of manipulation in a different context. In the process, Marguerite Mespoulet and Madeleine Mignon's motivations and qualities have been embellished, and the flaws of the collection have been hushed up. Yet it doesn't seem that Ireland left a deep impression on the two young women. In her later career, Marguerite Mespoulet, who became an academic, never published anything relating to Ireland. She emigrated to New York and became a professor of French literature at Columbia University, where she stayed until she retired. Her papers, which have been preserved by Barnard College,[83] prove her primary interest in nineteenth- and twentieth-century French writers. Before her departure for the United States, however, she issued a report on British women's efforts during the First World War,[84] a reminder of her feminist engagement and her interest in women's everyday life. Of this the reader does get a glimpse in her Irish travel diary. Perhaps she is at her most convincing when she comments on the plight of her Irish female contemporaries: the fringe maker who earns very little and can't work as much as she would like because of her seven 'kids';[85] or the spinners who gladly desert their spinning wheel for homespun fabric factories.[86] Women were her cause, but Ireland was merely the destination of a short mission. Nevertheless, her photographic creation has acquired a life of its own and has proved able to feed imaginary constructions in contemporary Ireland. At the two ends of the story, imagination has given birth to mythical Irelands. The contemporary reinvention of Mespoulet's Ireland strongly suggests that reimagining somehow involves remythifying.

83   'Marguerite Mespoulet papers', Columbia University Archival collections <http://
      www.columbia.edu/cu/lweb/archival/collections/ldpd_4079101/> accessed 4 March
      2012.

84   Marguerite Mespoulet and Esther Dumas, 'L'effort des femmes britanniques pendant
      la guerre' ['The efforts of British Women during the War'] [1918] <http://gallica.
      bnf. fr/ark:/12148/bpt6k5535215q> accessed 4 March 2012.

85   (My translation) ['mioches']. Beausoleil, Irlande 1913, 38.

86   Beausoleil, Irlande 1913, 58.

TINA O'TOOLE

3 Unregenerate Spirits: George Egerton and Elizabeth Bowen's Radical Irish Fiction

The experimental work of Irish writers George Egerton [Mary Chavelita Dunne] (1860–1945) and Elizabeth Bowen (1899–1973) presents an ideological challenge to the gender and sexual binaries of late nineteenth- and twentieth-century society. Their work may be compared to Monique Wittig's Trojan Horse framework, which she proposes as a model for counter-cultural movements and avant-garde writers at the end of the twentieth century. Wittig argues that, 'at the time it is produced, any work with a new form operates as a war machine, because its design and its goal is to pulverise the old forms and formal conventions. It is always produced in hostile territory'.[1] Bowen's life and work is relatively well known within the canon of both British and Irish literary scholarship but Egerton, on the other hand, is much less well known and has only recently begun to emerge in contemporary literary criticism, thanks to the pioneering early work of Margaret Diane Stetz, among others.

Focusing on her early fiction, I will consider the ways in which Egerton deployed protagonists who are clearly marked out as exiles, outsiders to the hegemonic order, partly as a means to destabilise that order. I will then move on to the work of Elizabeth Bowen and will contend that in her work, particularly in her 1968 novel *Eva Trout*, Bowen extends the blueprint forged by writers such as Egerton. I will argue that Bowen further develops the interrogation of gender and sexual identities developed by the 'New Woman' writers and female aesthetes of an earlier generation and that, in her last novel in particular, there is evidence of a gendered social

---

1 Monique Wittig, 'The Trojan Horse', in *The Straight Mind and Other Essays* (Boston: Beacon Press, 1992), 68–75.

world in a constant state of flux, rather than some kind of static account of immutable patriarchal oppression. Such an engagement with gender and sexual identities contributed to the contemporary work being carried out by 1960s feminist scholars, such as Wittig for example. Thus, by reading Bowen's fictional experiments in tandem with those of her peers, and as part of a continuum with the earlier experiments of Egerton and others, we may gain more insight into the cultural construction and deconstruction of gender and sexual identities in these two generations of feminist writers.

Born Mary Chavelita Dunne in Melbourne, the daughter of an Irish (Catholic) army captain, George Egerton spent her early childhood in various colonial outposts before 'moving home' with her family to Dublin. Creating a pseudonym from her mother's name, Isabel George, and that of her husband Egerton Clairmonte, she went on to become a writer whose work was linked with that of artists and activists such as Sarah Grand, Olive Schreiner, and George Gissing, among others, who were associated with 1890s literary decadence. The interrogation of sexuality was a central project shared by these 'New Women' and 'Aesthetes' of the 1890s, who sought to challenge the heterosocial status quo by addressing topics such as women's rights, gender roles, and sexual identities and expression (particularly in relation to women's sexuality). Sarah Grand is possibly the best-known New Woman writer, whose novel, *The Heavenly Twins* (1893) is one of the most important of this period. Grand began to publish in the 1870s and her influence on the work of later New Woman writers, as well as on other literary and political movements of the period, has been given much scholarly attention in studies of the period.[2] George Egerton's work came slightly later in the period and her work exhibits the influence of Grand, Mona Caird, and others, all of whom were striving at the time to develop a feminist literary aesthetic. To outline in brief the Irish context for this

---

2   Such as Lyn Pykett, *Engendering Fictions: The English Novel in the Early Twentieth Century* (London: Hodder and Arnold, 1995); Sally Ledger, *The New Woman: Fiction and Feminism at the Fin de Siècle* (Manchester: Manchester University Press, 1997); Teresa Lynn Mangum, *Married, Middlebrow, and Militant: Sarah Grand and the New Woman Novel* (Ann Arbor: University of Michigan Press, 1998).

material, it is acknowledged that the New Woman project has tended to be seen almost solely as a radical movement within the history of English literature, with its natural home in the 1890s London literary metropolis. Yet the number of authors involved in these radical cultural experiments who had Irish backgrounds is intriguing: Sarah Grand herself (1854–1943) was born in Donaghadee, Co. Down, and brought up in Co. Mayo, where she set one of her best-known works, *The Beth Book* (1894); 'Iota' [Kathleen Mannington Caffyn] (fl. 1893–1900), was born and brought up in Co. Tipperary; L. T. Meade (1844–1915) was born in Bandon, Co. Cork, and lived near Kinsale until her thirties; E. L. Voynich [Ethel Lillian Boole] (1864–1960), author of the best-selling novel *The Gadfly* (1897) was the daughter of mathematician George Boole and Mary Everest Boole, she was born and brought up in Cork; and Katherine Cecil Thurston [née Madden] (1875–1911), was the daughter of Paul Madden, the Home Rule Mayor of Cork, and spent most of her adult life in Waterford.[3] To go back to Egerton herself, her groundbreaking collection of short stories *Keynotes* (1893) was written while she lived in Millstreet, Co. Cork and, as I have discussed elsewhere, the local context to this apparently Scandinavian collection is evident in several of her narratives.[4] As I explain in *The Irish New Woman*[5] the Irish context within which these writers worked has been almost completely obscured by the predominantly nationalist character of Irish literary scholarship in the intervening century, which was coupled up until quite recently with a more general lack of interest in Irish feminist writings. This neglect has been particularly marked where nineteenth- and early twentieth-century literary culture is concerned, as Heidi Hansson has noted: 'Political considerations [...] intrude and a further difficulty when women's works are studied is that the focus on "national identity" in

---

3   For further biblio/biographical material on these writers, see Tina O'Toole, *Dictionary of Munster Women Writers* (Cork: Cork University Press, 2000).

4   For further discussion of this point, see Tina O'Toole, 'Ireland: The *terra incognita* of the New Woman Project', in Heidi Hansson (ed.), *New Contexts: Re-Framing Nineteenth-Century Irish Women's Prose* (Cork: Cork University Press, 2008), 125–41.

5   Tina O'Toole, *The Irish New Woman* (London: Palgrave Macmillan, 2013).

Irish criticism has made feminist approaches difficult'.[6] While this scholarly silence is evident in relation to the writers mentioned above, we can
see this phenomenon all the more clearly in relation to Elizabeth Bowen,
whose Anglo-Irish Planter background meant that she was constructed
as an outsider in Ireland during her own lifetime, and to some degree ever
since. Perhaps the 'political considerations' gestured to by Hansson above,
may explain the considerable attention paid to *The Last September*[7] by Irish
studies scholars to the almost complete exclusion of almost everything else
written by Bowen.

Egerton, having spent her formative years in a number of different
countries, sustained this *wanderlust* throughout her early adulthood. This
migrancy had a clear impact both on her writing and, ideologically, on her
sense of liminality in relation to the dominant culture of whichever country she happened to live in. In the late 1880s she spent some time living in
Scandinavia where the experiments of writers such as Ola Hansson, as well
as Ibsen and Nietzsche influenced her own writing, and her first publication was a translation of Knut Hamsun's *Sult* (1890). *Keynotes* (1893), her
celebrated first fiction collection certainly proved to be the 'keynote' of
this fin-de-siècle intellectual world. It was published by the Bodley Head
(a publishing house synonymous with aestheticism, particularly since their
publication of Oscar Wilde's *Salomé* in 1894) where publisher John Lane
clearly recognised his chance with this new author to develop links with the
New Woman writers of the period. Lavishly produced, *Keynotes* was also
illustrated by Beardsley, and launched the Bodley Head's Keynotes series,
publications by a range of different authors which included Grant Allen
and Richard Le Gallienne. Egerton's short stories, which reconstructed
women's subjectivity from their own perspective and tackled taboo subjects
such as women's sexual identities and autonomy, thus became synonymous
with the New Woman phenomenon. The toast of the 1890s literary set, she
contributed to *The Yellow Book*, that journal most closely associated with
literary aestheticism and she was lampooned by *Punch* in a series entitled

6   Heidi Hansson, *New Contexts: Re-Framing Nineteenth-Century Irish Women's Prose*
     (Cork: Cork University Press, 2008), 3.
7   Elizabeth Bowen, *The Last September* (Dublin: Constable, 1929).

'She-Notes' by 'Borgia Smudgiton'.[8] She mixed with other fin-de-siècle writers and intellectuals including Arthur Symons, Havelock Ellis, W. B. Yeats and Richard Le Gallienne. Described by William Frierson[9] as the first writer in English to delineate the 'sexual instinct' as experienced and expressed by women, Egerton interrogates desire and sexual identity from a woman's perspective. In her work, we find a whole range of transgressive relationships which disrupt the ideologies of the social contract and set her protagonists apart from nineteenth-century canonical heroines. Some of her short stories, notably 'The Marriage of Mary Ascension' and 'Gone Under' (from the *Discords* collection, 1894), focus on the social and economic reasons as to why women marry, just as Bowen would later do in *Eva Trout*. On the whole then, Egerton approves of those who defy the social contract and follow their instincts in relationship matters. It is worth speculating that Egerton's sense of her own outsider status enabled her to perceive 'natural' social relations as part of an oppressive hegemony. Her national identity and that early experience of having been uprooted several times to move with her family to a new barracks in another country or continent may have contributed to this perspective. More particularly, perhaps the fact that she herself lived outside of social norms, first as the mistress of a married man, and later as a single mother, enabled her to analyse the conventions oppressing her, and to deconstruct them.

We find Egerton's construction of the outsider figure in all of her texts. Having established the psychological depth of her protagonist in 'The Child', Egerton goes on to show that such awareness marks out the individual from the crowd. Among her playmates, the nameless child is a star: 'They are waiting for her, for is she not the most daring, the most individual amongst them?'.[10] However, this singularity ceases to be an asset as the child grows up. In the second part of this story, Egerton comments: '[The girl] is too sharp-tongued, too keen-eyed, too intolerant of meanness

8   *Punch* (10, 17 March and 8 December 1894).
9   William Frierson, *The English Novel in Transition* (Norman: University of Oklahoma Press, 1942).
10   George Egerton, 'The Child' from 'A Psychological Moment at Three Periods', in *Discords* (London: The Bodley Head, 1894), 6–7.

and untruth to be a favourite with her classmates – too independent a
thinker, with too dangerous an influence over weaker souls to find favour
with the nuns.'[11] The chance for an individual intellect to choose its own
path is seen as potentially seditious by one of the nuns. Egerton writes:
'For to the subdued soul of this still young woman who has disciplined
thoughts and feelings and soul and body into a machine in a habit, this
girl is a *bonnet-rouge*, an unregenerate spirit, the embodiment of all that is
dangerous.'[12] Juxtaposing this with Bowen's 'unregenerate spirit', Eva Trout,
who is a singular figure (even within the context of the radical educational
experiment which comprises her only experience of school), we can only
imagine how the nuns depicted in Egerton's narrative might have dealt
with such a child.

A key feature of New Woman texts is the depiction or creation of
unfamiliar worlds, thus Olive Schreiner's *The Story of an African Farm*
(1883) and Charlotte Perkins Gilman's *Herland* (1915) challenged social
mores by constructing new ideological relationships in alien landscapes.
Another way in which New Woman writers removed their readers from
the known social world and thereby challenged gender and sexual binaries
was through the introduction of untraditional or transgender figures. Much
scholarly attention has been paid to the Boy within the context of Wilde's
work and that of the aesthetes, however, we also find the Boy in some New
Woman fiction, and to some extent, we might argue that 'he' is a crossover
figure between these fin-de-siècle groups. To the New Woman writers the
Boy was one avenue through which they could access male privilege, at
least temporarily, as we find, for example, in several of Sarah Grand's novels
including *The Heavenly Twins* and *The Beth Book*. Some New Woman texts
address the possibilities for young women in carrying their exploration of
the role of Boy into adulthood, thus opening up a range of social roles for
female-to-male trans figures within their narratives. This deployment served
an important function within New Woman discourses, by demonstrating
that women were just as capable intellectually, emotionally, and physically,
to operate within the public sphere and to take on the responsibilities and

11   Egerton, 'The Child', 12.
12   Egerton, 'The Child', 13.

roles open only to men in that period. Furthermore, in exposing the ways in which gender is constructed *and* performed (to use Butler's formula), it pointed up the flaws within an essentialist, gender-divided system of social organisation. There were also those who carried their experiments with gender performance from the textual into the social world, of course, as Shari Benstock's research illustrates.[13] Laura Doan's[14] work on 1920s fashion illustrates the ways in which the visibility of masculine women in the European metropolis of the day influenced fashion in general, as women began to favour a masculine style of dress. In other words, this fictional phenomenon is not at odds with the contemporary social world.

There are a number of examples of New Woman texts that bring this kind of gender troubling into play. One such is Katherine Cecil Thurston's 1909 novel, *Max*, which explores the radical potential of the Boy figure and demonstrates the challenge posed by this fiction to the separate spheres of the contemporary social world. Max is a transgender figure who, in her former life as 'Maxine' ran away from her home in Russia and her marriage to a man she had come to despise, along with a place in the rigidly gender-segregated upper-caste world of her birth. Thurston's *Max* in several ways mirrors an earlier fictional episode in Grand's *The Heavenly Twins* when Angelica cross-dresses in order to gain access to the public world of men.[15] In both of Grand's excursions into gender-swap territory, she exposes the ways in which women deliberately construct themselves as Boys, detailing lovingly the exact process by which Angelica carries off her transvestism, from sending her measurements to a tailor to the way she hides her hands in order to distract attention from their diminutive size. With statements such as: 'isn't it surprising the difference dress makes? I should hardly have thought it possible to convert a substantial young woman into such a slender, delicate-looking boy as I make. But it just shows you how important

13   Shari Benstock, *Women of the Left Bank: Paris 1900–1940* (Austin: University of Texas Press, 1986).

14   Laura Doan, *Fashioning Sapphism: The Origins of a Modern English Lesbian Culture* (New York: Columbia University Press, 2001).

15   For further discussion of this point, see O'Toole, 'The New Woman and the Boy', in *The Irish New Woman*.

dress is,'[16] Grand underlines what Marjorie Garber defines as the 'resistance to the female-to-male transsexual'. Garber suggests that this results from 'a sneaking feeling that it should not be so easy to "construct" a man – which is to say, a male body'.[17] Just as in Grand's text, throughout Thurston's *Max* there are quite specific physical descriptions of the Boy, many of which incorporate traditionally masculine attributes in the description of how he projects himself:

> Zeal, endeavour, ambition in its youngest, divinest form [...] and none who had known Max [...] ever viewed him in more characteristic guise than he appeared on that February morning, clad in his painting smock, the lock of hair falling over his forehead, his hands trembling with excitement, as he executed the first bold line that meant the birth of his idea.[18]

As we do not at this point in the novel *know* the significance of this lock of hair, which symbolises the long tresses Max/ine left behind with his feminine identity, the potential for gender ambiguity built into this scene is lost in the first reading. Later in the novel when Max wishes to assert himself, the narrator describes the scene and his appearance in a way which leaves no room for ambiguity of any kind:

> The warm sun fell upon a rigid severity of aspect, as though the room had instinctively been bared for the enactment of some scene. Max himself, in a subtle manner, struck the same note. The old painting blouse [...] had been discarded for the blue serge suit, severely masculine in aspect; his hair had been reduced to an unusual order, his whole appearance was rigid, active, braced for the coming moment.[19]

This scene emphasises the need for Max to access and perform his masculinity to the utmost if he is to achieve his ambitions in a gender-divided social world.

---

16   Sarah Grand, *The Heavenly Twins* (Ann Arbor: University of Michigan Press, [1893] 1992), 452.

17   Marjorie Garber, *Vested Interests: Cross-Dressing and Cultural Anxiety* (London: Routledge, 1992), 102.

18   Katherine Cecil Thurston, *Max* (London: Hutchinson, 1909), 143.

19   Thurston, *Max*, 260.

The central character in Egerton's story 'The Spell of the White Elf' inscribes a character in a very similar situation, however in this case she does not resort to the full gender transition chosen by Max:

> A tall woman with very square shoulders, and gold-rimmed spectacles is passing us with two gentlemen. She is English by her tailor-made gown and little shirt-front, and noticeable anywhere [...] My compatriot is sitting comfortably with one leg crossed over the other, in the manner called 'shockingly unladylike' of my early lessons in deportment. The flame flickers over the patent leather of her neat low-heeled boot, and strikes a spark from the pin in her tie. There is something manlike about her. I don't know where it lies but it is there.[20]

At the beginning of the story, a male observer describes this character somewhat caustically as: 'a very learned lady; she has been looking up referats in the university bibliothek [...] I suppose her husband he stay at home and "keep the house" [*sic*]'.[21] Here, in other words, we find a modern career woman who chooses to project an ambiguous or transgressive gender identity but not to pass as male, as Max has done. Egerton's design here is not merely to subvert gender binaries in order to enable her character to access a profession, although she does disrupt the domestic setting just as suggested as the protagonist tells us: 'Positions are reversed, they often are nowadays. My husband stays at home and grows good things to eat and pretty things to look at, and I go out and win the bread and butter.'[22] Egerton extends this play with gender essentialism further in the text by introducing the theme of motherhood at its core.

The underlying belief that womanhood consists of a series of roles enforced by society is borne out in Egerton's narrative in which, as Adams and Tate point out: 'motherhood is posited as a social, not a biological role.'[23] Creating a somewhat irregular arrangement for the upbringing of a

---

20 Egerton, 'The Spell of the White Elf', in *Keynotes* (London: The Bodley Head, 1893), 72.

21 Egerton, 'The Spell of the White Elf', 72.

22 Egerton, 'The Spell of the White Elf', 80.

23 Brontë Adams and Trudi Tate (eds), *That Kind of Woman* (London: Virago, 1991), xiv.

child, who is raised by this childless couple who are completely unrelated to the birth mother, and adding to this by depicting the enmity between the two central women in the child's life, its birth and adoptive mothers, Egerton goes on to add to the oddness of their domestic arrangement through this deployment of a New Woman as mother. Certainly, the arrival of the child brings changes to the life of her central protagonist, but these do not include the denial of her professional aspirations, as she continues to travel widely and to publish her work, that is, she continues to engage with the public sphere rather than being silenced by the private sphere of motherhood and domesticity. Egerton's approval of this state of affairs permeates the narrative, and there are clear elements of projection here from what we know of her own biography. As I made clear above, this kind of gender trouble is not uncommon in New Woman fiction, however, it was more usual even within this utopian fiction for a career woman protagonist to be single and certainly childless. Iota's best-selling New Woman novel *A Yellow Aster* (1894), for example, turns on just such a point. The protagonist at the centre of *A Yellow Aster*, Gwen Waring, is a New Woman who is emotionally and sexually barren. In the absence of any *meaningful* work for women to do (one of the key rallying points of feminist campaigns of the period) Gwen's only vocation in life is marriage (which she undertakes as 'an experiment') to a young man who has been one of her intellectual companions. She soon discovers her mistake: 'You can't call your soul your own [...] it's bondage worse than death.'[24] However, rather than suggesting a radical shift in heterosocial mores, as Egerton proposes, Iota's solution is finally to reduce her character to an essentialist mother-figure. On giving birth to her first child, Gwen abandons her earlier desire for a career and embraces her higher role as mother, proclaiming: 'I am a woman at last, a full, complete, proper woman, and it is magnificent. No other living woman can feel as I do; other women absorb these feelings as they do their daily bread and butter [...] they slip into their womanhood; mine has rushed into me with a great torrent.'[25] The capitulation at the end of this novel to the

---

24   'Iota' [Kathleen Mannington Caffyn], *A Yellow Aster* (Leipzig: Bernhard Tauchnitz, 1894), 245.
25   'Iota', *A Yellow Aster*, 304.

sentimentality of nineteenth-century representations of the mother-child bond is depressing but perhaps predictable, indicative of the strength of hegemonic social identities. It also prefigures the ultimately anti-feminist message at the end of Grant Allen's *The Woman Who Did* (1895).[26] As I discuss below, Bowen arranges an equally 'odd' domestic scene around her central protagonist in *Eva Trout* who, much like Egerton's New Woman, takes a somewhat unconventional approach to motherhood, rejecting the hegemonic constraints of marriage and biological parenthood.

Unlike Egerton, Bowen grew up in Ireland (and spent more of her adult life living in Ireland than Egerton did) but she did so at a remove from what became, during her lifetime, the dominant culture of the Catholic nationalist majority, as I mentioned above. In *Pictures and Conversations* she discusses the impact this sense of difference had on her, describing her awareness even as a young child of different 'mythologies' at work in the culture and her realisation that she was differently placed in relation to these discourses.[27] It seems to me that this perspective on her relationship to different (and competing) national identities could be deployed to discuss identity formation more generally and it becomes clear in reading her fiction that Bowen's delineation of the 'mythologies' in relation to gender and sexuality was equally incisive, and divided in the same binary fashion. Thus, in several of her novels but particularly in *Eva Trout*, Bowen constructs the central character as an outsider in a gender-divided and heteronormative environment, who struggles to understand and assimilate to the dominant culture. Thus when Iseult, at a loss to understand Eva, exclaims: 'What caused the girl to express herself like a displaced person?'[28]; we may observe that this is precisely because she *is* displaced, although perhaps not

---

26   The New Woman figure in Allen's novel, Herminia Barton, conceived a child in a 'free union', in other words, she did not marry the child's father. In later life, her daughter reacts badly to the truth of her origins, and Herminia, unable to provide her daughter with the conventional background she needs in order to find a husband, commits suicide.

27   Elizabeth Bowen, *Pictures and Conversations* (London: Allen Lane, 1975), 23–4.

28   Elizabeth Bowen, *Eva Trout, or Changing Scenes* (London: Jonathan Cape, 1975 [1968]), 18.

quite in the way this term is usually meant. As the novel progresses, Eva's efforts to re-member herself, to match her own 'mythology' with that of the social world she moves through, result in a series of disjunctures, or ripples, in the surface of the dominant culture.

Rosi Braidotti's work on monsters usefully informs our reading of such outsider figures: 'The monstrous or deviant is a figure of abjection in so far as it trespasses and transgresses the barriers between recognisable norms or definitions.'[29] Everything about Eva Trout is monstrous and it is obvious from this first description of her that her large frame is somehow out of kilter in relation to those around her:

> The giantess, by now, was alone also [...] shoulders braced, hands interlocked behind her, feet in the costly, slovenly lambskin bootees planted apart. Back fell her cap of jaggedly cut hair from her raised profile, showing the still adolescent heaviness of the jawline [...]. Monolithic, Eva's attitude was. It was not, somehow, the attitude of a thinking person.[30]

More than just her size and shape, it is suggested, are monstrous. In attitude we are told that she is 'monolithic' and her physiognomy is indicative to Mrs Dancey, whose perspective this is, of someone who does not or cannot think as others do. The use of comparisons with immutable objects to describe Eva's thought processes continue throughout the text. We are told that at school, efforts had been made to 'induce flexibility' but in terms of both language and thought these attempts came too late; 'her outland-ish, cement-like conversational style had set'.[31] Thus, the outsized Eva is introduced in the text, with later accounts describing her as an 'Amazon at bay'[32] and a 'she-Cossack',[33] this from Mr Denge, following Eva's 'attack' on him. Discussing the genesis of the monster in European texts from the sixteenth century on, Braidotti tells us that the 'monstrous birth' is

---

29   Rosi Braidotti, *Nomadic Subjects: Embodiment and Sexual Difference in Contemporary Feminist Theory* (New York: Columbia University Press, 1994), 65.
30   Bowen, *Eva Trout*, 13.
31   Bowen, *Eva Trout*, 18.
32   Bowen, *Eva Trout*, 85.
33   Bowen, *Eva Trout*, 93.

commonly attributed to the sinfulness or guilt of the parents: 'The most common form of parental transgression concerns the norms for acceptable sexual practice [...] sexual excess, especially in the woman, is always a factor.'[34] The homosexuality of Willy, Eva's father, and his relationship with his boyfriend Constantine specifically, is presented as the 'cause' of much that is out-of-order in Eva's social context. Her mother, Cissie, had left her husband and baby two months after Eva's birth. As Cissie had also taken a lover, we may conclude that *both* of Eva's parents are guilty of the kind of sexual excess described by Braidotti. Following Cissie's departure, Willy and Constantine move in together, making themselves subject to a barrage of letters from Cissie's extended family who object to this 'unnatural' domestic setting for the raising of a child. When she is old enough to do so, Eva takes her father's side in this dispute, thus rejecting her kin and by extension, the social world. She later realises that: 'She had first been withheld from, then forfeited, her birthright of cricket matches and flower shows.'[35] In this way, we come to understand Eva's liminal position, her outsider status is confirmed.

To return to Eva's construction within the novel, having established a monstrous social identity for her central protagonist, Bowen demonstrates Eva's oddity in a number of key episodes. This is evidenced in particular when she moves into a new neighbourhood and rents a house. The experience of Denge, the letting agent, during this transaction, which is later relayed to Iseult, suggests that Eva has lost her mind completely:

> That a violent outbreak had caused him to flee the premises, into which you then barricaded yourself, *as* violently; that a messenger subsequently sent out by him with a kettle had turned tail, leaving the kettle to its fate, on being grimaced at 'hideously' from a window, and that no further sort or kind of any communication has been had from you since; though sallies into Broadstairs, in incomplete control of a powerful bicycle, have been reported.[36]

---

34   Rosi Braidotti, 'Signs of Wonder and Traces of Doubt: On Teratology and Embodied Differences', in Janet Price and Margrit Shildrick (eds), *Feminist Theory and the Body* (Edinburgh: Edinburgh University Press, 1999), 291.

35   Bowen, *Eva Trout*, 223–4.

36   Bowen, *Eva Trout*, 118.

Denge's fear of Eva and more specifically, his fear that she will burn his house down, extends to this manifestation of woman and bicycle somehow moulded together into a monstrous organism, or perhaps a cyborg, to use Donna Haraway's term (1984).[37] Jennifer González points out that:

> The image of the cyborg has historically recurred at moments of radical social and cultural change [...]. In other words, when the current ontological model of human beings does not fit a new paradigm, a hybrid model of existence is required to encompass a new, complex and contradictory lived experience.[38]

It seems to me that Bowen, particularly in episodes such as this, *is* attempting to forge a new paradigm, as I will discuss below.

While the perception of Eva's body is central to this text, she is rarely herself presented as one who is 'centred' in her own body, to the extent that in some episodes she does not appear to be at home within a human body at all. Eric Arble is the first person to come into close physical contact with this creature but his alcohol-fuelled attack on her heightens, more than anything else, the sense that Eva is somehow not-human. There is a strong suggestion in this passage that treating Eva badly, even violently, is not quite the same thing as abusing another human being:

> Eric got hold of Eva, by the pouchy front of her anorak and shook her. The easy articulation of her joints made this rewarding – her head rolled on her shoulders, her arms swung from them. Her teeth did not rattle, being firm in her gums, but coins and keys all over her clinked and jingled. Her hair flumped all ways like a fiddled-about-with-mop. The crisis became an experiment: he ended by keeping her rocking, at slowing tempo, left-right, left-right, off one heel on to the other, meanwhile pursing his lips, as though whistling, and frowning speculatively. The experiment interested Eva also. Did it gratify her too much? – he let go abruptly. 'That's all' he told her. 'But mind your own business next time.'[39]

---

37   See Donna Haraway, 'Manifesto for Cyborgs: Science, Technology and Socialist Feminism in the 1980s', in Jeff Escoffier (ed.), *Socialist Review* 15.2 (1985).

38   Jennifer González, 'Envisioning Cyborg Bodies: Notes from Current Research', in Kirkup et al. (eds), *The Gendered Cyborg* (London: Routledge, 2000), 61.

39   Bowen, *Eva Trout*, 101.

Crucially, even in such an acutely physical scene where one person lays hands on and violently shakes another, our attention is drawn not so much to Eva's physical body as to her inanimate aspects. She is shaken by the pouchy front of her anorak and, when shaken, she clinks and jingles suggesting a robot or again a cyborg, but certainly not something composed of human hair or flesh and blood but rather fabric, metal and mop-hair. If anything, she is transformed here into a large rag-doll, and like a child, Eric 'experiments' with the effect of his shaking her, apparently with no complaint from his human doll. Having sustained this for quite some time without any cry from her, Eric concludes that this abuse in some way gratifies Eva and it is only at this point that he stops abruptly, telling her sternly 'that's all'. In the aftermath of this violent scene, as both Eric and Constantine leave her alone in the house once more, we are told that there is 'not a trace left [of these various visitors] but for damage to Eva's frame ... *She* now yawned: so dismissive a yawn that it distended her rib-cage to cracking-point, just not dislocating her jaw by the grace of heaven'.[40] Again, the reference to 'frame' suggests the woman/bicycle cyborg, but her yawn, travelling as it does down through her body tissue and her bones, has quite a different effect. Both the flippancy of this gesture in the wake of the departing men, and Eva's ability to wrack her own body by the simple introduction of air into her lungs, is suggestive of someone reasserting herself bodily. That this effect is produced deep inside her rib-cage demonstrates the impact of Eric's actions as having merely affected the surface of her body, which is indicative of the effect of the opposite sex upon Eva throughout the novel.

Eva Trout's aberrant body image creates just such a reaction in those about her as did the 'learned lady' in Egerton's 'The Spell of the White Elf' or the unregenerate spirit of her protagonist in 'The Child'. When one of her schoolfellows asks 'Trout, are you a hermaphrodite?' she responds 'I don't know'.[41] This scene is not rendered negatively, however, as her classmates immediately begin to discuss the case of Joan of Arc, who was 'supposed to have been' a hermaphrodite. In other words, the possibility of having a transgender identity is dealt with in positive terms here, from

40   Bowen, *Eva Trout*, 126.
41   Bowen, *Eva Trout*, 58.

the perspective of the young Eva, made consistent with the identity of an idealised role model (albeit one who dies a tragic and untimely death, as will Eva). However, this episode causes us to examine more scrupulously our earlier impressions of Eva's bodily form: 'the giantess' described by Mrs Dancey now appears less 'monolithic' or monstrous, than masculinised. Judith Halberstam suggests that one reason for the kinds of reaction to female masculinity produced in the Mr Denges of contemporary society is that its manifestation undermines traditional notions of *masculinity* and thus patriarchal power. Furthermore, she notes that the masculine woman has tended not to be read as a 'historical figure, a character who has challenged gender systems for at least two centuries'.[42] This is a timely reminder in the context of our reading of *Eva Trout*, a novel now forty years old, enabling us to situate this discourse at the centre of a series of ongoing struggles in the arena of female masculinity.

Unlike the 'learned lady' of Egerton's short story, however, who assimilates to the heteronormative familial and social context, Eva takes the opposite course – attempting to bring the social context around to her way of seeing the world. Beginning with her removal to Cathay, the house in Broadstairs, she attempts to construct a life for herself on her own terms, refusing any interference from friends or family, and rejecting any imposition from the local community into her new world. Eva will not seek to reconstruct herself within the terms of the heterosexual contract, but instead by adopting Jeremy, she attempts to construct a family for herself without entering into marriage or domesticity; somewhat as Egerton's character had earlier done albeit within a slightly more conventional framework. Eva's struggle to establish her own identity in relation to the dominant culture derives from her own, sometimes mistaken, reading of the 'mythologies' which surround her and thus, as Hoogland points out, Bowen's text 'depicts what happens when a (female) subject does not effectively enter the phallogocentric order'.[43] In fact at times, Eva's readings of the social code turn

---

42   Judith Halberstam, *Female Masculinity* (Durham, NC: Duke University Press, 1998), 45.

43   Renée C. Hoogland, *Elizabeth Bowen: A Reputation in Writing* (New York: New York University Press, 1994), 209.

out to be more prescient than that of those around her, effectively disturbing the hegemony in ways which threaten to disrupt the code itself: 'expos[ing] that not only her own subjectivity, but subjectivity generally is no more than a necessary fiction with no meaning or essence.'[44] In a similar vein, Wittig observes:

> Whether we want it or not, we are living in society here and now, and proof is given that we say 'yes' to the social bond when we conform to the conventions and rules that were never formally enunciated but that nevertheless everybody knows and applies like magic.[45]

By rejecting a 'normal' heterosexual relationship as well as the family unit constructed around her by the Arbles, and finally, by rejecting a normative approach to motherhood, we can outline a range of ways in which Eva Trout rejects the social bond. Throughout *Eva Trout*, constant flux reshapes notions of a fixed family institution, and to some extent, redefines family as a communal commitment, the components of which are inclusive as opposed to exclusive, distinct units. However, unlike her 1890s predecessors, and also unlike her feminist contemporaries, whose project is the construction of a counter-culture, Bowen has an aversion to radical activism in the public domain. Her *Eva Trout* reimagines an affective life only at the level of the individual and we get little sense here of public discourses intruding upon or conditioning the private zone. Eva appears to operate in a completely free space outside of (or above?) the public domain which might, for example, reinforce gender and sexual norms, or refuse to condone her illegal adoption of Jeremy. Her wealth insulates Eva from the public world, keeping her safe from the legislation of any nation-state with a habit of intruding into the private lives of its citizens. Thus Bowen allows Eva free reign within the private sphere, traditionally a place where alternatives to the mainstream are possible. This enables the author on the one hand to establish a counter-cultural identity for her privileged protagonist while on the other preserving intact the social laws

---

44   Hoogland, *Elizabeth Bowen*, 241.
45   Monique Wittig, 'On the Social Contract', in *The Straight Mind and Other Essays*, 39.

Bowen likely deemed necessary for the regulation of the masses. Thus, when Wittig declares that her aim is to effect 'a whole conceptual reevaluation of the social world, its whole reorganisation with new concepts', we can clearly see how other Evas might benefit from such a utopian space. Bowen however, will never be amenable to the revolutionising of the social world on such a scale.[46] Having said that, bringing to mind Halberstam's comment that figures such as Eva Trout have 'challenged gender systems for at least two centuries',[47] it seems to me that Eva has been deliberately constructed as a challenge to the *status quo*, albeit in something of an exceptionalist way.

To return to Braidotti, whose 'monstrous other' encompasses both the divine and the abject,[48] it seems to me that we might read down through a line of these transgressive protagonists who emerge in the New Woman narratives of George Egerton and others, and are later reconfigured by Elizabeth Bowen, and see them as harbingers who open up a new space, and attempt to reconfigure notions of fixed gender and sexual identities. As Henry Dancey points out: 'Here's another thing about you, Miss Trout: you leave few lives unscathed. Or, at least, unchanged. [...] Ethically perhaps you're a Typhoid Mary. You [...] plunge people's ideas into deep confusion [...] you only have to pass.'[49] In the final scenes of the novel, Eva is described thus:

> Not far off, in one of those chance islands of space she stood tall as a candle, some accident of the light rendering her luminous from top to toe – in a pale suit, elongated by the elegance of its narrowness, and turned-back little hat of the same no-colour; no flowers, but on the lapel of the jacket a spraying-out subcontinent of diamonds; a great brooch.[50]

46   For further background on Bowen's political outlook, see Maud Ellmann, *Elizabeth Bowen, The Shadow Across the Page* (Edinburgh: Edinburgh University Press, 2004); Victoria Glendinning, *Elizabeth Bowen: Portrait of a Writer* (London: Weidenfeld and Nicholson, 1977).
47   Halberstam, *Female Masculinity*, 45.
48   Braidotti, 'Signs of Wonder and Traces of Doubt', 295.
49   Bowen, *Eva Trout*, 209–10.
50   Bowen, *Eva Trout*, 309–10.

Luce Irigaray posits the role of the angels, divine messengers, as a strategy to move beyond the prescribed roles allotted to sexual identity in Western culture. She reminds us that in Judaeo-Christian mythology, the angels act as mediators who 'circulate between God, who is the perfect immobile act, and woman, whose job it is to look after nature and procreation.'[51] Within this discourse, the angels open up the closed nature of the worlds of identity, action and history. At the end of Bowen's final novel this luminous Eva could be described as taking up the role of angel in the text, rejecting the use of woman-as-signifier to determine place (motherland, alma mater) and language (mother tongue) and project a moving-beyond the text into unknown and unknowable spaces.

51 Luce Irigaray, 'Sexual Difference', in *French Feminist Thought: A Reader*, ed. Toril Moi (Oxford: Basil Blackwell, 1987), 126.

4   Dublin, 1913: Irish Modernism and
     International Modernism

No sooner had I finished my book on 1913, *The Cradle of Modernism*, than myriads of files, issues and place names cropped up in a veritable deluge of little facts dating from this one year; all the facts that I had forgotten to include were brought to me. I had no doubt that if I wanted to present a cultural chronicle of the emergence of novelty in 1913, I could not avoid selecting, which meant eliminating countries, authors and topics. For instance, when I saw the 2007 publication of Amy Dockser Marcus's excellent *Jerusalem 1913: The Origins of the Arab–Israeli Conflict*, I regretted not having devoted at least a few paragraphs to the birth of Zionism and to the lineaments of a clash in Palestine between two communities, both of which saw in a new nationalism the only response to the dictatorial but crumbling rule of the Ottoman Empire. Moreover, this would have brought more grist to my mill, my major contention being that it was in 1913 that the world as we know it now was being ushered in. Thus, like a demented empiricist, I kept on collecting countless new data discovered after the publication, such as my encounter with George Loane Tucker's 1913 film *Traffic in Souls*. Set in New York, this film, one of the first American feature-length films (uncharacteristically, it lasts 90 minutes), sets out to expose the scandal of white slave traffic. The villain is an evil pimp, Trubus, who hides behind charity organisations while ruling over his denizens and prostitutes via technology. Trubus hides microphones everywhere and even disposes of a super slate that instantly delivers handwritten messages to his minions. Accordingly, he is defeated by technology when the heroes manage to record incriminating conversations on wax cylinders. This was not science fiction, however, since the invention of the portable Belinograph, the ancestor of today's fax machine, also dates from 1913.

However I can confess that among my numerous omissions, there was one that I made quite deliberately. I thought that this was for want of space first of all. It was the chapter that I would have entitled 'Dublin, 1913'. Was it because I had been impressed by the bulk of Pádraig Yeates's *Lockout: Dublin 1913*, whose 668 pages seemed hard to digest and condense in a few lines, or because I had opted earlier for a treatment of W. B. Yeats in connection with Ezra Pound? I had seen all too briefly the beautiful chapters on the Hugh Lane controversy and on the campaign of 'Save the Dublin kiddies' in Lucy McDiarmid's excellent *The Irish Art of Controversy* (2005). These dealt with important issues; I needed more time to process and integrate them in my general problematic, that is, my set of methodological questions. Whatever the main reason for my current hesitation, here is now a sketch of the chapter that is missing from my book.

I have to explain what I mean by my 'problematic'. The plan was simple enough: the idea was to encompass the culture of an entire year in a strict historical framework while highlighting the features that we tend to associate with modernity. This led me to understand that 'modernism', or the cult of the modern in all its forms, was inseparable from an early globalisation; the latter term suggested that technology, imperialism and nationalism would play a determining role in the modernisation of everyday life, but that this combination finally brought about the conditions of the outbreak of the First World War. Such a convergence of factors presupposes an earlier date for the emergence of globalisation than that commonly held, to the point that for some it may sound like an anachronism. Yet I believe that there is no anachronism in seeing globalisation as already present in 1913. It is true that, following Michael Hardt, Antonio Negri and many others, we conceive a late modernity entirely reshaped by globalised empires, dominated right now by an American axis, soon to be replaced by an Asian one.

Indeed, this has crucial relevance for the Irish situation at the time of its painful awakening and subsequent liberation from British imperialism. Critics have expressed scepticism about the alleged novelty of the phenomenon of globalisation, and Doug Henwood has provocatively pointed out that globalisation existed at least one century earlier, but under British domination. One might argue indeed that the world was more unified under British rule than in the second half of the twentieth century. In that case, Ireland would acquire an exemplary status, it would point to the first instance of decolonisation. To investigate these factors without falling too much into the wisdom of hindsight, I turned to a contemporary book written by Morton Fullerton. Fullerton noticed clearly that a unification of the world was taking place. A cosmopolitan intellectual and one-time lover and then close friend of the American novelist Edith Wharton, Fullerton published *Problems of Power* in 1913. In this prescient book, he sees a world war looming and attempts to find solutions that might avoid it.

Only an American could understand so well the complex tangle of rancours, jealousies, unstable alliances and proliferating aspirations that made central Europe such a powder keg. Count Aehrenthal, the Austro-Hungarian minister for foreign affairs, had described in April 1912 a new 'world-situation' generated by the alliance between England, France, Italy and Russia on the one hand, and Austria, Germany and Japan on the other. These alliances testified to an increasingly interconnected world as they all looked to Asia and Africa and brought about new 'zones of friction'.[1] The international treaties had generated an international 'dove-tailing'[2] of the nations of the world. Fullerton insisted upon a new economic 'dove-tailing' and gave the example of the Dardanelles Straits, which were closed for a few months in 1912 by the Turks during the Balkan War. Tons of Russian grain were to rot in the Black Sea; England, Romania, Bulgaria and Greece lost 20,000 pounds a day. Lord Lansdowne announced that it was intolerable to let a limited conflict strangle the trading interests of the whole world and thus the trading community forced the warring parties to reach a truce.[3] The view of the modern world sketched enacts with a vengeance the description famously given by Marx and Engels in their prophetic *Communist Manifesto* (1848): 'The need for a constantly expanding market for its products chases the bourgeoisie over the whole surface of the globe. It must nestle everywhere, settle everywhere, establish connections everywhere. The bourgeoisie has through its exploitation of the

1　　Morton Fullerton, *Problems of Power* (New York: Scribner's Sons, 1913), 6.
2　　Fullerton, *Problems of Power*, 62.
3　　Fullerton, *Problems of Power*, 7–8.

world-market given a cosmopolitan character to production and consumption in every country.'[4] Of course, they also saw a future 'world-literature'
as the outcome of such a process, in which the 'old local and national seclu-
sion and self-sufficiency' would be replaced by mutual interdependence.[5]
Those who doubted that there was any such world-literature must have
been shocked by the choice of Tagore as the recipient of the Nobel Prize
for literature in 1913. It was the first time that a non-European was granted
this distinction, and Yeats had a lot to do with it, as we will see.

The year 1913 was also when the American company AT&T pledged
that universal phone service would be available in all rural areas, when
the portable phonograph was manufactured and when radio broadcasts
were recorded on cylinders that gave fairly accurate renderings of political
speeches. One can date from 1913 the moment when today's global world
came of age, in the current intermeshing between technological inventions,
flows of international capital and the re-awakening of particularist claims,
whether religious or national or both, that saw in war the only solution
to their predicament.

Fullerton observed an upsurge of nationalisms everywhere: 'The
twentieth century tendency will almost uniformly be found to be towards
a greater "national" activity.'[6] What seems diminishing, he notes, is the
ancient 'passion for the planet' that still dominated in intellectual and
political circles a quarter of century earlier. He perceived clearly that the
reawakening of nationalism was a reaction to the encroachment of global
capitalism, a point that was brought home forcibly to the Dublin workers
in August 1913. For Fullerton, one solution lay in the awareness that the
United States had become a world power,[7] which entailed that it would
be unable to avoid being engulfed in a general conflagration, but which
may have compensated for some defects of the older British domination.
If, as he saw it, the geographical centre of gravity had shifted from the

4   Karl Marx and Friedrich Engels, *The Communist Manifesto*, in Karl Marx, *Selected Writings*, ed. David McLellan (Oxford: Oxford University Press, 1977), 224–5.
5   Marx and Engels, *The Communist Manifesto*, 224–5.
6   Fullerton, *Problems of Power*, 9.
7   Fullerton, *Problems of Power*, 23.

Mediterranean world to the Caribbean world,[8] the United States could not dismiss its responsibility facing emerging nations. The military and industrial rise of Japan, victorious over Russia in 1905, announced changes in the Asian world while Russia seemed closer to collapse like the Ottoman Empire.

Fullerton quotes the text of the *Internationale* and Karl Marx,[9] and describes the mounting tide of social unrest, workers' strikes and the new credit granted to the 'general strike' as not socialist, yet his vision of history, determined both by 'money' and 'public opinion'[10] is not incompatible with the main lessons of Marx and Engels. He is not blind to the combination of those two forces as he sees them merging in Germany: 'Germany is a parvenu Power and full of Pangermans who want to "make history," and not merely to "make money".'[11] He also observes that in October 1912, the mills in Gary, Indiana, had to close because 2,750 workers of Slavic origins decided all at once to join the crusade of the Balkan states against the Turks.[12]

Indeed, the Irish situation appeared to Marx and Engels as an interesting exception. They had advocated nationalism as an acceptable solution for Ireland in spite of their internationalist drift. Marx wrote to Kugelmann in April 1868 that 'The Irish question predominates here just now.'[13] He then analyses the overthrow of the church that the English had established in Ireland as a bulwark to landlordism. In December 1869, writing to Engels who was then preparing a monumental history of Ireland never to be completed, Marx stated that it was vital that the International Council of the Workers should discuss the Irish question: 'For a long time I believed that it would be possible to overthrow the Irish regime by English working-class ascendancy ... Deeper study has now convinced me of the opposite.

8   Fullerton, *Problems of Power*, 310.
9   Fullerton, *Problems of Power*, 196–7.
10   Fullerton, *Problems of Power*, 195.
11   Fullerton, *Problems of Power*, 210.
12   Fullerton, *Problems of Power*, 201, note 1.
13   Quoted in Karl Marx and Friedrich Engels, *Ireland and the Irish Question* (Moscow: Progress Publishers, 1971), 151.

The English working class will never accomplish anything before it has got rid of Ireland. The lever must be applied in Ireland. That is why the Irish question is so important for the social movement in general.'[14] One year before Marx's death, but just about the time of James Joyce's birth, Engels wrote to Kautsky that he held 'the view that two nations in Europe have not only the right but even the duty to be nationalistic before they become internationalistic: the Irish and the Poles. They are most internationalistic when they are genuinely nationalistic'.[15]

Engels remained unaware that a literary genius had just been born, a writer who did his best to link back the nationalistic urges of his country to international standards of culture, much as his role-model, Ibsen, had done for his native Norway. Besides, at the time, Engels had no patience with the anarchist deviation of armed nationalism or direct action as advocated by the Fenians. He condemned terrorist coups such as the Phoenix Park assassination of 1882: 'Thus the "heroic deed" in Phoenix Park appears if not as pure stupidity, then at least as pure Bakuninist, bragging, purposeless *"propagande par le fait"*.'[16] In the same letter, he urges Eduard Bernstein 'never [to] praise a single Irishman – a politician – unreservedly, and never identify yourself with him before he is dead' since 'Celtic blood and the customary exploitation of the peasant make Irish politicians very responsible to corruption.' Engels quotes O'Connell's acceptance of bribes and the famous rejoinder of one of the Land League leaders who was responding to the reproach that he had sold his country: 'Yes, and I was damned glad to have a country to sell.'

Yet, on the whole, Anglo-American as well as Irish modernism refused the collectivist drift of Marxists, futurists and unanimists in the name of individualism. One can apply to the ideology of the modern in the arts the paradox outlined by Morton Fullerton: individualism flares back most when it is threatened, exactly as nationalism returns under the repression either of the old empires such as the Austro-Hungarian double monarchy or of the new economic uniformisation of the world at the hands

14   Marx and Engels, *Ireland and the Irish Question*, 382.
15   7 February 1882. Marx and Engels, *Ireland and the Irish Question*, 432.
16   Marx and Engels, *Ireland and the Irish Question*, 436.

of international financiers. In this framework, modernist globalisation is not a recent factor associated with late capitalism but an older trend linked to the development of European and American imperialisms at the end of the nineteenth century. This development reached a climax when the competitive logic of international capital and the explosion of newly unleashed nationalisms led to a universal war. The worldwide web of the internet found its real birth certificate in the general rush to a worldwide war that took place so spontaneously in 1914.

It is nevertheless undeniable that in this global drift, Ireland was somewhat left behind, and that the main difference between Belfast and Dublin was the lack of a consistently organised industrial working class in the Irish capital. Yet, one can say that 1913 marks the beginning of the 'Irish revolution', as Joost Augusteijn and his collaborators depict it, or at least opens a revolutionary decade leading to independence.[17] What is really striking when one peruses the thick volume of *Lockout: Dublin 1913* is that Irish society was extremely stratified, with the upper class living mostly in the rich suburbs and thus barely affected by the transport workers' strike, but the ferocious and indiscriminate repression by British constables made most Dubliners aware of a new solidarity. Class divisions were not overcome overnight to be sure, but a common indignation against the might of the British Empire served as ideological cohesion. It was the shock of barely escaping police truncheons on 31 August 1913 (the Irish Labour movement's 'Bloody Sunday') that led Sean O'Casey to take a definitively socialist view of Irish politics. Thus Jim Larkin, Maud Gonne, Arthur Griffith, Constance Markievicz, James Connolly and Francis Sheehy-Skeffington were united in a struggle against the British despite important political disagreements.

Let us rehearse a few well-known facts. While Ulster resisted the possibility of Home Rule by creating the Ulster Volunteer Force in January 1913 (organised from the Ulster Volunteers), social unrest was brewing in Dublin, and the well-organised Irish Transport and General Workers' Union was being radicalised by its general secretary, Jim Larkin. Very much aware of

17   Joost Augusteijn (ed.), *The Irish Revolution 1913–1923* (Basingstoke: Palgrave, 2002).

the danger of sectarian violence in Ulster, Larkin was ready to retaliate, and
his rhetoric had an insurrectional tone. Larkin believed in the general strike
as a mass weapon, and he announced a 'lockout' on 26 August, just at the
beginning of the Horse Show week. His speech was typically incendiary:
'It is not a strike, it is a lockout of the men, who have been tyrannically
treated by a most unscrupulous scoundrel.' Larkin was attacking William
Murphy, who was president of the Dublin Chamber of Commerce and
served on the board of the Transport authority, who had promised that he
would break the strike. But Larkin was also telling his troops to emulate
Carson's Ulster armed volunteers: 'If Sir Edward Carson is right in telling
the men of Ulster to form a Provisional Government in Belfast, I think
I must be right too in telling you to form a Provisional Government in
Dublin. But whether you form a Provisional Government or not, you will
require arms, for Aberdeen has promised Murphy not only police but the
soldiers; and my advice to you is to be round the doors and corners, and
whenever one of our men is shot, shoot two of theirs.'[18]

The lockout was not very successful at first with just a few lines blocked,
but then Connolly was arrested as the socialist leader while Larkin went into
hiding. He was discovered near City Hall; the police charged everywhere
in the city centre, beating up bystanders including women and children;
two men who happened to pass by were killed by drunken constables. The
obvious use of excessive force by the police created widespread outrage and
was denounced in international newspapers. For the first time, one could
witness that there was no distinction to be made between the rioting slums
and the affluent Anglo-Irish bourgeoisie. Even though Griffith hated Larkin
for being too 'British' (that is, connected with English trade unions) and
too socialist (Keir Hardie had come to talk at a rally at Larkin's invitation),
he could not reject the popular movement of protest, and even a pacifist
like AE expressed solidarity with the strikers in the *Irish Homestead*.

It is in this pre-revolutionary context that one should reopen the debate
concerning an Irish-American modernism in which the two main actors
would be Yeats and Pound. Ezra Pound, who was twenty years younger,

18   Quoted in Pádraig Yeates, *Lockout: Dublin 1913* (Dublin: Gill & Macmillan, 2000),
      20–1.

had come to London in the hope of meeting his poetic mentor, and this he did in 1909. Soon, Pound was imitating the older man's Irish accent and poet's garb, but he also became indispensable to Yeats. His violence and arrogance would at times frighten the Irish poet, who was also flattered by Pound's utter devotion. It is usually believed that the raw energy of the young American poet pushed Yeats out of the 'nineties' and destroyed his mentor's complacency for Celtic twilights, theosophic séances, and hazy dreams of a Romantic Ireland. Pound would have pushed the older poet forward when they collaborated in the winter of 1913 as they worked together in Stone Cottage. However, it seems truer to say that Yeats's modernisation predated Pound's impact; at least, this was Pound's own view, since he wrote that the Irish poet's modernisation was due to Synge's example much more than to his own influence. Pound wrote in 1915 that the 'adorers of the Celtic twilight' were 'disturbed' by Yeats's 'gain in hardness' in the years 1910 to 1913. Pound alluded to poems like 'The Magi', 'The Scholars' and 'No Second Troy', adding: 'There is a new strength in the later Yeats on which he & Synge may have agreed.'[19]

The reference to Synge is crucial – he had died in 1909, leaving Yeats bereft, deprived of a friend and ally, a most important Irish voice. Much has been made of Pound's minor revisions of Yeats's poems that were sent to *Poetry* magazine in 1912. Yeats first dismissed them as mere 'misprints', but he came to accept Pound's suggestions. In January 1913, Yeats acted rather generously, writing that Pound's revisions were helpful. However, his careful choice of words emphasises the archaism of the young American poet: 'He is full of the middle ages and helps me get back to the definite and the concrete away from modern abstraction. To talk over a poem with him is like getting you to put it into dialect. All becomes clear and natural. Yet in his own work he is very uncertain, often very bad though very interesting sometimes. He spoils everything by too many experiments and has more sound principles than taste.'[20]

---

19   Quoted in James Longenbach, *Stone Cottage: Pound, Yeats and Modernism* (Oxford: Oxford University Press, 1988), 19.

20   Quoted in R. F. Foster, *W. B. Yeats: A Life, vol. 1: The Apprentice Mage 1865–1914* (Oxford: Oxford University Press, 1997), 476.

The sharp diagnosis shows that Yeats had kept his critical faculties intact. For him, taking Pound's advice and returning to the medieval or Renaissance virtues extolled by Pound, whose troubadours were the models of a simple, direct and musical expression, was a paradoxical way of modernising himself. Yeats's new tone came to the fore in *Responsibilities* from 1914. Its poems are noticeably stronger in tone and diction, they are pared down, often colloquial, at times truculently topical or violently political. The new tone which I connect with an early modernism is not yet free from the hangover of the past – indeed, in 'September 1913' Yeats laments the passing of 'Romantic Ireland' ('Romantic Ireland's dead and gone / It's with O'Leary in the grave'), in the poetic tract by which he denounces the rejection of Sir Hugh Lane's gift to the Municipal Gallery. But this is precisely what defines early modernism: as Stanley Cavell stated in *Must We Mean What We Say?*, the most important fact of the modern 'lies in the relation between the present practice of an enterprise and the history of the enterprise, in the fact that this relation has become problematic'.[21] He adds that modernism not only contains history (as Pound would later insist) but contains a history that has become self-conscious, problematic and reflexive. History is seen as a doubtful narrative made up of myth and illegible facts, and can no longer be taken for granted unless it is reappropriated by a deliberate creative effort. This is what Yeats set out to do.

Yeats's models were first found in the Italian Renaissance, a Renaissance which chimes with the heroism of nineteenth-century Irish patriots who had sacrificed their lives for the nationalist cause. Yeats attacked the materialism of the middle class, suggesting that the new heroes of Irish nationalism should not be miserly but spendthrift and sacrificial. In brief, it was under the pressure of burning Irish issues such as Parnell's legacy, the controversy triggered by Synge's *Playboy of the Western World* and the scandal surrounding Lane's bequest, that Yeats was pushed forward to the idea of the modern.

Meanwhile, it was in London that Pound was making a major discovery, that of China. Ernest Fenollosa, who had spent most of his career

21   Stanley Cavell, *Must We Mean What We Say? A Book of Essays* (Cambridge: Cambridge University Press, 2002), xxxiii.

teaching philosophy in Japan, died suddenly in London in 1908. He left unpublished notes that his widow Mary wanted to edit. She began the task with her late husband's *Epochs of Chinese and Japanese Art*, published in 1912. By then, she had no money left and was exhausted. Mary Fenollosa contacted Ezra Pound in whom she recognised an emerging leader of poetic modernism with an interest in the East, and asked him to edit her late husband's remaining manuscripts in September 1913. Pound accepted, and was given the mass of notebooks and manuscripts. There were notes on the Japanese language, translations from various poems and Noh plays. Pound had expressed some interest in Chinese poetry earlier, but the gift propelled modernism into uncharted seas.

Fenollosa's posthumous notes had the effect of pushing Imagism beyond itself, making an Eastern literature suddenly accessible to enthusiastic non-specialists. Pound's relative incompetence caused many blunders (for instance, he never realised that Li Po and Rihaku Po referred to the same poet, one name being in Chinese, the other in Japanese transliteration) but these very limitations prevented him from falling into the staid orientalism of British Museum sinologists. Pound wrote excitedly to William Carlos Williams in December 1913: 'Dorothy is learning Chinese. I've an old Fenollosa treasure in mss.'[22] The consequences of the unexpected gift of the Asian 'treasure' were momentous. Pound spent the winter of 1913–14, from November to January, with Yeats in a cottage near Coleman's Hatch on the outskirts of Ashdown Forest. Pound acted as a secretary, taking dictation, classifying correspondence, reading aloud to the Irish poet at night. They shared stories, discussed translations, examined drafts of poems, and also started sorting out Fenollosa's notes. Pound sent his version of Nishikigi to *Poetry* at the end of January 1914, using Fenollosa's rough crib. He later published '*Noh*' *or Accomplishment*, which contains Fenollosa's essays on Noh, along with a selection of canonical Noh plays translated from his papers while Yeats wrote the introduction to the book.

Pound also worked on Fenollosa's translations of Chinese poems accompanied by Japanese glosses. *Cathay* (1915) was the result of these

---

22   Ezra Pound, *Selected Letters 1907–1941*, ed. D. D. Paige (New York: New Directions, 1971), 27.

several collaborations and these poems reinvented Chinese poetry, as Eliot was to say. 'The River-Merchant's Wife', 'The Jewel Stairs' Grievance' and 'Exile's letters' are masterpieces of creative translation. Even his earlier 'In a Station of the Metro' was construed as being a Japanese haiku or hokku. Finally, Pound tackled Fenollosa's notes on the Chinese ideogram ('The Chinese Written Character as a Medium for Poetry'), in which he saw the foundation of new poetics. Yeats could also find his own in these notes. This is the argument of a Noh play, *Nishikigi*, as presented by Fenollosa: 'Among the most weird and delicately poetic pieces is Nishikigi, in which the hero and heroine are the ghosts of two lovers who died unmarried a hundred years before.'[23] The haunted and magical world of Noh could be easily assimilated to the Irish folklore explored by Yeats. While Noh is an elite art devised for the aristocracy, its themes are pastoral and its characters priests, fairies, ghosts and peasants.

If Pound took the initiative with China and Japan, it was Yeats who was responsible for the discovery of Tagore. When the Nobel Prize for literature was handed to Rabindranath Tagore in 1913, he appeared above all as a poet, playwright, educator and religious leader whose work had a strong impact on Yeats. Yeats was credited with the glory granted to Tagore in a gesture that seemed to pre-announce his own Nobel Prize. Tagore was the author of *Gitanjali: Song Offerings* (translated into English in 1912). *Gitanjali* soon went through a dozen printings in London just after its publication. In his telegram of acceptance, Tagore thanked the Nobel committee for having 'brought the distant near, and made a stranger a brother'. Such optimism may seem unfounded just one year before the outbreak of a world war, but it is consistent with Tagore's friendship with Gandhi. Both of them looked beyond the ugly European military confrontation to a post-colonial stage. Tagore had been visiting London in the spring of 1912, and had been launched and feted by Yeats. Yeats said at a banquet in July: 'To take part in honouring Mr Rabindranath Tagore is one of the great events of my artistic life. I have been carrying about me a book of translation into English prose of a hundred of his Bengali lyrics written within the last ten

---

23   'Noh' or Accomplishment, in Ezra Pound, *Poems and Translations*, ed. Richard Sieburth (New York: Library of America, 2003), 402.

years; I know of no one in my time who has done anything in the English language to equal these lyrics.'[24]

The translations were prose translations, and Pound, who had heard Tagore sing the poems to a musical accompaniment, knew how different they sounded in the original. The prose paraphrase kept little of this melodic charm. A typical section from *Gitanjali* illustrates well the neo-Whitmanian unanimism of Tagore's songs: 'The same stream of life that runs through my veins night and day runs through the world and dances in rhythmic measures. / It is the same life that shoots in joy through the dust of the earth in numberless blades of grass and breaks into tumultuous waves of leaves and flowers. / It is the same life that is rocked in the ocean-cradle of birth and of death, in ebb and flow. / I feel my limbs made glorious by the touch of this world of life. And my pride is from the life-throb of ages dancing in my blood this moment.' Pound initially shared Yeats's infatuation with the Bengali poet, and wrote two pages of introduction to the six poems by Tagore published in the December 1912 issue of *Poetry*. There, he asserted that he felt that 'world-fellowship' had become 'nearer' because of this visit, and he stressed the refinement of the poet, who, he said, made him feel 'like a painted Pict with a stone war club' by comparison.[25]

Meanwhile, Tagore took a trip to the United States in November 1912. He first visited Urbana, Champaign, where his son was doing agronomical research. He wrote to Pound from there, complaining of his solitude. Pound narrates an anecdote about Tagore in January 1913: someone has asked how Tagore could be taken as a Bengali patriot, when he had written an ode to the King. A student of Tagore explained that his master had tried to write a nationalist poem, that he had failed and then given a poem previously written and said: 'It's addressed to the deity. But you may give it to the national committee. Perhaps it will content them.'[26] Witty as this is,

24   Quoted in Probhat Kumar Mukherji, *Life of Tagore* (New Delhi: Indian Book Company, 1975), 111.

25   Humphrey Carpenter, *A Serious Character: The Life of Ezra Pound* (London: Faber & Faber, 1988), 186.

26   Pound, *Selected Letters 1907–1941*, 14.

it is the aspect with which Pound grew disenchanted, and he would often make fun of the hazy syncretism of Tagore, which as Foster notes, anticipated the later craze for Khalil Gibran's vague spiritualism. 'As a religious preacher [Tagore] is superfluous', Pound wrote to Harriet Monroe. He added: 'We've got Lao Tse. And his [Tagore's] philosophy hasn't much in it for a man who has "felt the pangs" or been pestered with Western civilization. I don't mean quite that, but he isn't either Villon or Leopardi, and the modern demands just a dash of their insight.'[27] This remained the view taken by Pound afterwards: Tagore was good, but only if one considered him as a foreign lyrical voice, a contemporary Kabir. Above all, he should never be taken seriously as a thinker, especially when he pretended to be a sage with a mission, disseminating a universal message of peace. This aspect of Tagore sounded very much like theosophy, which was one reason why Yeats had been drawn to it. But there was also the nationalist aspiration of Bengalis and Hindus striving to achieve independence from Britain, or at least some form of Home Rule. Even if Tagore, because of his religiosity and universalism, was not a staunch nationalist, Yeats projected on him his own resistance to English imperialism.

It was in Urbana that Tagore wrote 'Highest Price', a poem in which he imagines a hawker who cries out (this is the first line): 'Who will buy me, who will buy me, rid me of my cares?' The hawker's load gets heavier, and the king tries to 'buy it by force' but the hawker struggles and gets free. An old man in an alley buys some of it with gold. Then it is a beautiful young woman who buys some of the load with a smile. The last stanza offers a startling resolution:

> Along the sea-shore the sun shines, the sea breaks and rolls.
> A child is on the sandy beach: he sits playing with shells.
> He seems to know me: he says,
> 'I'll buy your cares
> for nothing.' Suddenly, I am released
> From my heavy load; his playful face has won me free of cost.[28]

27   Pound, *Selected Letters 1907–1941*, 19.
28   Rabindranath Tagore, *Selected Poems*, trans. William Radice (Harmondsworth: Penguin, 1993), 73.

This calls up Nietzsche's famous parable of the three metamorphoses in *Thus Spake Zarathustra*. The spirit is really free after having carried heavy loads, not by turning into a lion embodying negation but when it can become a child, the image of 'innocence and forgetfulness'.[29] Tagore meant to suggest that we do not only desire freedom but also hanker after servitude. Like Joyce's Stephen Dedalus, he is aware that it is in his mind that he has to free himself of the slavery imposed by priests and kings. The hawker is the poet who is tired of a freedom that he finds too difficult to bear, and he recovers it only when disinterested love and childish play merge; then the dual burden of the self and of the works is lifted. The poem was written one month before *Gitanjali* was published, at a time when the Nobel Prize looked like a wishful fantasy.

In January 1913, Tagore travelled to Chicago where he met Harriet Monroe and lectured on India and the problem of evil. He then went to Rochester, where he gave a lecture on 'Race conflict', a symptomatic theme that he thought relevant for an American audience. During this trip to America and when he was returning to London, his prose translation of *Gitanjali* (retouched by Yeats) along with two plays, *The King of the Dark Chamber* and *The Post Office* had been published. Their success in England and elsewhere was such that Tagore was short-listed by the Nobel committee, a success that was partly due to Yeats's vigorous campaign of promotion. Tagore returned to India in September 1913; he was in Calcutta when he heard that he had been awarded the Prize. Although celebrated by friends, he took the opportunity to settle old accounts in a speech he gave, infuriating many former partisans. By then, Tagore had begun distancing himself from Yeats, whose patronising attitude he politely bore but resented. Symptomatically, it was also in 1913 that Tagore sent a message of welcome to Gandhi who had begun preaching non-violent resistance of the Indian minority in South Africa.

Thus for Pound, the distinction granted to Tagore was just a further proof that he had lost any relevance. He judged everyone severely in 1917: 'Tagore got the Nobel Prize because, after the cleverest boom of our

---

29   Friedrich Nietzsche, *Thus Spake Zarathustra: A Book for Everyone and No One*, trans. R. J. Hollingdale (London: Penguin, [1909] 1961; 1969), 55.

day, after the fiat of the omnipotent literati of distinction, he lapsed into
religion and optimism and was boomed by the pious non-conformists.
Also because it got the Swedish academy out of the difficulty of deciding
between European writers whose claims appeared to conflict [sic]. Hardy
or Henry James?' He notes, however, with evident glee that this had been
a 'damn good smack' for the British Academic Committee led by Gosse
who had turned down Tagore 'on account of his biscuit complexion' and
elected two non-entities instead.[30] Like Yeats, Pound had read Tagore's religious rhapsodies as another variation on theosophic rhetoric, whereas the
Upanishads were a serious and essential part of his culture. Tagore belonged
to the reformist Hindu sect founded by Rammohun Roy, Brahmo Samaj.
It rejected ordinary Hinduism and embraced a 'deity' that was purposely
left vague and formless. This religion was an aesthetic at the same time,
in a fusion or confusion which prevented Tagore from calling himself a
modernist. As we have seen with Cavell, modernism is not necessarily
divorced from history, but rather questions the values associated with
history. Tagore steadily refused the accolade of modernist masters that
he felt somewhat condescending. In several essays of the 1920s and 1930s,
Tagore criticised Eliot, Pound and their followers for being too alienated,
despairing and nihilistic. In his vision, the poet was to become the god of
his universe, thus feeling ethically responsible for all other creatures. Indeed,
he embodied the Romantic ideal of the poet as priest and prophet with
a vengeance. Culturally it blended an older Romanticism and typically
modernist features: the age of the masses had come, a new beauty marked
by technology displaced the older ideals.

Yeats saw in 1913 the combination of violent energies coming both
from the side of the 'people' and of the intelligentsia – dashing to the ground
the hopes of a peaceful Home Rule that looked realistic despite staunch
opposition in Ulster. If one can indeed say that 1913 marks the beginning
of the Irish Revolution, a revolution that took a whole decade, from 1913
to 1923, then it is also fair to say that the advent of the First World War
forestalled a civil war in Ireland – a revolution which kept a socialist aspect,
pitting the workers against the capitalists.

30   Pound, Selected Letters 1907 1941, 106.

Thus the Irish ended up following the general European pattern and even, as we have seen, heralding a pattern that became general only after the Second World War, namely decolonisation with all its painful wars from India to Indochina, from Algeria to many countries in Africa. But in 1913, the link between the past and history still bore the name of Romanticism, already itself a reaction formation against the Enlightenment. It was the old European Romanticism that was to find a specific outlet in the Great War, and there was no dearth of Romanticism in Ireland. What seems to have struck most historians is the sudden spreading of bellicose enthusiasm that took by storm advanced countries like France, England, Italy and Germany in the summer of 1914. Sophisticated, cosmopolitan and internationalist artists and writers such as Cendrars, Gaudier and Apollinaire expressed the same wish to go crush the enemy at once, while all three could have avoided the draft, for reasons of nationality (Cendrars and Apollinaire only received French nationality after they had enlisted) or distance (Gaudier was living in London and could have avoided being drafted because of his family situation). Thus Romanticism was not dead yet, but also, more tellingly, modernism itself contributed to the general unleashing of passionate aggression (at least, that would be Tagore's view).

European-centred modernism should be seen in the larger picture of a world caught in the throes of early globalisation. The American public remained at some distance from the European conflagration, split between republican interventionism and Wilson's reluctance to join the war. Yet, it was informed of the crisis that was brewing in Europe. The newspapers reported the race in naval building and new armaments between Britain, Germany and France. In May, Winston Churchill offered a one-year truce only to be rebuked when the Kaiser announced plans to build an even stronger armada. Some sought reassurance in the belief that socialist leaders such as Jaures in France and Liebknecht in Germany would oppose the war and call for a general strike. The outcome of the Dublin lockout could have made them more cautious. Meanwhile in August 1914, Tom Kettle, a onetime friend of James Joyce, was in Ostend buying guns for the Irish volunteers. His being in Belgium forced him to see first-hand the ravages of war and German atrocities in Mechelen. He finally enlisted and was killed in action with the British army in 1916. He had hoped that the Irish solidarity would lead the British to grant independence to Ireland after the war.

The causes of the war were explained in an article published in January 1913 by the *Atlantic Monthly*. It was penned by the Italian journalist and prolific cultural critic Guglielmo Ferrero, whom Joyce had read closely when in Rome and Trieste. In 'The Dangers of War in Europe', written while the Tripoli campaign was still under way, Ferrero contrasted the optimism of the nineteenth century, marked by struggles against absolutism and the rise of liberalism, to the first decade of the twentieth century, which saw the rise of nationalism. Ferrero's thesis came close enough to that of Fullerton although he paid little attention to the economic factor. For Ferrero, it was the triumph of post-1848 liberalism that led directly to the current bellicose situation. Democracy had come too quickly or not at all, thus preventing public opinion from maturing. This, coupled with the increased power of the press, had unleashed a sentimental and Romantic nationalism that infected populations much more than their rulers. Italy's war against the Turkish Empire in Libya had been launched by popular assent defended by a massive press campaign, while the King had remained reluctant. Similarly, in Germany it was Kaiser Wilhelm II who had saved international peace during the 1905 Moroccan crisis with France, and this he did against German public opinion. In the new century, masses appeared more conservative, more entranced by tradition, more easily swayed by nationalistic frenzy, whereas political rulers tended to be realistic and cautious. Such a view would have been shared by Yeats, whose snobbism and class prejudice never dulled a finely tuned perception of Irish political antagonisms.

Ideals inherited from the Enlightenment were shared by educated groups only, and these tended to lose touch with the excitable majority. Thus Ferrero foresaw the rise of fascism after the war, a fascism which, as we know, deeply attracted both Pound and Yeats. Bellicism seemed to derive from an ineradicable populist Romanticism, and the combination was powerful enough to blind people to the pain inflicted by war. Ferrero's main example was the Abyssinian War covered by the Italian press: magnified as an epic legend, it became a lurid romance full of patriotic fervour. What was never mentioned were the dire realities of mass slaughter, of civilians' extermination and general devastation. In this view, war would be the consequence of the paradoxical conflation of a modern evolution towards democracy in a period of industrial revolution and scientific progress, and the spectral resurgence of an ancient heroic Romanticism, a compromise between the fruits of the French Revolution and the return of nationalist myths. Democracy had not succeeded in educating the masses or raising their political consciousness. The huge reshuffling of Europe begun by Napoleon had been completed in 1913, and its outcome looked terrifying. This diagnosis helps us understand the plight of the modernists: they could not revert to the old rationalism debunked by Nietzsche, Bergson, and the Marxists, and they could not believe wholeheartedly in the Romantic myths of blood, the earth and the land.

Thus the clash of 1914 managed to stifle the progressive tendencies that had erupted in the previous year. One can verify this in Walter Heape's hugely popular *Sex Antagonism*, which begins by analysing what he calls a 'sexual discontent' permeating liberal societies. Anticipating Freud's *Civilization and Its Discontents*, Heape listed three main sources of unrest and places of antagonism in civilisation: class, sex and race. Heape sketched the organisation of three levels of struggles, passing rapidly on racial conflicts, while seeing class antagonism as a positive feature. He added pointedly: 'this is a class war that we are experiencing',[31] and he saw no immediate end to this phenomenon. By contrast with the first two, 'sex antagonism' was a more recent phenomenon, although Heape demonstrated that it had always existed by deploying the genealogy of exogamy and totemism. Heape asserted the pre-eminence of biology over history (he deemed women inferior because of a different sexual constitution) but his work remains important in the context of 1913. Moreover, his research was rigorously parallel to the work of early sexologists such as Eugen Steinach – who famously transformed male guinea pigs into female guinea pigs and also, somewhat later, performed the operation that was instrumental in rejuvenating Yeats: the vasectomy called the 'Steinach operation' performed in 1934 brought renewed vigour to Yeats who experienced rebirth at the blessed age of sixty-nine.

Heape's highlighting of the trinity of race, class and gender as the three main domains of social struggle should remind us that the outbreak of the Great War in 1914 temporarily put an end to these unresolved quarrels. Actual war silenced or suppressed them, until they came back in the 1920s –

31   Walter Heape, *Sex Antagonism* (New York: Putnam's Sons, 1913), 2.

this time, women gained the right to vote in most advanced countries, even if there was a lot to be desired on the fronts of race and class. In 1913, however, class war seemed incompatible with nationalistic war, and this was clearly felt in Ireland. This proved to be a decisive factor in the policy of the German intelligence services facing Stalin, Trotsky and Lenin; they helped these revolutionaries, allowing them to go back to Russia so as to preach class warfare, bring about a revolution and prevent the tsarist regime from waging war on the Eastern front.

It would be an unfair exaggeration to say that most modernists were bellicists: Pound, Broch, Joyce, D. H. Lawrence and others voiced their rejection of militarism, their suspicion of the 'red herring' of nationalism, as Pound said. Pound was immediately struck by the enormity of the loss when friends like T. E. Hulme and Gaudier-Brzeska were killed. Those who resisted the drift to war usually did so because their internationalist ethos led to a double critique of Romanticism and modernity. But the war also forestalled something.

On the whole, one might say that the writers I have focused on define a moment of hesitation facing modernism: Tagore is praised for qualities that are more generic than specific to his writing, whereas Yeats and Pound are two unlikely revolutionaries, with their irrepressible admiration for enlightened princes and their cult of stately order. Yet, taken together, they define a moment of early modernism that shows that the achievements of 1912–13 had merely been delayed by the war. They were modernist not because of an elitism that would force them to be above the fray, or because of their lack of political commitment. On the contrary, they evinced that subtle combination of cultural elitism that aims at educating an entire generation, and a concern for the evolution of a whole culture, whether it be that of Ireland, India or the United States. All three see the need to open their cultures to otherness, in different directions of course – Tagore's religious syncretism, Yeats's fusion of pre-Christian ritual, occultism and lyrical self-regeneration, Pound discovering China allied with the rituals of ancient Greece. In typically modernist fashion, all three insisted on the autonomy of art, but this never meant that they saw art as divorced from ethics, politics and national issues. Early and late modernism shared a concern for the health of language and therefore the welfare of society at large.

5   'To Sleep is Safe, To Dream is Dangerous': Catholicism on Stage in Independent Ireland[1]

Because we cannot go back, we are forced to go on. The counter-revolution is forced upon us because the spiritual and moral are real. They insist upon being in spite of all denials whether implicit or explicit.[2]

For most of the twentieth century the accumulation of religious capital was central to the creation and maintenance of an Irish Catholic social elite that permeated the fields of commerce, government, the civil service, the professions and the semi-state sector. The history of this linkage and how it operated has yet to be written.[3]

In March 2003, Gerard Mannix Flynn presented *James X*, an account of a childhood and adolescence stolen by Church and State, at the Project Arts Centre in Dublin.[4] *James X* is a solo performance, set in the ante room of a state tribunal inquiring into the abuse of young people in church-run state institutions. At the play's end, James X makes the decision not to participate in the tribunal, and explicitly confronts Inglis's 'Irish Catholic social elite':

1   Paul Vincent Carroll, *Shadow and Substance*, in George Cusack (ed.), *Selected Plays of Paul Vincent Carroll* (Gerrard's Cross: Colin Smythe, 2014), 130.

2   Desmond FitzGerald, cited in John M. Regan [1932], *The Irish Counter-Revolution 1921–1936* (Dublin: Gill & Macmillan, 2001), vi.

3   Tom Inglis, 'The Religious Field in Contemporary Ireland: Identity, Being Religious and Symbolic Domination', in Liam Harte and Yvonne Whelan, *Ireland Beyond Boundaries: Mapping Irish Studies in the Twenty-first Century* (London, Dublin, Ann Arbor, 2007), 119.

4   <http://www.irishplayography.com> records an earlier version presented at the Temple Bar Music Centre in 2002.

Holding up the [official] file about his past, he describes it as the property of 'the state, the church, their servants and agents, and you the citizens'. He flings it to the ground and walks out amongst the audience.[5]

In this gestural sequence, Flynn encapsulates the principal contribution of dramatic art to public understanding of Irish experiences: it takes statements ('This file contains the story of my life.') and turns them into questions ('Who says this file contains the story of my life, and in whose interests is that statement made?'). *James X* is a moment in which the victim repositions himself as a target, exposes the deliberate quality of the actions of those who violated him, and inaugurates a moral imperative for Irish people to excavate the motivation for those actions. Flynn's work marks a specific cultural moment, the emergence into public space of persons devastated by a theocratic compact entered into during the Irish counter-revolution.[6] This unholy alliance was forged between a church in the grip of a fantasy of manifest destiny, and an emergent political elite of 'men who freed their nation, but who could never free their souls from the ill-effects of having been in slavery'.[7] As a result of this arrangement, for most of the twentieth century, 'in order to gain access to proper housing, a decent education, a good job or membership of a social club',[8] a citizen of Independent Ireland had to perform unquestioning fealty to the Catholic Church. By vesting schools, hospitals, sporting and leisure facilities in the hands of the Catholic Church, the State gifted to that church extraordinary power over people's intimate lives. *James X* stages 'the tribulations that beset a child's passage through a country that is portrayed as grim, authoritarian and deeply prejudiced against him and his kind'.[9]

Ongoing revelations of the scale of sustained and violent theft of the dignity of vulnerable people suggest that the field exposed by Inglis is in

---

5   Patrick Lonergan, *Theatre and Globalization: Irish Drama in the Celtic Tiger Era* (Basingstoke: Palgrave Macmillan, 2009), 167.

6   See Regan, *Irish Counter-Revolution*.

7   M. J. Molloy, 'Preface to *The Wood of the Whispering*', ed. Robert O'Driscoll, *Selected Plays of M. J. Molloy* (Gerrard's Cross: Colin Smythe, 1998), 111.

8   Inglis, 'The Religious Field', 133.

9   Bruce Arnold, cited on <http://www.abbeytheatre.ie/whats_on/event/1187>,

urgent need, not only of mapping, but of excavation. Where Ireland's social historians have been reluctant to tread, however, its dramatic artists have long been busy. In 1906, Bernard Shaw commented acidly on an immanent tendency in anti-colonial Catholic nationalism toward theocratic domination of the majority population, post-independence: 'The British Government and the Vatican may differ very vehemently as to whose subject the Irishman is to be; but they are quite agreed as to the propriety of his being a subject.'[10] The notorious riots which greeted the original production of J. M. Synge's *The Playboy of the Western World* (Abbey Theatre, 1907) were seen as a response to the play's perceived blasphemous slurs on the unique modesty of Irish Catholic womanhood. To that extent, in the ferment of the theatre auditorium, the outraged audience acts as a surrogate for a prudish church, and plays out the cultural logic of the power relations described by Shaw. More generally, the *Playboy* riots offer a telling performative example of what would deteriorate during the first half-century of independence into a social order in which critique and progress are silenced by reactionary voices which 'continually shout down others'.[11] The calcified and fearful environment thus generated guaranteed a society in which J. J. Lee remarked, there was little or no market for ideas. In such an environment, what Inglis identifies as a paucity of historiographical interest in the interpenetration of economic, religious and political elites in Independent Ireland comes as no surprise. Silence is not neutrality, however, as Peadar Kirby observes: 'far too much academic output in Ireland is functional to the persistence of a highly inequitable society and to the requirements of the elites who benefit from it'.[12] Benefitting from a public culture of silence, and despite the critical dramas of Shaw, Synge and others, the reactionary Church／ State arrangement had remarkable success in domesticating its claims and

10　G. B. Shaw, 'Preface for Politicians', in Shaw, *John Bull's Other Island* (London and New York: Penguin, 1984), 19.

11　Luke Gibbons, 'Narratives of the Nation: Fact, Fiction and Irish Cinema', in *Theorizing Ireland*, ed. Claire Connolly (Basingstoke: Palgrave Macmillan, 2002), 75.

12　Peadar Kirby, *The Celtic Tiger in Distress: Growth with Inequality in Ireland* (Basingstoke: Palgrave, 2002), 204.

practices as an unquestionable status quo, post-independence.[13] The bitter
continuity between Synge's and Shaw's prophetic insights and Flynn's historical witness foregrounds two important features of Irish experience in
the twentieth century: by substituting control by a nexus of Church, State
and commerce for colonial domination, Independent Ireland postponed
decolonisation; dramatic representations of Irish reality, both prophetic
and testimonial, offer Ireland a resource for critical self-understanding
which is ignored only at great cost.

The dramatic world of *The Playboy of the Western World* is set in the
storied West of Ireland among a peasantry posited by nationalist myth-
making as 'native subject(s) locked in a prehistoric and hence apolitical
past'.[14] The play stages a paradox: the social order is rigorously structured
around Catholic religious capital, and the people adhere to cultural practices which Catholicism is radically unable to control. This paradox is
inscribed in the figure of Father Reilly, whose influence is ubiquitous, but
who never appears on stage. His creature is Shawn Keogh, who is to marry
the vigorous Pegeen Mike, only child of Michael James O'Flaherty, in
whose shebeen the dramatic action takes place. Shawn's nemesis is Christy
Mahon, a young stranger who purports to have killed his own father. The
gulf between the kind of respectability emerging in the nascent Church/
State compact, embodied in the unequal relationship of Shawn and Father
Reilly, and the everyday proclivities of Michael James and his cronies is
evident from the beginning of the play. The men are eager to be off to
Kate Cassidy's wake, and have been delayed because of Pegeen's refusal
to be left alone. Paralysed by the prospect of scandal, Shawn Keogh will
not remain unsupervised in the house with his intended before they are
married. Christy stumbles in to look for shelter, and unmasks himself as
a passionate, fearsome, patricide. At Pegeen's prompting, he is offered a
position as pot-boy to the shebeen, and settles in for the night. This solution enables Michael James to travel to the wake:

13   As one senior clergyman in the now notorious diocese of Ferns put it, over thirty
      years ago, 'There are three institutions in Ireland that will never fail: the Church,
      the GAA and the Fianna Fáil party; because they're all run by the same people.'
14   Chris Tiffin and Alan Lawson (eds), *De-scribing Empire: Post-colonialism and
      Textuality* (London and New York: Routledge, 1994), 233.

MICHAEL: Well, God bless you Christy, and a good rest till we meet again when
               the sun'll be rising to the noon of the day.
CHRISTY: God bless you all.
MEN: God bless you. [They go out except Shawn who lingers at door]
SHAWN: [*To Pegeen*] Are you wanting me to stop along with you and keep
               you from harm?
PEGEEN: [*gruffly*] Didn't you say you were fearing Father Reilly?
SHAWN: There's be no harm staying now, I'm thinking, and himself in it too.
PEGEEN: You wouldn't stay when there was need for you, and let you step off
               nimble this time when there's none.
SHAWN: Didn't I say it was Father Reilly ...
PEGEEN: Go on then to Father Reilly [*in a jeering tone*], and let him put you
               in the holy brotherhoods and leave that lad to me.[15]

Shawn's craven pursuit of clerical approval over the pleasures of the wake
or Pegeen's company specifically locates him as an internal outsider in
this economy of revelry and desire. Despite their ostentatious usage of
the language of benediction, the wake to which the men are going is a
site of pagan excess, involving the ingestion of inordinate amounts of
alcohol:

MICHAEL: ... wasn't it a shame I didn't bear you along to Kate Cassidy's wake,
               a fine, stout lad, the like of you, for you'd never see the match of it
               for flows of drink, the way when we sunk her bones at noonday in
               her narrow grave, there were five men, aye, and six men, stretched
               out retching speechless on the holy stones.[16]

Even more transgressively, Act III stages what amounts to the pagan
wedding of Christy and Pegeen, at which her father, Michael James
O'Flaherty, officiates:

PEGEEN: Bless us now, for I swear to God I'll wed him, and I'll not renege.
MICHAEL: [*standing up in the centre, holding on to both of them*] It's the will of
               God, I'm thinking, that all should win an easy or a cruel end, and
               it's the will of God that all should rear up lengthy families for the

15   Ann Saddlemyer (ed.), *J. M. Synge, The Playboy of the Western World and Other Plays*
     (Oxford: Oxford University Press, 1995), 107–8.
16   Synge, *Playboy*, 138.

nurture of the earth. What's a single man, I ask you, eating a bit in one house and drinking a sup in another, and he with no place of his own, like an old braying jackass strayed upon the rocks? [*To Christy*] It's many would be in dread to bring your like into their house for an end to them maybe with a sudden end; but I'm a decent man of Ireland, and I'd liefer face the grave untimely and I seeing a score of grandsons growing up gallant little swearers by the name of God, than go peopling my bedside with puny weeds the like of what you'd breed, I'm thinking, out of Shawneen Keogh. [*He joins their hands*] A daring fellow is the jewel of the world, and a man did split his father's middle with a single clout should have the bravery of ten, so may God and St Mary and St Patrick bless you, and increase you from this mortal day.

CHRISTY and
PEGEEN: Amen, O Lord![17]

The stage directions which organise Michael James's gestures here position him unambiguously in a sacerdotal capacity. Marriage may be blessed by God, the mother of Christ and the patron saint, but it is profoundly a matter of the body, its temporal and economic contingency and corporeal needs. These three episodes put in question Inglis's characterisation of vernacular practices as vestiges of a 'type of magical-devotional oriented religion associated with traditional forms of Catholicism'.[18] The 'traditional forms' staged here predate formal religious prescriptions and attract popular allegiance on the basis of appeal to a sensual life. In this way, Synge's dramaturgy resonates with Yeats's idea that people turn to the drama in search of 'a fuller, more opulent life'. The fictional world stages a tense standoff between the codifications of the institutional Church, Irish people's spiritual and corporeal needs, and the rituals and practices by means of which those needs are expressed. In the description of Kate Cassidy's interment, the sacred – 'holy stones' – is wholly compatible with excess of the flesh; indeed, the presence of the sacred is signified by ritual drunkenness. In a clear repudiation of the Jansenist tone of the Irish Church, God's blessings and God's will are evoked to dignify manifestations of specifically carnal

17   Synge, *Playboy*, 140.
18   Inglis, 'The Religious Field', 111.

practices – the funeral bacchanal, and the coupling of male and female. The offspring of the most ostentatiously devotional person in the community will be 'puny weeds', and those issuing from the patricide will be 'gallant little swearers by the name of God'. Among these embedded cultural contradictions, Shawn Keogh is Shaw's pusillanimous Catholic incarnate.[19] Nonetheless, he reads the coming times astutely, and by the play's end, will possess Pegeen by default.

As the twentieth century progresses this 'type of magical-devotional oriented religion'[20] retains, in the theatre at least, a potent charge. Synge's social and spiritual standoff re-emerges in the dramatic action of the iconic play of the early 1990s, Brian Friel's *Dancing at Lughnasa* (Abbey Theatre, 1990). The play was an instant success in Ireland, where it seemed perfectly in tune with President Mary Robinson's invitation, 'Come dance with me in Ireland.' It toured internationally, extensively and at length, and received many accolades, including a Tony Award for director, Patrick Mason. *Dancing at Lughnasa* dramatises women's experiences as a function of remembrances formed when Christina's son, Michael, the play's narrator, was seven years of age. In production, however, its elegiac tone – and remarkable dance sequence – tends to blur the contours of the ideological warfare under way in the actual world out of which the dramatic action emerges. Popular reception of the dance sequence at the play's core, which has tended to misrecognise it as a celebration, exemplifies the problem:

> Audiences usually perceive this dance ... in wholly positive terms as a liberating outburst of repressed energy that expresses the pent-up protests of the sisters against De Valera's Ireland ... The dance is a sensual frenzy, then, but its rapture is not a wholly positive one: there are suggestions of a disfiguring surrender to cruelty and pain as well.[21]

---

19   'The Catholic is theoretically a Collectivist, a self-abnegator, a Tory, a Conservative, a supporter of Church and State one and indivisible, an obeyer.' Shaw, 'Preface for Politicians', 18.

20   Inglis, 'The Religious Field', 111.

21   Joe Cleary, 'Modernization and Aesthetic Ideology in Contemporary Irish Culture', in *Writing in the Irish Republic: Literature, Culture, Politics 1949–1999*, ed. Ray Ryan (Basingstoke: Macmillan, 2000), 124–5.

The dance is a frenzied 'Yes!' to life desired: a physicalisation of the terrifying recognition that postponement of desire has institutionalised conditions in which it will never be fulfilled. This crucial misreading disables the critical charge of the play's pivotal moment, and is compounded in Frank McGuinness's screenplay,[22] which moves this most private frenzy out of doors, framing it as an affirmation of sisterhood rather than a cry of pain. This is not the only instance in which the screenplay alters the dramatic narrative significantly. In another case, however, McGuinness interpolates a scene which overcomes the play's tendency to place the audience at a distance from the social context in which the intimate narrative is embedded. The camera is taken into the outhouse where Christina's occasional lover, Gerry Evans – Michael's father – is obliged by the matriarchal Kate to spend the night. Christina goes to the outhouse to join him, and the 'poor lovers' are overlooked by a photograph of massed and marshalled throngs of Irish people assembled in the Phoenix Park in Dublin in obeisance to Rome, on the occasion of the Eucharistic Congress in 1932, four years before the remembered action of the play occurs: 'All Ireland', as Austin Clarke put it, 'keeping company with them'.[23] There is a terrible pathos in that moment, as it dramatises the awful difficulty of living an ordinary life in the gap between Catholic Ireland's 'grim, authoritarian and deeply prejudiced'[24] corporate mind, and the embodied desires of lived experienced. And yet, the episode has the power to reveal not domination, but contestation and contradiction. The controlling gaze of the Church Triumphant penetrates through to the outbuildings of a frugal homestead, to disrupt moments of human intimacy. The memento of the triumphalist ceremony hangs, however, not in the parlour or the hallway, but in a debased apartment at one remove from family life. The pomp and circumstance of a rampant clerical aristocracy is thus ironically juxtaposed with the stable at Bethlehem, mapping Chris and Gerry's unorthodox arrangements on to the 'basic unit' of Irish state ideology – the (holy) family. Thirty years on from Christy and

---

22   Pat O'Connor, *Dancing At Lughnasa* (Ferndale Films, 1998).

23   Austin Clarke, 'The Envy of Poor Lovers', *Irish Poetry After Yeats*, ed. Maurice Harmon (Dublin: Wolfhound Press, 1979), 39.

24   Arnold, <https://www.abbeytheatre.ie>.

Pegeen's pagan wedding, the lovers' recalcitrance to Catholic orthodoxy yields, not benediction and the promise of human continuity, but stigma and internal exile. However, this image, and all reservations notwithstanding, Friel's drama makes clear that their story will join the list of 'silenced voices [which] inevitably emerge'.[25]

The year is 1936, and, in Dublin, De Valera's draughtsmen are moving to and fro between state buildings and Archbishop's House in Drumcondra, the better to align the document that will become *Bunreacht na h-Éireann/The Irish Constitution* (1937) with Archbishop McQuaid's version of Catholic social doctrine. Apart from Christina and Michael, the Mundy household shelters the unorthodox figure of Father Jack, ailing brother of the five sisters. He has returned from missionary work in Uganda, and it gradually emerges that he pursued, and still clings to a preference for African animist spirituality over corporate Vatican discipline. His presence in the household places the family increasingly beyond the pale inscribed by Church, State and Commerce, exemplified in the ideal family of the prosperous and pious Austin Morgan, once a suitor to Kate. The price of perceived recalcitrance plays out in Kate's expulsion from her post in the local, Catholic-controlled state primary school, and the loss of her modest income brings about the destruction of the extended family unit. The women's gradual degradation is not staged, but is sublimated in the lyricism of the closing monologue, in which the deliberate cruelty of their fates disappears in the warm glow of their remembered pre-lapsarian presence around which the adult Michael's nostalgia is woven. For Cleary, the problematic relationship between historical reality and theatrical representation to which *Dancing at Lughnasa* points speaks of a society 'with neither the imaginative resources nor the strategies required to meet the challenges of the future'.[26] There is indeed a risk with so compelling an artefact that it becomes, as it were, the exemplary script by which popular memory narrates 1936–37. To the extent that it diverts the gaze from

25   Edward Said, 'Afterword: Reflections on Ireland and Postcolonialism', in Clare Carroll and Patricia King (eds), *Ireland and Postcolonial Theory* (Cork: Cork University Press, 2003), 182.
26   Cleary, 'Modernization and Aesthetic Ideology', 126–7.

the social reality of that time, it re-mystifies history as simple quaintness, and generates, not anger at the betrayal of generations of Irish people by a Church/State compact, but nostalgic mourning for an innocence – if not a paradise – lost.

One year after *Dancing at Lughnasa* opened at the Abbey, Druid Theatre Company staged *Shadow and Substance*, by Paul Vincent Carroll, which had premiered at the Abbey Theatre, on 6 May 1937. Carroll, 'the first major Catholic playwright of post-Treaty Ireland',[27] was a fierce critic of a philistine church's grip on the intimate lives of Irish people, and his plays were hugely popular in the 1930s. In *The Things That Are Caesar's* (1932):

> A father and mother fight for the soul of their daughter. The mother wants her to marry a wealthy local, a match which would bring money to renovate her pub and prestige to her family. The father has always instilled in his daughter a fierce sense of independence and distrust of religion and much of society's prevailing values. She is much more her father's daughter, but ultimately accepts that she must deal with the opportunities she has, not ones she would hope for.[28]

This drama stages a 1930s version of the vernacular resistance captured in the image of Christina and Gerry in McGuinness's outhouse, and contests clerical triumphalism in its defining moment: the Eucharistic Congress of 1932. Ultimately, Church power rested in its dual character as both 'a conduit for the supernatural and a source of religious capital'.[29] Its impact on public life in Independent Ireland was decisive, and intellectual life declined to such an extent that the president of University College Dublin banned a performance of *The Importance of Being Earnest* during the early 1930s.[30] The impact of the Censorship of Publications Act (1929) was so severe that W. B. Yeats, in 1928, 'left politics, disillusioned at the manner in which

---

27   Christopher Murray, *Twentieth-Century Irish Drama: Mirror up to Nation* (Manchester and New York: Manchester University Press, 1997), 129.

28   <https://www.irishplayography.com>

29   Inglis, 'The Religious Field', 125.

30   Diarmaid Ferriter, *The Transformation of Ireland 1900–2000* (London: Profile Books, 2004), 431.

a prohibition ethos was developing',[31] and 'formed the anti-censorship Irish Academy of Letters in 1932'.[32] Against this tidal wave of repression of critical consciousness, *Shadow and Substance* confronts the social and personal consequences of the dramatic upward revaluation of religious capital in Independent Ireland. The play also explores the problem posed for the Church's hegemony over the supernatural by the endurance of 'magical-devotional oriented religion'[33] in the central figure of Brigid, a poorly educated young woman in service to Canon Skerritt, the Parish Priest of Ardmahone. Brigid has visions of St Brigid, a local saint with strong pre-Christian associations, and her obsessive attachment to her patron at a time of local cultural ferment will cost her life, by the play's end.

The canon regards himself as a cultivated, scholarly gentleman, and a connoisseur of life's finer things: classical music, quality wines and Spanish culture. In all of these matters he is the polar opposite of his curates, Father Corr and Father Kirwan, who embody the kind of ostentatiously peasant[34] curate which will staff the Irish Church for the next half-century:

FATHER KIRWAN:	Is he an Irishman at all?
FATHER CORR:	His father was Irish. It's his mother was the Spaniard.[35] They met in Brussels.
FATHER KIRWAN:	It's a pity she didn't stay at home instead of gallivantin' about the Continent. Sure you'd think he hadn't a drop of Irish Ireland blood in his veins. I'll bet me boots he'll side with that book agin the Confraternity and the Football Club.[36]

In 1937, however, Spain was a figure which defined in Ireland a stark politico-religious cleavage. Spain's tragedy remains, in Carroll's play, as in *Dancing at Lughnasa*, at the level of shadow, while the substance of both plays – Brigid's

31   Ferriter, *Transformation of Ireland*, 343.
32   Ferriter, *Transformation of Ireland*, 343.
33   Inglis, 'The Religious Field', p. 111.
34   'FATHER CORR: (*rising with fire*) I'm a farmer's son, Canon, and I'm not ashamed of it.' Carroll, *Shadow and Substance*, 107.
35   It is worth noting the playful performative potential of the use of the epithet, 'the Spaniard', which was freely applied to Eamon De Valera.
36   Carroll, *Shadow and Substance*, 121.

turmoil and Michael's memories – remains relentlessly local. Skerritt is, after all, the parish priest of Ardmahone, which translates as 'Up my own backside.' In his office as parish priest, Skerritt is *de jure* manager of the local primary school, of which his nemesis, Dermot Francis O'Flingsley, is principal teacher. The immediate *casus belli* between them is the canon's disgraceful neglect of his responsibilities to maintain the school buildings in good order. O'Flingsley's explicit refusal to accept the degradation of children and teachers by an arrogant and undemocratic church lies at the heart of Murray's view that in Carroll's work, 'the early Joycean, Catholic *non serviam* is heard in the theatre for the first time'.[37]

CANON:	*You* have complaints, O'Flingsley? I did not think it was considered a – a suitable attitude in a teacher to have complaints.
O'FLINGSLEY:	You forget, Canon, that I am 'that man O'Flingsley' first, and your schoolmaster second.
CANON:	Very novel, and shall we use that hateful word, modern?
O'FLINGSLEY:	If it's something ancient, very ancient you want, here you are: No coal, no handle on sweeping-brush, no caretaker for the school, no windows that aren't stuck fast; eighteen crumbling desks, six broken panes of glass, no lighting on dark days, and the public highway of Saorstát Éireann for a playground. And these complaints render my attitude – unsuitable.
CANON:	… These alleged deficiencies are not complaints. They are officially termed 'Recommendations in Writing to the Very Reverend Manager.'
O'FLINGSLEY:	Or alternatively, 'Words Scrawled on the Sands by an Innocent.'[38]

The play's dramatic standoff is enhanced by the fact that, while he may be right on important matters, O'Flingsley is otherwise not particularly appealing. Like Skerritt, he affects a superior air, and is both arrogant and vain. These traits enable him, however, to oppose the monstrous clericalism of the Catholic Church, and he has published a polemic against its excesses, *I Am Sir Oracle*, under the pseudonym Eugene Gibney. As the play opens, the curates are busy inciting local worthies to burn copies of

37   Murray, *Twentieth-Century Irish Drama*, 9.
38   Carroll, *Shadow and Substance*, 141.

the book and to plan retributive action against the author, should he be identified. Corr and Kirwan are graceless individuals, whose attraction to modernity and its passing fancies – motor cars, for example – affronts Skerritt's veneration of the enduring monuments of European culture.[39] While for most of the play's action curates and people cower before Skerritt's merciless disapproval, the tragic denouement delivers to their militant, reactionary conservatism, the future. Following O'Flingsley's dismissal from his teaching post for authoring *I Am Sir Oracle*, the curates incite a mob to attack him at his home. Brigid, wandering ecstatically toward the shrine of St Brigid on the saint's feast day, is caught in the violence, struck by a brick, and mortally wounded. The play ends as O'Flingsley and Skerritt:

> draw the coverlet over Brigid's face. Their eyes meet fully for the first time, and hold each other over BRIGID's body. Then each moves slowly back in different directions.[40]

While the dramatic narrative – and Brigid's fate – centres on the playing out of O'Flingsley's well-founded antipathy toward the canon, the script indicates from the outset that, in moral terms he may be less Skerritt's opponent than his doppelganger:

BRIGID:	Yous hate one another. Sure I know, be now ...
O'FLINGSLEY:	I suppose we do.
BRIGID:	Isn't it funny now that I think there's no one like aythur of yous? Would that not mean that the two of yous are maybe the wan? Or am I blatherin'?
O'FLINGSLEY:	You certainly *are* blatherin', Brigid. If you love *him*, you hate *me*; and if you love *me*, you hate *him*.[41]

---

39 This places Skerritt as a neo-Thomist, and, in Regan's analysis, aligns him with a studied antipathy to modernity which exerted, via the writings of Maritian, 'an important influence over a limited but influential number of right-wing political Catholics in Ireland, as well as in France, Spain and Belgium between the wars'. Regan, *Irish Counter-Revolution*, 281.
40 Carroll, *Shadow and Substance*, 163.
41 Carroll, *Shadow and Substance*, 94.

Brigid's choice here is posited in absolute terms: hers is the duty of loyalty to male authority; the only decision to be made is to which version of paternalistic direction and control she will offer allegiance. O'Flingsley, a fictive surname with echoes of 'unflinching' about it, suggests the moral steel of the man, the only person in the hinterland who is the canon's intellectual match. His decision, as a citizen, to call Skerritt to account for his failings aligns O'Flingsley with a kind of protestant sensibility which was finding Independent Ireland to be a very cold house indeed:

> many of the instances of religious discrimination that have punctuated the history of post-independence Ireland, such as the appointment of a Protestant librarian in County Mayo in 1931 ... can be seen as attempts by the Irish Catholic Church to symbolically dominate Protestants.[42]

In the person of O'Flingsley, *Shadow and Substance* dramatises the reality that a great deal of energy went into curbing and coercing recalcitrant Catholic minds also. The antagonism to Protestantism was always also a way of establishing an absolute right to social domination *tout court*, and was as much about internal church discipline as it ever was about primacy in a theological contest. Skerritt explicitly condemns a request from a local deputation to meet with him to discuss *I Am Sir Oracle* as an invitation to 'agree to a – a descent into Lutheranism and a sort of a Kirk session'.[43] O'Flingsley's dismissal from his position, and his replacement by the pusillanimous laughing-stock that is Francis Ignatius O'Connor[44] suggests that Skerritt's immersion in European high culture is a gesture both elitist and cynical:

> O'FLINGSLEY: As a scholar who knows what he won't publicly admit, you loathe and detest the whole miserable fabric of things here. You detest that disgraceful apology of a school down there, even more than *I* do.

---

42 Inglis, 'The Religious Field', 127.
43 Carroll, *Shadow and Substance*, 122.
44 The stage direction for Francis's entrance in Act II reads: 'Francis is a sheepish, obsequious youth, his whole being in the grip of an inferiority complex. He is awkward and without confidence.' Carroll, *Shadow and Substance*, 115.

... Why then do you deliberately prepare to perpetuate it through that poor spineless imbecile there beside you?[45]

In terms of theatre history, his dismissal aligns O'Flingsley with Christy Mahon, usurped in a place he no longer wishes to remain, by a puny weed 'the like of what you'd breed, I'm thinking, out of Shawneen Keogh'.[46] O'Connor, who 'know(s) Lord Macaulay inside out',[47] seems perfectly aligned with the kind of social quietism encapsulated in Skerritt's admonition to Brigid, 'To sleep is safe, to dream is dangerous.'[48] He is lifted by clerical power into a position O'Flingsley has come to hold in contempt: 'an Irish schoolmaster ... a clerical handyman, a piece of furniture in a chapel house, a brusher-out of barn schools, a Canon's yesman'.[49] O'Flingsley, like Christy Mahon before him, will face 'hog, dog or divil on the highway of the road'.[50] He does so with some equanimity, however, as he realises his fall from security into uncertainty brings with it the restoration of a human dignity he had subordinated to protecting his position in the education system of the Catholic State:

> O'FLINGSLEY: I'll always owe you something for taking me by the scruff of the neck out of a mouse's hiding place and putting me back on the high road.[51]

The social world of Ardmahone is revealed as a rural Irish microcosm of a place produced by and for 'a new establishment of Church and state in which imagination would play no part and young men and women would emigrate to the ends of the earth not because the country was poor, but because it was mediocre'.[52] Synge's prophetic adumbration of a lifeless

45   Carroll, Shadow and Substance, 143.
46   Synge, Playboy, 140.
47   Carroll, Shadow and Substance, 136.
48   Carroll, Shadow and Substance, 130.
49   Carroll, Shadow and Substance, 143.
50   Synge, Playboy, 106.
51   Carroll, Shadow and Substance, 143–4.
52   Frank O'Connor, cited in Ferriter, Transformation of Ireland, 344.

people in a famished place, in *The Playboy of the Western World* is made flesh, thirty years later, in Ardmahone.

Postcolonial readings of cultural production in Independent Ireland frequently attempt to tease out narratives and images of consciousness resistant to the repressions of the successor state. O'Flingsley's story is a very clear example of such a narrative. Of his replacement by O'Connor, who is to marry Skerritt's preposterous niece, Thomasina, he remarks:

> O'FLINGSLEY: Hurrah for the Catholic ideal! A rebel knocked out; a niece mar-
> ried off; and a school made safe for a stagnant tradition all in one
> move! Canon, you deserve a seat in Maynooth.[53]

In the figure of Brigid, what is important is not what is absent, repressed or unwelcome, but that which endures and cannot be eradicated. Hers is a consciousness recalcitrant to either of the cultural formations at war over the soul of Ireland in the 1930s, either Skerritt's theocratic fantasy of pre-modern refinement, or O'Flingsley's democratic utopianism. Ultimately, her story is one which counterpoints their versions of 'modernity critically by representing, however weakly or even self-destructively, alternative ways of living'.[54] When Michael James O'Flaherty blesses the union of Pegeen and Christy Mahon, he does so in the names of God and St Mary and St Patrick. The Mother of Christ is given the archaic appellation, St Mary, and the national patron saint, Patrick, is included. Mary's presence alongside Patrick draws attention to the exclusion of St Brigid, co-opted to Catholic nationalism as the latter's female equivalent, and 'Mary of the Gael.' In *Shadow and Substance*, Brigid recognises in St Brigid a prototypical nun, and expresses her desire to enter a convent. This dismays Skerritt, and when, at the end of Act II, an agitated Brigid discloses that she is in daily conversation with St Brigid, he prescribes a rest cure:

> CANON: Rest to the body, Brigid, is like prayer to the soul. And you will then
> forget these imaginings of yours.

53   Carroll, *Shadow and Substance*, 142–3.
54   David Lloyd, *Irish Times: Temporalities of Modernity* (Dublin: Field Day, 2008), 3.

BRIGID:	But in bed, how can I forget, if her face is there in the curtains and the mark on her cheek where she struck the loveliness out of her face?
CANON:	Now, now, now! I am trying not to be angry. There is no historical authority for that at all. The Church in its wisdom does not confirm it. It is probably just a myth. A myth, Brigid ...
BRIGID:	What is a myth, Canon?
CANON:	A legend, child.
BRIGID:	And what is a – a legend, Canon?
CANON:	Brigid, this is very trying! An old tale, that may or may not be true.
BRIGID:	Then – it could be true, Canon?
CANON:	Now, which of us knows best about these things, Brigid?
BRIGID:	You, Canon.[55]

This dialogue turns on the tale of St Brigid's voluntary disfiguration in refusal of the world, and her many suitors, marriage to whom would have confined her within the limits set for her gender. When Brigid is fatally injured, O'Flingsley describes her wound as 'side of the head and upper part of the face'.[56] The centrality of the saint's story to the dramatic action is flagged in Carroll's epigraph to the published script:

SPECIAL NOTE
A legend connected with St Brigid relates how in order to escape the attentions of persistent suitors, she disfigured the loveliness of her face at Faughart, her birthplace, near Dundalk, Ireland.[57]

As an abbess, St Brigid is said to have been a formidable figure, the match for any male with authority in the Ireland of her time. As such, she is an exemplary figure of female capacity, at some remove from the docile nuns of the nineteenth and twentieth centuries. Both the imperative to control her, and her power to disturb, is evident in the dialogue cited. Skerritt dismisses St Brigid as insubstantial, but in order to do so, he must submit to Brigid's catechism, which raises the substance of shadows, and the politics around the right, not only to narrate but to interpret realities. In the end, Skerritt

---

55   Carroll, *Shadow and Substance*, 129–30.
56   Carroll, *Shadow and Substance*, 161.
57   Carroll, *Shadow and Substance*, 92.

asserts the mystique of his clerical authority to terminate the discussion. He imposes an ending that fails to bring Brigid's search to a conclusion, as the tragic denouement confirms, for the simple reason that he lacks the power to do so. He may force O'Flingsley onto the highway of the road, to confront his terrors 'that I'd have no money and be hungry',[58] but in the face of Brigid's utopian desires, he is helpless.

Rhetorically, the fabric of life in Independent Ireland is woven from the cloth of State Catholicism. As that cloth becomes threadbare, the cultural prescience of Synge's dramaturgy and Shaw's criticism has, in stark contrast, worn well. What Synge stages goes beyond illustrating Shaw's cultural politics, as the dramaturgy contains within it evidence of a living consciousness not easily cowed by colonial modernity, either British or Roman. As the twentieth century progresses, the Abbey stages 'generations of playwrights', of whom Carroll is acknowledged as the first and most significant author of Catholic experience from the inside, as it were. It is equally clear, in the distance travelled between Christy Mahon and James X, that images and narratives are worked and re-worked in an effort to arrive at what Seamus Heaney calls 'symbols adequate to our predicament'.[59] Performance efficacy is not solely a function of words or of stage action, and has a great deal to do with audience response and expectation. In 1907, the stage was eclipsed by pandemonium in the auditorium, and the *dramatis personae* of *The Playboy of the Western World* were silenced by the servants of a nascent theocratic successor state. Almost a century later the descendants of those who founded and shaped that state through counter-revolution, and of those who had to endure its furtive cruelties, are left together alone in an auditorium by James X. His walk-out on official Ireland asserts that the dignity of refusal remains available as a 'weapon of the weak' even to the most abject. It is precisely their damaged quality that establishes the credentials of survivors of the various crimes of State and Church as a cultural resource:

---

58   Carroll, *Shadow and Substance*, 97.
59   Seamus Heaney, *Preoccupations* (London: Faber, 1980), 56.

Paradoxically, the very acknowledgement that they have suffered damage and were prevented from unfolding the extent of their potential guards against nostalgic projection: these remnants are not the regressive images of some impossible golden age, and their promise of alternatives could only be realised with the advent of the justice whose absence they protest.[60]

As Catholic Ireland implodes, and Ireland Successful crumbles, perhaps the damaged histories of James X, Brigid and the Mundy sisters re-emerge as exemplary narratives, not of defeat, but of struggle. In Irish theatre, even as an aggressive theocratic version of anti-colonial nationalism gets into its stride in the early twentieth century, a pattern of representing intimidating clerical power as always contested is established. Critical interrogation of theatrical representations offers insight into Catholic supremacy and the social and political arrangements which enabled it. In addition, it draws attention to popular resources with the potential – if mobilised – to set a different direction for what may need to be re-imagined and re-wrought, a century later, as a Second Republic. In such an entity, to dream would not be dangerous, but would be valued as a form of critical consciousness indispensable to the common good.

60   Lloyd, *Irish Times*, 3.

6 From *Borstal Boy* and *Ginger Man* to *Kitty Stobling*: A Brief Look Back at the 1950s

The 1950s are very personal to me because I was born then, in 1952. Now, sixty years later, I realise that the 1950s represent the end of a way of life and the beginning of the world that we live in today.

The industrial civilisation of the British imperial project, of which Ireland had been an intrinsic if unstable part, finally started to run aground in the 1950s: a culture that had spanned the globe and had produced an extraordinary legacy – of great modernising achievement on one hand, and, on the other, a battle ground of colonialism. Post-Second World War, these two powerful forces would clash in localised struggle in various parts of the remaining British Empire or countries under British influence. 'When [Harold] Macmillan became Prime Minister in 1957', writes the social historian Dominic Sandbrook, 'no fewer that forty-five different countries were still governed by the Colonial Office, but during the next seven years Ghana, Malaya, Cyprus, Nigeria, Sierre Leone, Tanganyika, Western Samoa, Jamaica, Trinidad and Tobago, Uganda, Zanzibar and Kenya were all granted their independence.'[1]

These struggles would form the political and ultimately the social backdrop to a generation of young men and women who, in the 1950s, were starting to break free from the conventional and prescribed ways of living and working: the context to much of the best in English fiction of the period such as *Room at the Top* (1957), *This Sporting Life* (1960) and *Absolute Beginners* (1959) as well as the 'group' known as 'The Movement' poets.

---

1   Dominic Sandbrook, *Never Had It So Good: A History of Britain from Suez to The Beatles* (London: Abacus, 2006), 282.

In Britain the welfare state and the democratic opening up of educational possibilities created the foundations for a new *kind* of society that would finally emerge in the 1960s.

The transformation of England, in particular, into a consumerist society provided Ireland with the safety valve that the truly conservative nature of the Irish State and the fragility of its traditional economy obviously needed. Emigration to England, and further afield, was both a forced and elegiac comment on the failure of De Valera's nationalism. It was also an opportunity to see the wider world and play some part in the cultural and economic changes that were taking place. Although how this would have been viewed at the time is clearly a matter of perspective and of how individuals fared in their new lives 'across the water'.

The following statistic is a stark reminder of how things were: 'Of every 100 girls in Connacht in 1946, forty-two had left by 1951.'[2] To what kind of life and loving one wonders. Indeed the statistics become a story in themselves: 'About 400,000 souls left in ten years for Britain, and to a lesser extent, for Canada, the United States, Australia and New Zealand.'[3] During post-war reconstruction in the UK, 634,000 Irish men and women settled there; but if one stretches this figure to include the period 1931–61, 'Irish-born' residents in Britain increased from 505,000 to 951,000 which, considering the numbers of those who *returned* to Ireland during the Second World War, is really quite staggering.

On a wider front, though, 1950s America and the momentum that was building up throughout that society, as well as the first mass moves towards civil rights and an end to apartheid in the States, would politicise the English-speaking world by the end of the decade. The example of the civil rights movement in the States would create an unstoppable cultural dynamic towards equality of races and religions with the separation of

2   See Joseph Lee, *Ireland 1912–1985: Politics and Society* (Cambridge: Cambridge University Press, 1990), 377; and James Ryan, 'Inadmissible Departures: Why did the emigrant experience feature so infrequently in the fiction of the mid-twentieth century?', in *The Lost Decade: Ireland in the 1950s* (Cork: Mercier Press, 2004), 228.

3   Dermot Keogh, 'Introduction: The Vanishing Irish', in *The Lost Decade: Ireland in the 1950s*, 18.

Church and State. The 1950s in Ireland was probably the last decade in which both parts of the island, the ruling political parties and the pre-eminent role of the Churches, could withstand this shifting of power in the Western world. In a sense, 1950s Ireland was the beginning of the end too for that largely unhealthy relationship. In Thomas Kilroy's view, the literature and drama of the period marks a threshold between the short-lived past of an independent Catholic Ireland and the emergence of a modern-ising free state or republic that simply had to reconnect with Europe and, more pressingly, its British neighbours, if it ('Ireland') was to survive. This is exactly what started to happen under the strategic shifts of economic policy initiated by T. K. Whitaker and others within the Department of Finance and in the mostly Dublin-based intellectual and political elite.[4] A process poetically dramatised in retrospect in 1968 in Thomas Kinsella's meditative masterpiece, 'Nightwalker'.[5]

In Northern Ireland, still marked by war and its after-effects (Belfast had been blitzed in 1941 with the loss of approximately 1,000 people) but a landscape scarred by the German bombers – the momentary possibility of opening up and producing an egalitarian civic society (notwithstanding 'Operation Harvest', the abortive IRA campaign) – stuttered and stumbled into the mid-1960s before the hope of a just society was snuffed out with the eruption of the Troubles.[6]

There are two parts to the story of the Irish 1950s – a northern and southern dual-narrative that sometimes inter-connects but more often diverges. It is a story that has not really been told before.

From a personal point of view, growing up in 1950s Belfast, the stability and quality of life that many enjoyed there – of good schools, functioning,

---

4   Terence Brown, *Ireland: A Social and Cultural History 1922–2002* (London: Harper Perennial, 2004), 201–6. See also Tom Garvin, 'Dublin Newspapers and the Crisis of the Fifties', *News from a New Republic: Ireland in the 1950s* (Dublin: Gill & Macmillan, 2010), 61–77.

5   Thomas Kinsella, 'Nightwalker', in *Nightwalker and Other Poems* (Dublin: Dolmen Press, 1968).

6   Jonathan Bardon, *A History of Ulster* (Belfast: Blackstaff Press, 1992), 569–74, gives a succinct portrait of the bombings and after-effects. See also Bardon's definitive *Belfast: An Illustrated History* (Belfast: Blackstaff Press, 1983), 234–45.

well-run hospitals, new roads leading into blossoming suburbs, diversify-
ing new 'tec' factories – sat alongside the traditional heavy industries of
shipbuilding, aircraft manufacture, tobacco, mills, and such like.[7]

These industries, we now know, were becoming increasingly unten-
able and in a couple of decades would be extinct – a complete traditional
way of industrial life, with its customs, work practises, housing, and expectations – literally everything, gone. And along with this disappearance,
the exposure, almost at exactly the same time, of a bigoted and repressive
system of government which had shown itself to be blindly indifferent to
the poverty and inequality in its treatment of its Catholic minority and
the urban poor of both religions.

The wider political world was redefining the power blocs of the Cold
War – in Korea, in Suez, and in what became known as The Iron Curtain
behind which previously autonomous states had been colonised by the
Soviet Union and would remain so for fifty years, despite attempts at liberation, such as in Hungary, that were ruthlessly repressed.

In Ireland, north and south, the old wounding partition aside, the
ingrained grievances of poverty, injustice and the dreadful inner-city housing conditions in both capitals, seemed beyond the ability of either Church
or State to remedy. Ireland's difficulty became England's opportunity and
as we know, emigration flourished into a way of life. The statistics say it all.

On the cultural front, much was happening in Ireland and to Irish
writers based abroad. Alongside the list Brian Fallon provides in his essential portrait, *An Age of Innocence: Irish Culture 1930–1960*,[8] one can add
the achievements of Elizabeth Bowen, Mary Lavin and Kate O'Brien.
While the early fiction of Edna O'Brien, in *The Country Girls* (1960) and
The Lonely Girl (1962) charts, according to Terence Brown's insightful
study, *Ireland: A Social and Cultural History 1922–2001*, a pattern emerges
of 'a brief idyll of youthful discovery followed by disillusionment before
sending them [O'Brien's country girls] on to the more exotic attractions
of London, but the young woman or man from a rural background who

7   See Gerald Dawe, *My Mother-City* (Belfast: Lagan Press, 2007).
8   Brian Fallon, *An Age of Innocence: Irish Culture 1930–1960* (Dublin: Gill & Macmillan,
     1998), 263–5.

sought to establish a family in the city was confronted there by adjustment to the novel ways of urban family life.'[9] Brown goes on to point out that by the 1950s, 'despite the slow rate of economic growth in the country as a whole, Dublin has been transformed from the elegant, colourful, and decaying colonial centre of English rule in Ireland into a modern if rather dull administrative and commercial capital'.[10]

This change would work its way into the livelihoods of many but it would also impel others into a kind of subculture: a halfway house between the past and the emerging present. The setting for such 'hesitancy and uncertainty' was the public house.

The subculture for writers has been explored with intimate detail and knowledge in memoirs such as John Ryan's *Remembering How We Stood* (1975) and the excellent *Dead as Doornails* (1976) by Anthony Cronin. The local rows and gossip and personality clashes between Dublin-based writers such as Patrick Kavanagh and the younger Brendan Behan were more often than not drink-related.

Drink became the arbiter of authenticity; a counter-cultural shelter, literally a public house for private lives, with its holy hours, after hours, Sunday closings and other licensing controls creating a lifestyle all of its own, as well as lasting mythologies. Footage of a drunken Flann O'Brien being interviewed one Bloomsday bears the marks of an embittered and caustic self-regard that is itself tragi-comic. *Such-and-such is a terrible man for the gargle.* Alcoholism, an affliction of the 1950s, was as much a tragic feature of the time as the polio epidemic of 1956 or the political collapse some years earlier of the Mother & Child Scheme in 1951.

Behan's success in the 1950s – indeed the 1950s was very much *his* decade with the success of *The Quare Fellow* (1956), *Borstal Boy* (1958) and *The Hostage* (1958) – was based upon an ebullient verbal art that seemed to challenge the official sentiments of the time, both in Ireland but also in Britain and in the United States. As his *Borstal Boy* hit the note of a kind of 1950s break-through, shared in novels of the period, or in a play such as John Osborne's *Look Back in Anger* (1956), *Borstal Boy* turned the tide on

9   Brown, *Ireland: A Social and Cultural History*, 206.
10   Brown, *Ireland: A Social and Cultural History*, 206–7.

English complacency and through the sheer energetic verve of his English, Behan manages to sound like a Beat poet in full flow – one minute irreverent, aggressive, the next meditative and accepting, while displaying an almost Wildean play of paradoxical grievance and entitlement:

> Jesus, if they'd only let me sit there and sew away, I could be looking down at the canvas and watching my stitches and seeing them four to an inch, and passing the time myself by thinking about Ireland and forgetting even where I was, and, Jesus, wasn't that little enough to ask? What harm would I be doing them? If any of them was in Mountjoy, say, and I was there with a crowd of Dublin fellows, I wouldn't mess them about, honest to Jesus Christ I wouldn't, no matter what they were in for. And that James, that was a proper white-livered whore's melt.[11]

If the 1950s were Behan's, the militant republican, jailed at age sixteen in England in the late 1930s and who came to understand England and condemn much of what was hypocritical in the Irish, his death in 1964 in his early forties makes its own telling point about the traps that were on offer in the decade of television and mass-produced populist magazines. For like Dylan Thomas who had died as a result of alcoholism before him in 1953 and Elvis Presley, who died after him, Behan had become that modern phenomenon – a *celebrity*; one of the very first Irish celebrities on the Anglo-American stage.

In the infamous live interview with Malcom Muggeridge on the prestigious BBC '*Panorama*' programme, cursing and swearing and obviously the worse for drink; in his brawling, binge-fuelled lifestyle, Behan was bizarrely anticipating the rock-star fate of the present day. Even though it was his 'Irish' stereotype that probably fitted in with 'English' prejudice and American expectation. 'The English hoard words like misers', wrote Kenneth Tynan in his review of Behan's *Quare Fellow*, 'the Irish spend them like sailors and in Brendan Behan's new play language is out on a spree, ribald, dauntless and spoiling for a fight. It is Ireland's sacred duty to send over, every few years, a playwright to save the English theatre from inarticulate glumness.'[12] Shaped in such 'national' terms, it's precious wonder that

11   Brendan Behan, *Borstal Boy* (London: Arrow Books, 1990), 77.
12   *The Observer* (27 May 1956), quoted in Michael O'Sullivan, *Brendan Behan. A Life* (Dublin: Blackwater Press, 1997). For review and BBC Interview see pp. 208–11.

Behan's death as a result of diabetes and alcoholism was viewed almost as a semi-state funeral. But in a curious way too one of the leading roles offered to the Irish writer of the time – as a 'character' – was buried with him; few serious writers since Behan would follow in his footsteps.

Behan had been memorialised *before* his death, however, in J. P. Donleavy's *The Ginger Man* (1955). Behan and the Catacombs feature in this richly cruel comedy of manners set in drink-besotted 1950s Dublin, in which the reek and customs of the period are relentlessly exposed in Donleavy's unstoppable saga of the life of one Sebastian Dangerfield and his numbered days as a law student at Trinity College.

This is how Behan turns up at one of the gatherings of the time:

> There was suddenly a crash at the door, the centre boards giving way and a huge head came through singing.
> > Mary Maloney's beautiful arse
> > Is a sweet apple of sin.
> > Give me Mary's beautiful arse
> > And a full bottle of gin.
> A man, his hair congealed by stout and human grease, a red chest blazing from his black coat, stumpy fists rotating around his rocky skull, plunged into the room of tortured souls with a flood of song.[13]

Like *Borstal Boy* and Behan's plays, Donleavy's prose catches the absurdly mischievous, mocking, feckless playing with reality as his main characters brazen their way through the city life of the capital. It is a novel literally seeping with a Dublin that has disappeared; something of which we see in the photographs of Nevill Johnson. Interesting therefore to consider how, in looking back at his experience of living in 1950s Dublin, one of Ireland's best-known novelists, John McGahern, interprets the scene in the posthumously published collection of his autobiographical essays, *Love of the World: Essays* (2009).[14] In speaking of his own generation of young aspiring writers, born in the provincial 1930s (Tom Murphy, Kilroy, Mac Intyre) and who, by the 1950s, were based in Dublin, McGahern is

---

13　J. P. Donleavy, *The Ginger Man* (London: Abacus, 1996), 157.
14　John McGahern, 'The Solitary Reader', in *Love of the World: Essays* (London: Faber and Faber, 2009).

unambiguous: 'The two living writers who meant most to us were Samuel Beckett and Patrick Kavanagh.'[15]

Both Beckett and Kavanagh were hugely influential in different ways. It is interesting to recall just what they stood for, on the ground, so to speak. McGahern states:

> They belonged to no establishment and some of their best work was appearing in the little magazines that could be found at the Eblana Bookshop on Grafton Street. Beckett was in Paris. The large, hated figure of Kavanagh was an inescapable sight around Grafton Street, his hands often clasped behind his back, muttering hoarsely to himself as he passed. Both, through their work, were living, exciting presences in the city.[16]

Indeed Patrick Kavanagh would become a significant figure in McGahern's own fiction while Beckett's influence on another writer who emerged out of the 1950s, Brian Friel, is important to note here. Friel's early drama, such as *Philadelphia Here I Come!* (1964), has Beckettian undertones in the play's view of language and memory – the father's inability to recall details that matter to the departing (emigrating) son, the twenty-five-year-old Gar.

Friel's play also echoes many of the themes that dominated 1950s Ireland: the allure of American popular culture – 'I'll come home when I make my first million', Gar protests, 'driving a Cadillac and smoking cigars and taking movie films',[17] as well as the sense of 'having to' leave Ireland with its claustrophobic provincialism.[18] As Gar puts it, picking up terms he has heard earlier from his drunken old schoolmaster:

15   McGahern, 'The Solitary Reader', 92. Interesting to note that in his memoir of mid-1950s Ireland, *Irish Journal*, the German novelist Heinrich Boll remarked about how the 'utterly un-uniform unity that is Ireland has spoken to me most clearly of all through its literature. Beckett, Joyce and Behan – all three are intensely Irish, yet each is far removed from the other, farther than Australia from Europe.' 'Epilogue', *Irish Journal* (Illinois: Northwestern University Press, 1967), 123.

16   McGahern, 'The Solitary Reader', 92.

17   Brian Friel, *Philadelphia Here I Come!* (London: Faber and Faber, 1965), 68.

18   Friel, the penultimate line: 'God, boy, why do you have to leave?.' *Philadelphia, Here I Come!*, 96.

All this bloody yap about father and son and all this sentimental rubbish about 'homeland' and 'birthplace' – yap! Bloody yap! Impermanence – anonymity – that's what I'm looking for; a vast restless place that doesn't give a damn about the past. To hell with Ballybeg, that's what I say![19]

In his short story, 'High Ground', set in the 1950s but published in 1982 and collected in *High Ground* (1985), John McGahern puts in the mouths of his timber-workers and another alcoholic old school-master a complicated complex of self-recognition and ironic delusion, as the men sup their pints after hours in Ryan's Pub. The young Moran (a literary brother to Gar in *Philadelphia*) eavesdrops outside the pub by the church, having gone to the well for spring water, the pressure of having been offered his old teacher's job pressing upon his mind:

> 'Ye were toppers, now. Ye were all toppers', the Master said diplomatically.
> 'One thing sure is that you made a great job of us, Master. You were a powerful teacher. I remember to this day everything you told us about the Orinoca River.'
> 'It was no trouble. Ye had the brains. There are people in this part of the country digging ditches who could have been engineers or doctors or judges or philosophers had they been given the opportunity. But the opportunity was all that was lacking.' The Master spoke again with great authority.[20]

Patrick Kavanagh could well have been one of those voices, indeed in some of his poems he seems to be deliberately improvising the innocent circumspection similar to these characters' knowledge, intimacy and understanding.

After years of hard dedication to his craft, that would produce one of the mid-century Irish writing 'classics' in *The Great Hunger* (1942), and having fought against what he saw as the establishment in Dublin, Kavanagh's health like Behan's, gave out. But out of his illness – lung cancer and the complications of an unsteady lifestyle based around the

---

19   Friel, *Philadelphia Here I Come!*, 69.
20   John McGahern, 'High Ground', in *High Ground* (London: Faber and Faber, 1985), 102.

pub – Kavanagh's rebirth took place in mid-1950s, as he was to remake his writing life by the Grand Canal:

> So it was that on the banks of the Grand Canal between Baggot and Leeson Street bridges in the warm summer of 1955, I lay and watched the green waters of the canal. [...] I was born in or about nineteen-fifty-five, the place of my birth being the banks of the Grand Canal.[21]

Come Dance with Kitty Stobling,[22] which was finally published in 1960 after an arduous period of seeking a publisher, is addressed to his muse and contains great lyrical lightness of touch, surrounded by some scars of struggle, as health and moral freedom are restored.

I think it is a great book, as important in its way as W. B. Yeats's magnificent volume of a preceding generation, *The Tower* (1928). *Come Dance with Kitty Stobling* is a hymn to rebirth but it is also a remarkable poetic testament to the resilience of the imagination and the ability of Kavanagh to transcend the demeaning, niggardly and cramped atmosphere that had contaminated so much of the Irish literary scene by the 1950s.

As the Northern Irish, London-based poet Louis MacNeice remarked of the Dublin scene of a decade and a half beforehand, when he arrived in from Galway in 1939 after just hearing about the declaration of the Second World War:

> I was alone with the catastrophe, spent Saturday drinking in a bar with the Dublin literati; they hardly mentioned the war but debated the correct versions of Dublin street songs. Sunday morning the hotel man woke (I was sleeping late and sodden), said, 'England has declared war.'[23]

Kavanagh's *Kitty Stobling* takes on in 'The Paddiad: Or the Devil as a Patron of Irish Letters' what remains of this 'literary world' while caustically pointing his finger at those who promote it outside the country. This is the prefacing 'Note' to the poem:

21   Patrick Kavanagh, *Self Portrait* (Dublin: The Dolmen Press, 1964), 25–8.
22   Patrick Kavanagh, *Come Dance with Kitty Stobling & Other Poems* (London: Longmans, Green and Co. Ltd, 1960).
23   Louis MacNeice, *The String are False* (London: Faber and Faber, 1965), 212.

> This satire is based on the sad notion with which my youth was infected that Ireland was a spiritual entity. I had a good deal to do with putting an end to this foolishness, for as soon as I found out I reported the news widely. It is now only propagated by the B.B.C. in England and in the Bronx in New York and in the departments of Irish literature at Princeton, Yale, Harvard and New York universities.
>
> I have included this satire but wish to warn the reader that it is based on the above-mentioned false and ridiculous premises.[24]

A timely warning for those today uncritically advancing the notion that Ireland is some kind of 'cultural nirvana'. But the poems kick free of this kind of polemic and become, if you like, 'spiritualized' – airy contemplations on the meaning of being; a cumbersome phrase for what is, in Kavanagh's idiomatic English, so deceptively easy on the ear.

The sonnets, opening with 'Canal Bank Walk' and 'Lines Written on a Seat on the Grand Canal, Dublin' continue throughout the collection with 'October', 'Dear Folks', 'Yellow Vestment', 'Come Dance with Kitty Stobling', 'Miss Universe', 'Epic', 'Winter', 'Question to Life', 'Peace', 'Nineteen Fifty Four' and 'Hospital'. They form the poetic core of the collection. And in this re-centred world of his imagination, Kavanagh created what, in John McGahern's opinion, was a lasting vision, one of the great legacies of the period.

'Kavanagh had in *The Great Hunger*', McGahern remarks, 'brought a world of his own vividly to life. The dumb world of de Valera's dream had been given a true voice'. Kavanagh, McGahern continues, 'had an individual vision, a vigorous gift for catching the rhythms of ordinary speech, and he was able to bring the images that move us into the light without patronage and on an equal footing with any great work'.[25]

Patrick Kavanagh's is a truly pitch-perfect Irish-inflected voice, talking away to itself and is no longer troubled with the literary business of reputation and/or recognition. It is a wonderful achievement of the 1950s which Kavanagh would bequeath to a later generation of poets coming behind him who would, ironically, unlike Kavanagh, achieve international acknowledgement. Alongside the early books of Thomas Kinsella and John

24   Kavanagh, *Come Dance with Kitty Stobling*, 38.
25   McGahern, 'Journey along the Canal Bank', in *Love of the World: Essays*, 330–1.

Montague, and the breakthrough of Austin Clarke's *Ancient Lights* (1955), *Come Dance with Kitty Stobling* set a high watermark for Irish poetry, particularly when placed alongside the achievements of, say, Philip Larkin's *The Less Deceived* (1955) or Robert Lowell's masterful, shape-changing volume, *Life Studies* (1959). In poems such as 'The Hospital' or in 'Lines Written on a Seat on the Grand Canal, Dublin', Kavanagh's imagination declares a revelation earned and honoured through hard won experience:

> And look! a barge comes bringing from Athy
> And other far-flung towns mythologies.
> O commemorate me with no hero-courageous
> Tomb – just a canal-bank seat for the passer-by.[26]

But perhaps the best way to draw this reflection on the 1950s to a close is to refer to a poem in *Come Dance With Kitty Stobling* (published, we should recall, in the first year of the 1960s) in which Kavanagh himself ponders the past decade from its mid-point. The poem is 'Nineteen Fifty Four.'

Kavanagh had been through a lot – lost a court case against the *Leinster Leader*, experienced increasing ill-health, and cancer would be later diagnosed. He was fifty at the time, a relatively young man to our way of thinking; yet in a poignant sense 'Nineteen Fifty Four' is a reflection, as is much else in *Come Dance with Kitty Stobling*, on Kavanagh's surviving his own life and times. The last line carries with it an elegiac realisation of freedom that carries to this very day:

> But tonight I cannot sleep;
> Two hours ago I heard the late homing dancers.
> O Nineteen Fifty Four you leave and will not listen,
> And do not care whether I curse or weep.[27]

Whether to 'curse or weep' as time passes is a perennial question. But perhaps Brian Fallon has defined best, as we look back from the vantage point of sixty years, the legacy of the 1950s:

26   Kavanagh, *Come Dance with Kitty Stobling*, 1.
27   Kavanagh, *Come Dance with Kitty Stobling*, 33.

Yet many still remember the Fifties as a grim, grey, rather bitter decade, which no doubting some respects they were. Internationally the Cold War had reached a stage of permafrost, and the mushroom-shadow of the Atomic Bomb hung over Europe, though there was still real faith in the capacity of the United Nations [Ireland was admitted in 1955] to maintain an international balance of power. Money was short, so too were jobs, and writers and artists in particular were badly paid; it was a period when many of them had to take casual employment of all kinds to tide them over until better times, and a number emigrated temporarily to London ... Yet underneath it all there was in fact a considerable life force.[28]

If lessons are ever learnt from history, the 1950s show how best to counter the understandable anger and rage about political chicanery and moral failure of the Church in contemporary Ireland. The 1950s are a kind of alter-image of today when what we now know was happening was *not* exposed publicly or challenged politically. In 1950s Ireland we can see our younger selves reflected as an age of innocence but also one full of dark secrets and wrongs.

This proves the incontestable point that we neither need to go, nor should even consider going, backwards to realise that a soft-centred remodelled nationalism – the very thing that Patrick Kavanagh railed against – is not what is needed today to rectify Ireland's problems, simply because it does not work.

If the 1950s prove anything in *Ireland* it is by way of a rebuke and an inspiration; about the political need for a level-headed Mark 2 of the Whitaker generation who will coolly and calmly focus upon the historical fault-lines and fissures in this society in an effort to work through and plan how best to fix these while, at the same time, trying to realistically appraise Ireland's standing in the rest of the world.

28   Fallon, *The Age of Innocence*, 262.

CAROLINE MAGENNIS

7 Sexual Dissidents and Queer Space in Northern Irish Fiction

The ways by which Northern Irish society has preserved its boundaries and cohesion in the maintenance of certain forms of sectarian identity are in unnerving correspondence with the ways in which it has repressed homosexuality through law, protests and intimidation. For each subversion of the norm, it seems, there is a tactic of marginalisation against those who dare dissent. Space is a critical issue for the study of both ethno-sectarian conflict and the queer experience. This chapter takes a number of theoretical cues from the work of the sociologist Rob Kitchin, whose essay 'Sexing the City' (2002) describes Belfast as having a 'homophobic hyper-hetero masculinity.'[1] Kitchin, working with Karen Lysaght, employs the term 'sexual dissidents'[2] and remarks that:

> It is clear that Belfast, as expressed through legislation and political policy, and institutional and public attitudes and practises, is on the whole a sexually conservative and homophobic society.[3]

Space is a critical issue for both gay activists and for queer theory. As Kitchin and Lysaght note, there is a growing academic interest in the provision and maintenance of 'queer space' and debate on the necessity of a separate space. These debates, in Northern Ireland, are inflected with political consequences.

1   Rob Kitchin, 'Sexing The City: The Sexual Production Of Non-Heterosexual Space In Belfast, Manchester And San Francisco', *City* 6.2 (2002), 205–18.
2   Kitchin and Lysaght use this term to 'represent all those people who do not perform as "good" heterosexuals' (23) in the formulation set out by Gayle Rubin (1989). See Kitchin and Lysaght, 'Queering Belfast, Some Thoughts on the Sexing of Space', NIRSA Working Paper Series, NIRSA, Maynooth.
3   Kitchin and Lysaght, 'Queering Belfast', 215.

This chapter will focus on the representation of homosexuality and homophobia in Northern Irish fiction, with particular reference to Maurice Leitch's *The Liberty Lad* (1965) and Glenn Patterson's *The International* (1999). Both of these novels are set in pre-Troubles Northern Ireland, where bisexuality appears to correspond with an ambivalent attitude to sectarian politics. Patterson's novel was published in 1999, over thirty years after *The Liberty Lad*, and so allows a more knowing glance at the era's sexual politics. There will be an emphasis on the spatial tensions in Northern Irish gay life rendered in fiction, particularly the inscribing of a sexual status to space, and how this intersects with sectarian violence.

Representations of homosexuality in Northern Irish fiction are notable by their absence. The work of Forrest Reid, particularly *Uncle Stephen* (1931), explores the potential for quasi-Hellenistic relations between man and boy. Tom refers to his uncle as 'his master' and understands his role as a 'pupil'.[4] After this, one of the earliest mentions of homosexuality in Northern Irish fiction is in the prolific Brian Moore's novel *The Emperor of Ice Cream* (1965). Gavin and Freddy meet Maurice Markham, a friend of a poet whom Freddy admires. When Freddy implies that there is homosexuality in their local community a shocked Gavin retorts 'You mean they're *fruits*?'[5] Freddy acts nonplussed, nonchalantly cleaning his glasses and asking Gavin if he had never met an actual 'fruit' in a Catholic school. Gavin retorts that boys often tried to 'grab you in the jakes' but they weren't 'real pansies'.[6] His 'good' side, manifested in the novel by the 'white angel', is shocked and sees Freddy as introducing him to deviants and degenerates. He muses:

> What did homos *do*, anyway? What repulsive couplings took place between Reverend McMurty and Maurice? There was something about the thought which made him physically sick. O God, he did not want to be like Maurice or Matthew. How could he have ever admired those effeminate twerps? *He* had never felt homo, never. Still, if you lusted after girls but had never actually slept with one, then how could you be sure you mightn't be homo at a future date?[7]

4   Forrest Reid, *Uncle Stephen* (London: Faber and Faber, 1931), 268.
5   Brian Moore, *The Emperor of Ice Cream* (1965) (London: Deutsch, 1966), 96.
6   Moore, *The Emperor of Ice Cream*, 96.
7   Moore, *The Emperor of Ice Cream*, 96.

It is important, though, to note the critical voice with which Moore addresses the Catholic Church and the prejudices it has instilled in him, in this novel and others. This passage, written as the gay movement began to gain consciousness, can be read as a satire on heterosexual panic. The Belfast-born singer Brian Kennedy has written two novels, *The Arrival of Fergal Flynn* (2004) and *Roman Song* (2005) about a young homosexual man growing up in war-torn 1980s Falls Road. These present us with a loose fictionalisation of Kennedy's own upbringing. Also featuring a gay sexually active priest is Damian McNicholl's *A Son Called Gabriel* (2004), set in the 1960s and 1970s in a working-class Catholic community in Northern Ireland. This novel centres on the adolescence and sexual awakening of Gabriel Harkin. It is worth noting, though that while the gay male experience has been under-represented in Northern Irish literature the lesbian experience is almost completely absent from Ulster writing.

So, why this barely audible queer Ulster voice? Northern Ireland has a long history of homophobia, the apex of which was Ian Paisley's Save Ulster from Sodomy Campaign, which was launched in 1977. This was a response to the decriminalisation of homosexual acts between men in England and Wales in 1967 and subsequent attempts to extend the laws to Northern Ireland. The European Court of Human Rights ensured that this campaign failed in 1982 as homosexual acts were decriminalised. However, Alan Bairner, drawing our attention back to issues of space, notes that

> when a young policeman was shot dead in a Belfast pub during the final stages of the conflict, more attention was paid to the fact that he had been drinking in a gay bar than that he had been killed. Similarly, one of the main complaints levelled at the film *Resurrection Man* ... was not that the leading character was portrayed as a sociopath but that homosexual tendencies were ascribed to him and one of the other loyalist paramilitaries. In a climate, which allows such attitudes to persist, it is by no means only women who should be frightened of hegemonic masculinity.[8]

These attitudes are evidenced by Martin's father in David Park's *Swallowing the Sun* (2004) as he tells his sons 'It's fuckin' dresses they ought to be wearing. It's handbags they should be carrying. Bloody nancy boys the

---

8   Alan Bairner (1999), 'Masculinity, Violence and the Irish Peace Protest', *Capital and Class, Northern Ireland Between Peace and War* 69 (Autumn), 125–44.

pair of them'.[9] A more progressive picture emerged in a survey conducted by Ipsos-Mori on behalf of the Lesbian Advocacy Services Initiative, and reported in *The Observer*.[10] According to this survey, three-quarters of the Northern Irish people say they are tolerant of gay men, lesbians and bisexuals, and 88 per cent believe there should be no discrimination against them. However, despite these figures, they still perceive the Province as a homophobic place. Fifty-nine per cent said they considered the north 'either not very or not at all accepting' of lesbians, gay men and bisexuals, yet only 21 per cent of the same people hold such views themselves. Catholics perceive themselves as less homophobic than Protestants do. Eighty-three per cent of Catholics said they were 'very accepting' of gays, lesbians and bisexuals compared with 70 per cent of Protestants. The new mood of tolerance this survey conveys is in sharp contrast to the findings for the Belfast-based Institute for Conflict Research in 2006. Their research found that 82 per cent of gay men had suffered harassment, usually at the hands of young men, reminding us of the five gay men who have been killed in Northern Ireland since 1997, and contrasted this with the fact that only 42 per cent of declared victims had notified the police of the crime committed against them.

In Eoin McNamee's work, references to homosexuality are refracted through the same dark lens applied to all sexuality in his novels. His characters' sexual encounters, whether gay or straight, are joyless and serve as portrayals of hierarchical structures of power. In *The Blue Tango* (2002) the barber, Wesley Courtney, is homosexual and this marks him out as deviant to the police officers who are investigating the death of Patricia Curran. This is an indication how sexuality, or at least the appearance of heterosexuality, is integral to the masculine collective. Due to his deviance, the hairdresser is singled out for investigation by the police over the murder, and is considered to have knowledge of any sexually deviant activity in the area, homosexual or not. There are echoes of Judith Butler's idea on the penalties for not performing your gender as expected by the

9   David Park, *Swallowing the Sun* (London: Bloomsbury, 2004), 1.
10   Henry McDonald, 'Hain moves to outlaw prejudice against gays', *The Observer*, 30 July 2006.

society in which you live. When Patricia jokes about 'Fruity Wesley's demon barber shop',[11] his space is marked as queer, therefore taboo and deviant. In *The Blue Tango*, in a similar manner to the work of Italian physiognomist Cesare Lombroso, homosexuality was believed to have physiological manifestations: 'It was widely believed that they could be singled out by their high-pitched effeminate speaking voices, their weak handshakes, their poor eyesight.'[12] In this novel, homosexuality is the rampant, unruly, Other which conflicts with upstanding Protestant Ulster. The 'Sons of Ulster' must always be on their guard.

An interesting account of homosexuality and homophobia in a Northern Irish paramilitary comes from Brendí McClenaghan in his 'Letter from a Gay Republican: H-Block 5.' McClenaghan tells his story of trying to be both republican and gay, and how these two discourses of masculinity at first seemed irreconcilable. In a return to our concern of space, he had been in prison for seventeen years at the time of writing his letter, and was on blanket protest in the early 1980s. These facts point to his participation in republicanism as severe and bloody. In prison, he was ostracised and contemplated moving to a non-paramilitary wing and even suicide. The leader of his wing was made aware of the situation and offered his full support; McClenaghan then published an article 'Invisible Comrades: Gays and Lesbians in the Struggle' in *An Glór Gafa*, the republican prisoners' quarterly magazine. The response was diverse, as he notes: 'Reactions to the piece were many and varied, ranging from blatant homophobia to solid support.'[13] Vincent Quinn has drawn more specific parallels between the politics of sectarian and gay identity in Northern Ireland:

> If gay space exists what does it look like? Shops and houses marked with emblems? Banners bearing provocative slogans? Marches? Demos? Clubs and bars with particular clienteles? Flags? Bodies declaring their allegiance via dress codes and styles

---

11   Eoin McNamee, *The Blue Tango* (London: Faber, 2005), 28.

12   McNamee, *The Blue Tango*, 124.

13   Brendí McClenaghan, 'Letter from a Gay Republican: H-Block 5', in *Lesbian and Gay Visions Of Ireland*, ed. Íde O'Carroll and Eoin Collins (London: Cassell, 1995), 122–30.

of personal adornment? Resistance? Pride? A statement of identity in the face of public hostility?[14]

Like Brendí McClenaghan, Quinn asks if one can both be homosexual and accepted as a member of a loyalist or republican community. Quinn also asks important questions about the gendering of the conflict in Northern Irish literature, and the consequences this has for non-traditional sexual identities.

Both McNamee and McClenaghan examined the reaction to homosexuality in a Northern Irish paramilitary organisation. However, there is also some representation of non-violent gay men in Northern Irish novels, even if they are rarely protagonists. *Eureka Street* (1996) by Robert McLiam Wilson features a number of interesting depictions of the ways in which men function together in social settings; in homosocial rather than homoerotic groupings. Jake's group of friends is one of his few stable relationships in the text. The sincere affection this cross-community group of men has for each other is palpable, despite their ribald banter. This novel features a small number of 'out' gay characters. When Jake's friend Donal announces that he is gay, his friends are remarkably accepting of both him and his new partner. Jake muses that: 'Donal was there with his new boyfriend. Pablo seemed a nice young man, if pointlessly good looking and well muscled.'[15] While this is a discussion of male sexuality, it is worth pointing out that this text also features a lesbian relationship between two older women, Chuckie's mother and her neighbour. Jake's romantic tendencies are also applied to men, as an acne-ridden youth who works in the local corner shop incurs his reveries: 'This kid just blushed because he thought he was generally a crap idea, a big mistake. It made me want to kiss his lumpy neck. It made me want to die of love.'[16] It is only Roche, the abused child who befriends Jake, who brings any real homophobia into the text. 'You're not going to fruit me up, are you? You're going to try and fuck my bum,

---

14   Vincent Quinn, 'On the Borders of Allegiance: Identity Politics in Ulster', in Richard Philips et al. (eds), *Decentring Sexualities* (London: Routledge, 2000), 258–77: 258.
15   Robert McLiam Wilson, *Eureka Street* [1996] (London: Minerva, 1997), 353.
16   McLiam Wilson, *Eureka Street*, 171.

you dirty poof.'[17] While the boy states 'No handjobs, remember?'[18] Jake wryly tells Roche: 'You're much less sexually attractive than you believe.'[19] This child is abandoned by his parents, and his tough exterior masks his ill treatment and abuse.

Maurice Leitch's *The Liberty Lad* centres on a young teacher, Frank, and the fractured relationship he has with the place in which he has grown up and still lives – rural Northern Ireland. His best friend is a gay man, Terry, with whom he has a number of encounters and whose lifestyle fascinates him. Frank begins a flirtation with a local married woman whom he later chides for lack of imagination whilst being drawn to the furtiveness of the encounter: 'Wonder would she perform, extra-maritally, as they say in the News of the World?.'[20] Belfast, for Frank, represents erotic potentiality, with the rural figured as a parochial, non-sexual site. However, the homoerotic elements of Frank's experience provide the most telling comment on the relationship between sex and space in Northern Ireland. The youthful play between Frank and Terry arouses conflicting feelings in Frank. One August afternoon while wrestling with Terry they point 'mockingly at the bulges that had suddenly appeared in our trunks. And I suppose before that there must have been other times too when we fumbled innocently with each other. Just how *normal* was our relationship anyway?'[21]

Frank's education leads him often to theorise in depth about the nature of his encounters with Terry. He is aware of psychoanalysis and is fascinated by the erotic: 'A clear case of fetishism of erotic symbolism', I said. 'If you'd read your Krafft-Ebing you'd know that.'[22] Frank has obviously read extensively into the psychology of sexuality, which at this point was booming after the Kinsey Reports. One would consider this unusual reading for a primary school teacher in rural Northern Ireland. When Terry and Frank visit the Isle of Man, it is the first time out of the safely regimented space

17   McLiam Wilson, *Eureka Street*, 166.
18   McLiam Wilson, *Eureka Street*, 247.
19   McLiam Wilson, *Eureka Street*, 301.
20   Maurice Leitch, *The Liberty Lad* [1965] (Belfast: Blackstaff, 1985), 80.
21   Leitch, *The Liberty Lad*, 27.
22   Leitch, *The Liberty Lad*, 29.

of Northern Ireland for either of them. Having booked a double room in order to save money, Frank wakes up with Terry lying behind him, pressed into his back, with Terry's hand on his genitals:

> Everything left my mind except the pleasure that came from the deft fingers ... I was turned round and pulled roughly towards him. His arms went round me and I felt the rasp of his male face against the side of mine. I think it was that which brought me to my senses.[23]

This leads to a frank exchange between the pair that begins with Frank asking him 'point-blank if he was a homosexual'.[24] Terry is remarkably candid about his previous sexual escapades and offers Frank a glimpse into a world he hardly dared think of:

> The flood-gates were up, all the secrets and private feelings he had been guarding for years he poured out for me and I listened, fascinated, by the strange new underground world of an in-between sex. Many of the things he told me I had read about, tantalisingly in novels or clinically in textbook, but there were other things that struck me with a hammer-like force.[25]

Frank is surprised when Terry recounts the names of men he has been intimate with and men he knows to be homosexual: '(H)e listed me film stars, actors, writers and celebrities he knew about and some he had slept with, and he told me of local men, some of whom I knew and some of them married.'[26] Frank is fascinated by these new codes of behaviour, admitting that 'it was a new world for me, with its own languages and laws, and I was greedy for knowledge'.[27] After Mona rejects his attempts at a sexual encounter in a house for sale he goes to a bar named Delargy's in the Docks Area of Belfast with Terry and some of Terry's friends. Frank begins the evening unsettled by the effeminate manner in which these men are acting, and slowly comes round to the idea that he is drinking in a bar frequented

23   Leitch, *The Liberty Lad*, 39.
24   Leitch, *The Liberty Lad*, 39.
25   Leitch, *The Liberty Lad*, 39.
26   Leitch, *The Liberty Lad*, 40.
27   Leitch, *The Liberty Lad*, 40.

by homosexuals. He notices the shift in Terry's behaviour: 'Here he was with his own kind. Before that night I'd always thought of *him* as being different ... but now it was me who has out of place.'[28] Bradley, Terry's MP friend, is a predatory gay man, despite being a married father. When they first meet, Bradley and Terry leave Frank at the end of the evening with a few pleasantries that barely conceal their intentions. Frank is disconcerted by Bradley's charm and charisma, believing his personal traits to be studied. Frank remarks that: 'I became aware for the first time of his trick – if it was a trick – of concentrating all his attention on the person he was speaking to at the time, and when he shifted to someone else it was like being deprived of the glow of a powerful searchlight.'[29]

In a comedic scene, Frank offers himself up to Bradley. Frank is being considered for the post of head-teacher of the school where he works, and Bradley is on the interview panel. Frank is reluctant at the beginning to give himself to Bradley in return for his influence but he changes his mind, and it is not clear whether he is career or sexually motivated. Bradley is in full control of the situation, which plays like a seduction scene from a bad movie. Leitch again feminises the homosexual figure, casting Frank in the role of supplicant: 'And so now I was to be the fatalistic pea-hen awaiting king cobra. The desire to squawk arose in me.'[30] The licentiousness is temporarily halted by Bradley's young son, but carries on with Frank, terrified and reluctant, unfamiliar with the codes of homosexual seduction. In his encounters with women in the text, he endeavours to be the aggressor. This role reversal troubles his masculine sense of self. However, when Bradley reaches to feel if Frank is aroused, he finds that Frank is not and their encounter ends with both parties covering their obvious embarrassment with pleasantries. When Frank is driving home, he feels sexual stirrings, which are couched in euphemism: 'I felt a sudden delayed tightening and stirring between my legs. In the words of our local delicate turn of phrase I was "touching cloth".'[31] His body fails him again at his father's funeral when

28   Leitch, *The Liberty Lad*, 160.
29   Leitch, *The Liberty Lad*, 53.
30   Leitch, *The Liberty Lad*, 184.
31   Leitch, *The Liberty Lad*, 190.

he cannot cry: 'My eyes were like two cinders. Truthfully, I was obsessed more with the fact that people might notice my absence of external grief than any personal worries.'[32]

Glenn Patterson's *The International* tells the story of Danny, a bisexual barman in a Belfast hotel. Patterson's collected non-fiction writing, *Lapsed Protestant* (2006), describes the hostility to any behaviour that deviates from hegemonic masculinity. On returning home from university in England, local 'hard men' loyalists refer to him as 'Glenda' due to his appearance, which was presumably the height of new wave fashion at the time:

> I had taken to wearing nail varnish while I was away, dyeing my hair and crimping it. I had taken to wearing tight black leggings and carrying a shoulder bag (handbag, these people preferred to think of it as), sometimes black, sometimes pink. I kept my hairspray in it.[33]

This could be a description of an early sartorial creation of Patrick Brady from Patrick McCabe's *Breakfast on Pluto* (1998). In a Northern Ireland consumed with extreme violence and a Save Ulster from Sodomy campaign it is not hard to see why this performance can be read as so subversive and disruptive to normative Northern Irish masculinity. Patterson offers his opinion on the derision he receives:

> Of course, back then, their ridicule didn't bother me. I invited it. Their ridicule was a measure of the difference between us and I was determined to be as different as I could possibly be from the people I had left behind.[34]

Patterson maintains the importance of identity markers as he grew up during the Troubles: 'I had spent most of my late teens trying to distinguish myself from the people in had grown up with, the place I had grown up in' (Appendix). This performance alienates Patterson from a sectarian identity, aligning him with a third category of Northern Irish identity, one

32   Leitch, *The Liberty Lad*, 194.
33   Glenn Patterson, *Lapsed Protestant* (Dublin: New Island, 2006), 30.
34   Patterson, *Lapsed Protestant*, 30.

that disrupts both communities' sense of self. This category is populated by those who, like Stephen Dedalus in *A Portrait of the Artist as a Young Man* (1916), decide that '*non serviam: I will not serve*'.[35]

In Patterson's *The International*, Danny's first homosexual experiences are marked by shame and lead to rebuke and censure. He is also the subject of homophobic abuse in the street, as men call after him '"Fruit!"... "He's not denying it. Bum boy!"' He kisses another boy while he is still in school,[36] who claims Danny got him drunk and forced his affections. Danny is expelled from school and his parents refer to the incident as 'the unpleasantness'.[37] One must bear in mind that the novel sets these instances in the 1960s long before homosexuality was decriminalised. Patterson cites part of his inspiration for the novel to be a gay actor he worked with on his monologue play *Monday Night Little Ireland North of England* (1994). According to Patterson, he 'was gay, in his fifties and had told me something about going to a bar, about the gay scene in the late 1950s'. Patterson speaks about 'camp' as a subject position outside of normative sexuality, one could, of course, substitute 'queer' for 'camp'. Camp allows Patterson to step outside of the Northern Irish mainstream and commentate. It is an authorial decision, with camp/queer as a vantage point: 'I am interested in 'camp'; there is a sort of positioning of yourself, a stepping outside. A positioning of yourself in a place where you can commentate.' There is a 'stepping outside' inherent in Patterson's choice to set this novel in pre-Troubles Northern Ireland, the vantage point of history.

In *The International*, Danny has sex with a girl[38] while thinking about a classmate Gregory, who he has a crush on and who, Danny notes, plays the tuba. Danny finds the subversive nature of his sexuality exhilarating.

> Some part of me even enjoyed the subterfuge. That what I was doing was illegal did cross my mind, but it was the Sack, not the Law I most feared, Anyway, I had

---

35 James Joyce, *A Portrait Of The Artist As A Young Man* (New York: Barnes & Noble, 1992), 124.

36 Glenn Patterson, *The International* (London: Anchor, 1999), 47.

37 Patterson, *The International*, 47.

38 Patterson, *The International*, 45.

grown up in a place where all sex was considered dirty; furtiveness seemed a necessary part of it.[39]

This clandestine approach to sex may be a contributing factor to Patterson's
comment in *Lapsed Protestant* that 'Were you aware that, despite our
old fashioned attitudes to sex, there are men on the London gay scene
who will *only* sleep with men from here?'[40] Patterson, by his own admis-
sion a 'white heterosexual male', uses a character with ambiguous
sexuality as a metaphor for his belief in the fluidity of identity. That is,
in employing a bisexual leading man he queers Northern Irish identity.
Patterson states that:

> I don't feel like it's fixed, I don't feel our identities are fixed, and I think that
> most identities are limiting positions. In *The International*, Danny is simply who
> he is, you know, he doesn't really even call himself gay; he was alive to anything
> that went on ... I deliberately didn't make an issue of it because I didn't want it
> to be an identity.[41]

Patterson is aware of homoerotic moments in his fiction: 'I am aware that
there are other bits and pieces right through the fiction, like the scene in
the toilet in *Black Night at Big Thunder Mountain*. It's "speeded" up, but
there's something there. There's also in *Number 5* a "homo-fascinated"
thing going on.'[42] Danny gains employment at a hotel in Belfast city
centre, and this allows him to be promiscuous with the hotel guests. He
becomes '... champion of the one-night hand-stand'[43] and admits, wryly,
that there 'had been women as well, the odd time'.[44] In their study, Kitchin
and Lysaght detail their interview with a young Belfast gay man called
Anthony, discussing how 'the dominant heterosexuality of the bar can be

---

39   Patterson, *The International*, 100.
40   Patterson, *Lapsed Protestant*, 13.
41   Caroline Magennis, 'Interview with Glenn Patterson', in Paddy Lyons and Alison
      O'Malley-Younger (eds), *No Country for Old Men* (Bern: Peter Lang, 2008), 115–21.
42   'Interview with Glenn Patterson'.
43   Patterson, *The International*, 101.
44   Patterson, *The International*, 101.

subverted by using it as a place to pick up sexual partners'.[45] His conquests, of both sexes and religions, signify a pre-Troubles pre-AIDS innocence and naiveté.

The so-called Swinging Sixties never quite made the impact in Belfast that they made elsewhere. Two politically yet equally morally conservative traditions in Northern Ireland ensured that Danny's sexual liberation was a rare thing indeed. Danny states: 'In those days in Belfast the Sabbath was kept wholly. This was the town where swings were chained to their frames on Saturday night and not let down till Monday morning'.[46] Although the sexually permissive 1960s, cultural myth or not, never quite made the same impact in Northern Ireland as elsewhere, Patterson allows Danny no small amount of erotic freedom as prospective partners take his eye with a surprising regularity. Danny considers why he is so successful in his conquests, admitting '... there was nothing attractive about me, save this one thing: I worked in a hotel and I looked as if, were you to ask me, I wouldn't say no'.[47] Like the protagonists in Robert McLiam Wilson's novels *Ripley Bogle* and *Eureka Street*, he is prone to romantic reveries, falling in love with both genders in the course of one day: '... In any case I had worked a fourteen-hour shift the day before and had fallen in love twice and twice been rebuffed'.[48] Danny ends up having a threesome with an older but attractive American couple who are staying at the hotel. There is extreme awkwardness when Danny bumps into the couple the next day. The scene at the hotel is decadent: '... I didn't know suddenly whether I wanted to push him aside or her aside or push them both together but I was over by the bed myself and Natalie's hands were tugging my belt and Bob said shit and fuck and baby and Natalie said shush, over and over again'.[49]

When space is inscribed with violent and sectarian resonances, as it has been in Northern Ireland, it limits the possibility of that space being gay. As Anne Enright states in her endnote to the novel:

45   Kitchin and Lysaght, 'Queering Belfast', 18.
46   Patterson, *The International*, 15.
47   Patterson, *The International*, 101.
48   Patterson, *The International*, 9.
49   Patterson, *The International*, 115.

[*The International*] says that there are different ways to describe people's lives – different maps, if you like – and those maps can be stolen. And so the man who describes himself as gay becomes a Catholic gay or a Protestant gay, but only if he wants his knees capped for deviant sexual behaviour. ... So it was another heist to make your narrator gay – and easily, naturally gay; like a wildflower growing from the cracks in concrete; gay without anguish or blame. It is another insistence on things being as they are.[50]

When space is inscribed with violent and sectarian resonances, it makes it more difficult to queer. There is the oft-used public/private, male/female dichotomy to be considered. Public houses and betting shops offered almost 'legitimate' targets for paramilitaries, so imbued were they with sectarianism and masculinity. Bars were often strongly aligned with a community, and seen as non-neutral space. Doorstep shootings were seen as an utter violation as they broke down the barriers between home and violence. Peter Ward, whose job the fictional Danny gets, was one of the first civilian victims in the wrong part of the city at the wrong time. A making sectarian of space had begun which, during the Troubles, left little possibility for a queering of space in Northern Ireland. When other cities were developing their own gay areas with the decriminalisation of homosexuality, every inch of Belfast was carved up along ethno-religious lines. Gay Belfast would always be in the divided city.

The International is set at a time when these spatial divisions are becoming more fixed. The novel represents a pre-Troubles moment when a bar could be seen as a decent cross-section of Northern Irish masculinity. The pre-eminence of space in gender and sectarian relations offers us an interesting dynamic in *The International* where a hotel offers both public space (the bar) and private space (guests' rooms) and Danny performs differently in both. In their analysis, their 'queer reading of the city' Lysaght and Kitchin 'posit that all space is queered, that the sexing of space is always partial and contested, always in the process of becoming; that heterosexist spatiality, for example, is profoundly unstable, consciously engaged in the process of reproducing itself'.[51] Their study found that, like Danny,

50   Enright, 'Endnote', *The International*, 258.
51   Kitchin and Lysaght, 'Queering Belfast', 3.

most of their interviewees 'lead double or compartmentalized lives, "out" in some spaces ... but "closeted" in others'.[52] Thus, in *The Liberty Lad* the split between the erotic and the repressed is fundamentally along city lines, whereas *The International* explores the possibility of space to be inscribed with sexualised meaning, and how sectarian conflict stems the fluidity of a gendered subjectivity. Both texts, with their rejection of the violent and embracing of the erotic, offer new potential for Northern Irish masculine identity. They point to the ways in which the queer landscape of Belfast is changing, and one can only hope Northern Irish fiction can represent these changes.

---

52   Kitchin and Lysaght, 'Queering Belfast', 1.

8 'Kicking Bishop Brennan up the Arse': Catholicism, Deconstruction and Postmodernity in Contemporary Irish Culture

The title of this chapter refers to the television programme *Father Ted*, and specifically to Episode 6 in Season 3 where Ted, having lost a bet to his arch-enemy Father Dick Roche, is forced to kick his very critical boss, Bishop Len Brennan, a Limerick man, 'up the arse'.[1] In a series of hilarious misadventures, Ted finally accomplishes this feat, being photographed in the act by his friend, Father Dougal. The popularity of this anarchic programme has been huge, but what is of particular interest to me is the deconstruction of attitudes about the Church that it has exemplified. What is perhaps most interesting about the genesis of this programme is that it was offered to Radio Teilifís Éireann (RTÉ), the Irish television broadcasting service, who refused to take it up, before buying it to show on their station on which it became one of the most popular comedies in the TAM ratings.

This comedy could be read as being profoundly anti-Catholic – portraying the classic stereotypes of the wheeler-dealer priest (Ted himself, albeit not an especially successful wheeler-dealer); the alcoholic priest (Father Jack – whose four-word mantra 'feck-arse-girls-drink' became the show's catchphrase); the idiot-savant (but mostly idiot) priest (Father Dougal); and of course, that metonym of the role of women in the Church, the housekeeper Mrs Doyle (provider of another catch-phrase in terms of her urgings of cups of tea on unfortunate guests: 'Ah you will, you will, you will ...!'). And yet the programme avoids any real criticism of the Church as an organisation. None of the major church scandals of the past number

---

1   Arthur Mathews and Graham Linehan, *Father Ted* (London: Hat Trick Productions for Channel 4, 1995–8).

of years has been directly dealt with, and all of the clerical characters are, in different ways, likeable. The eponymous Bishop Brennan, who, it is discovered, has a son, is obviously an allusion to Bishop Eamon Casey, but that aside, there is little direct attack on the Church; indeed, there is a fondness for the priests as flawed individuals who are, in their limited way, doing their best.

What is groundbreaking about this programme, however, is the placing of the institutional Church as a target of satire, however gentle that satire may be. For so long, the Church had been the sacred cow of Irish media coverage, but *Father Ted* levels that playing field as the Church, like the family, the law, the world of work and politics, becomes subject to a ludic glance. The Church is now seen as just another organisation, as part of the way in which society and culture are ordered, and which is subject to the same rules, regulations and expectations as the other societal structures with which it competes.

In other words, the Church is just one more way in which society structures itself: it is another example of the interaction of the system and the subject; in a way that parallels politics, ethnicity, ideology and community, religion as an organisation is a system which provides support, stability and a place for the subject. It provides a structure within which the individual can exist; it provides sets of rules and guidelines which structure the individual; and also provides a sense of teleology, in the provision of a set of answers to the questions posed by existence.

This chapter will examine the changing role of the Catholic Church as structure in contemporary Ireland, seeing this altered role as part of a larger process of societal change across the Western world. It will stress the power of culture to act as an agent of change, and as a way of transforming the role of institutions by altering our perception of those institutions. It will contend that fiction – be it a television series, a film or a novel – accesses a mode of truth that is potent and highly valuable. There is a strong tradition of seeing the aesthetic as a mode of truth in continental philosophy. Jacques Lacan sees that 'truth shows itself [*s'avere*] in a fictional structure',[2] while

2   Jacques Lacan, *Écrits: The First Complete Edition in English*, trans. Bruce Fink in collaboration with Héloïse Fink and Russell Grigg (London: W. W. Norton, 2006), 625.

Martin Heidegger also focuses on the truth-telling qualities of the aesthetic. For Heidegger, art, and especially poetry, is a gateway towards this access to the truth of being fully human, and truth, '*all art* as the letting happen of the advent of the truth of what is, is, as such, *essentially poetry*' [italics original].[3] This aspect of television, film and fiction will be explored with respect to the loss of hegemonic status of the Catholic Church in Ireland. Indeed, what is remarkable is not that the Church has lost its hegemonic status, but rather that this process has been so belated.

The reason for this is that one of the central facts in any position of social and cultural power is epistemology or the theory of knowledge which is hegemonic in a society. In Ireland, health and education were under the control of the Church since independence. As George Bernard Shaw acerbically put it:

> Under the feeble and apologetic tyranny of Dublin Castle we Irish were forced to endure a considerable degree of compulsory freedom. The moment we got rid of that tyranny we rushed to enslave ourselves.[4]

Instead of a debate regarding the future direction of our society in terms of the major issues of land ownership, legal and societal rights and social justice, there ensued a process of adaptation of hierarchical British models of government, judiciary, legislature and civil service, adding the additional layer of the Roman Catholic Church. The fact that both of these institutions were imperial in design, and therefore designed to restrict debate and enforce compliance with the existing structures was not taken into consideration. The Dáil and Seanad were a carbon copy of the structures of Westminster, and despite the default position of republicanism, there was little or no effort to emulate the ringing assertions of the American Bill of Rights, or the French declaration of the Rights of Man and the Citizen, 27 August 1789. Instead the imprimatur of the Catholic Church was sought by de Valera in the run up to the drafting of the constitution in 1937.

---

3   Martin Heidegger, *Poetry, Language, Thought*, trans. Albert Hofstadter (New York: Harper & Row, 1971), 70.

4   George Bernard Shaw, 'The Censorship', *Irish Statesman* 11 (1928), 206–8: 206.

In a manner that has become a locus classicus of a postcolonial state, British rule was replaced with home rule, but this was a home rule that was unselfconfident and based on non-existent intellectual foundations. All of the social and political thinking was based on Roman Catholic doctrine, and significantly, Catholic political influence was also pervasive in the country. As John A. Costello, leader of the inter-party government, declared: 'I am an Irishman second; I am a Catholic first',[5] and it was this attitude that created a hierarchically driven model of society in which the parallel and coterminous structures of Church and State ruled, with comparatively little criticism from those being ruled. Cultural and intellectual diversity were the agents of change in this situation, and I will trace the analysis of such structural dissemination briefly through the work of Jean-François Lyotard, Jacques Lacan and Jacques Derrida, before locating the iconographic image of Bishop Brennan being kicked up the arse in a quadriptych with two other images which graphically illustrate this process of structural dissemination that I see as typical of the condition of contemporary postmodern culture.

Jean-François Lyotard, in his book *The Postmodern Condition*, has defined postmodernism as a process whereby the grand narratives of culture have become broken down. He makes the point that while a self does not amount to much, nevertheless 'no self is an island; each exists in a fabric of relations that is now more complex and mobile than ever before. Young or old, man or woman, rich or poor, a person is always located at "nodal points" of specific communication circuits, however tiny these may be'.[6] As he goes on to add, one is always located at a post through which various kinds of messages pass. No one, not even the least privileged among us, is ever entirely powerless over the messages that traverse and position him or her at the posts of sender, addressee, or referent. His point is that one's mobility in relation to these language-game effects is tolerable, at

5   Dermot Keogh, *Twentieth Century Ireland: Nation and State* (Dublin: Gill and Macmillan, 1994), 208.

6   Jean-Francois Lyotard, *The Postmodern Condition: A Report on Knowledge*, trans. Geoff Bennington and Brian Massumi (Minneapolis: University of Minnesota Press, 1984), 15.

least within certain limits (and the limits are vague); it is even solicited by regulatory mechanisms, and in particular by the self-adjustments the system undertakes in order to improve its performance. He goes on:

> It may even be said that the system can and must encourage such movement to the extent that it combats its own entropy, the novelty of an unexpected 'move', with its correlative displacement of a partner or group of partners, can supply the system with that increased performativity it forever demands and consumes.[7]

His argument here is telling in a contemporary context. He is suggesting that the ability of a single overarching structure to answer all the questions, and provide the epistemological structures wherewith to organise a contemporary complex society has been deconstructed by the fractured nature of selfhood, and consequently, what has emerged is a number of smaller narratives, both complimentary and contradictory, which compete for the attention and loyalty of the subject.

This is in accordance with the psychoanalytic theory of Jacques Lacan, who sees the self as split, and as motivated by a desire to in some way heal this split. Lacan, developing the work of Freud, undercut the notion of rationality as the dominant factor in our humanity and instead began to examine language as an index of the unconscious processes of the mind. He also coined the phrase that the 'unconscious is structured like a language,'[8] which brought the study of structures to the fore in continental thought. For Lacan, the unconscious and language could no longer be seen as givens, or as natural; instead, they were structures which required investigation. In this model, language, no matter what the mode of enunciation, was shot through with metaphors, metonymies and complex codifications which often masked, as opposed to revealed, the real self. Taking the structuralist ideas of the word as divided into signifier and signified, he stressed the lack of correlation between the two, adding that meaning is always fraught with slippage, lack of clarity and play.

7   Lyotard, *Postmodern Condition*, 15.
8   Jacques Lacan, *The Four Fundamental Concepts of Psychoanalysis* (Harmondsworth: Penguin, 1977), 20.

His recasting of 'I think, therefore I am' into 'I desire, therefore I am' has led to a revision of the primacy of reason in the human sciences. He also suggested that selfhood was a complex construct in which the self took on reflections and refractions from the societal context in which it was placed. His notion of the 'mirror stage' stressed the imaginary and fictive nature of the ideal-self, which he saw as predicated on a desire for an unattainable ideal which could never be actualised. In a culture where repression of desire was very much part of the socio-religious mindset, this view of language and desire would have revolutionary implications for any analysis of culture and sexuality. By stressing the primacy of desire, psychoanalysis conflicts directly with the tenets of the Church.

Catholicism has generally seen desire, especially sexual desire, as a negative human quality in need of repression. The adequation of desire with sin has long been part of the Irish psyche: the corollary of this ethico-moral equation (desire + sin = guilt), has led to serious consequences for individual development in Ireland. Indeed, it is in relation to desire that the contemporary difficulties of the Church can best be understood. The capitalist, or post-capitalist, cultures of Western Europe and the developed world are in many ways, the enactment of desire: capitalism is the political system which accedes to the importance of desire in the human psyche. One need only recall the fall of the Berlin Wall – there was never any great rush of people from West Germany to East Germany; the traffic was all one-way, another index of the primacy of desire. Despite the radical uncertainty of moving to a capitalist system, the desire for possessions, for a better life, for personal freedom, was the motive force in determining the direction of traffic across the ruins of that forbidding wall. Indeed, commodity fetishism, the engine which drives capitalist economies, is the practical embodiment of desire – I need a new smartphone, a bigger PC, or tablet, with more RAM and an Intel core i7 processor. Secular Western society is really structured by this form of reified desire, and the Catholic Church, with a different attitude to the satisfaction of desire, is very much out of step with this culture, and with the postmodern concept of the secular self, a self which is firmly located in history and in material culture.

By dividing human subjectivity into three orders, the imaginary, symbolic and real, Lacan offered an historical and social dimension to psychoanalytic studies, the effect of which is still being felt today, and the primacy of language is central to his work. Until then, the individual was being examined very much in isolation, with the psyche being the object of analysis in terms of how the unconscious influences the self. In fact, in a Lacanian context, all subjectivity is defined in terms of what is called the symbolic order, and this order is the structural matrix through which our grasp of the word is shaped and enunciated. For Lacan, the symbolic order is what actually constitutes our subjectivity 'man speaks, then, but it is because the symbol has made him man'.[9] It is the matrix of culture and the locus through which individual desire is expressed: 'the moment in which the desire becomes human is also that in which the child is born into language'.[10] The social world of linguistic communication, intersubjective relations, knowledge of ideological conventions, and the acceptance of the law are all connected with the acquisition of language.

Once a child enters into language and accepts the rules and dictates of society, it is able to deal with others. The symbolic, then, is made up of those laws and restrictions that control both desire and the rules of communication, which are perpetuated through societal and cultural hegemonic modes. Lacan condenses this function in the term the 'Name of the Father'. Once a child enters into language and accepts the rules and dictates of society, it is able to deal with others. The symbolic is made possible because of the acceptance of the 'Name of the Father', those laws and restrictions that control both desire and the rules of communication: 'It is in the *Name of the Father* that we must recognize the basis of the symbolic function which, since the dawn of historical time, has identified his person with the figure of the law.'[11] Through recognition of the 'Name of the Father', one is able to enter into a community of others. The symbolic, through language, is 'the pact which links ... subjects together in one action. The human action

9   Jacques Lacan, *Écrits: The First Complete Edition in English*, trans. Bruce Fink in collaboration with Héloïse Fink and Russell Grigg (London: W. W. Norton, 2006), 229.
10 Lacan, *Écrits*, 262.
11 Lacan, *Écrits*, 230.

par excellence is originally founded on the existence of the world of the symbol, namely on laws and contracts'.[12]

The connection with Religion here is all too clear. Catholicism, as a subset of Christianity, is a patristic, and patriarchal, Religion where the Name of the Father is a central signifier. Indeed, one of the most universal of the Catholic prayers is the blessing of the self, beginning, as we all know: 'In the Name of the Father, and of the son, and of the holy spirit.' Lacan, writing from within a French *milieu*, profoundly influenced by a Catholic symbolic order, uses this phrase as an index of the law into which an individual, as Lyotard has pointed out, is born, and which, in many ways, reconfigures that individual. This order is patriarchal, fixed and stratified, within a given temporal and spatial structure, not unlike the hierarchy of the Church itself.

What separates this order from mere notions of peer-pressure is the fact that it exerts a huge influence on the unconscious as well as the conscious self. These influences are not obvious at times, and form part of the inchoate but influential series of seemingly core values which drive our personalities. And of course, the crucial point here is that the very notion of the *Name of the Father*, of cultural construction, law, language, societal norms is one which is constantly subject to change. The symbolic order of 2017 is vastly different from that of 1904, to take a broad sweep, as we will see in terms of a contrast between *Ulysses* and *American Beauty* later in this chapter. These text both reflect some of the changes in attitude that began to deconstruct the power of the Church, and are also agents of change in that process. At the level of structure and control, religious interdiction of sexual practices such as sex outside marriage and same-sex marriage, which would have been well-nigh absolute in 1904, has been almost completely deconstructed by a contemporary secular society which has passed referendums on issues such as same sex marriage and wherein contraception is now freely available. Civil partnerships are on the increase, and religious control over health and education is coming under increased critique and

12   Jacques Lacan, *Freud's Papers on Technique 1953–1954. The Seminar of Jacques Lacan, Book 1*, trans. John Forrester, ed. Jacques-Alain Miller (New York: Norton, 1991), 230.

scrutiny. Clearly, the Ireland of 2017 has a very different symbolic order to that of 2005.

This view of the socio-symbolic order, itself hugely formative of the individual that we become, as subject to change, is important in terms of the politics of theory. In fact, Lacan sees the *relationship* between language and reality as constantly in flux, and only kept in place by specific nodal connections, what he terms *points de capiton*, quilting points (a metaphor drawn from the points in a mattress which are nailed down for stability), where signifier, signified and referent are in some form of stasis and harmony.[13] These anchoring points, which he also calls Master Signifiers, are our key to some form of certainty: in language, for example, they are to be found in punctuation, which guarantees the stability of the sentence and allows us to retroactively make sense of what we have been reading. The particular symbolic order of a culture, a language, a temporal period, is an important aspect of any Lacanian analysis of individuality. The key question, of course, is how such structures change? If the symbolic order is different in different times and places, how does it change? These very *points de capiton*, which keep a structure in place, must be dislodged in some way. Thus if the connection between language and what it represents is controlled by the Catholic Church, through education, then the resulting worldview that is taught will be, by definition, Catholic, society will be structured according to Catholic principles, and there will be little change. It is here that we come to the work of Derrida.

It was with this same issue of structurality that Derrida's work was concerned, as he presented a critique of 'logocentrism' (the central set of beliefs or truth-claims around which a culture revolves) and introduces his strategy of deconstruction (the dismantling of the underlying structure of a text to expose its grounding in logocentrism). Derrida postulates that the history of any process of meaning or signification is always predicated on some 'centre', some validating point seen as a 'full presence which is beyond play'.[14] Derrida, and perhaps specifically his neologism 'deconstruction', has

13   See the translator's notes in *Écrits*, 808.
14   Jacques Derrida, *Writing and Difference*, trans. Alan Bass (London: Routledge, 1978), 280.

become a synecdoche of this process of theoretical critique. At its most basic, deconstruction involves the reversing the binary oppositions which are constructive of the epistemological paradigm of Western philosophy for, as Derrida notes: 'to deconstruct the opposition, first of all, is to overturn the hierarchy at a given moment'.[15]

Some of these centres or, to use the Lacanian term, *points de capiton*, can be traced as follows: in early Christian times, the centre was a single God who was seen as the origin and source of all things. In the eighteenth century, during the Enlightenment period, this centre was displaced by the notion of human rationality and the search for a knowledge that was immanent and not transcendent. In the contemporary era, rationality is still a central tenant of our culture, but now, the unconscious, as set out by Sigmund Freud, has become a new centre of our system of thought and politics. The initial step in these changes was the privileging of the opposite term, so God was replaced with human thought, and rationality with the unconscious. However, this reversal is only the first step in the deconstructive project. Making the point that an opposition of metaphysical concepts is never the face-to-face opposition of two terms, but a hierarchy and an order of subordination, Derrida goes on to say that deconstruction 'does not consist in passing from one concept to another, but in overturning and displacing a conceptual order, as well as the non-conceptual order with which the conceptual order is articulated'.[16] It is this sense of displacement of the static oppositional criteria that is important in the context of the present discussion. What Derrida has termed the 'structurality of structure' stresses that very little in human culture is 'natural' or 'given'; instead, all structurations are created from an ideological standpoint which, and here we would again be in Foucault territory, is governed by power relationships. What we might term the 'politics of deconstruction' exerts a loosening force on these relationships by suggesting the necessity for alternative structures which are self-aware in terms of the power relationships.

15   Jacques Derrida, *Positions*, trans. Alan Bass (Chicago: University of Chicago Press, 1981), 41.
16   Jacques Derrida, *Margins of Philosophy*, trans. Alan Bass (Chicago: Chicago University Press, 1982), 329.

For Derrida, the teleology of deconstructive critique involves the imbrication of text with context. He is unwilling to bracket any field of cultural endeavour within its own self-defined parameters. We have already noted his comment that deconstruction consists of transference, and of a thinking through of transference, and I have already cited his almost gnomic definition of deconstruction as '*plus d'une langue* – both more than a language and no more of *a* language'.[17] The ideas of hermetically sealed-off cultures, national languages and ideologies are deconstructed to reveal a broader context of comparison and contrast, a process which will have ramifications for any exploration of Irish social, cultural and political mores, and in this context, it is interesting that *Father Ted* was produced by Hat Trick productions for Channel 4, as opposed to any of the Irish television stations. For structures to be decentred, the impetus must come from outside the structure itself.

While these theories referred initially to academic texts, and were presented in language that could be described at best as opaque and at worst as unreadable, their political subtext was subversive in the extreme. In Derridean terms, the imbrication of text and context stresses the constructedness of almost all socio-cultural and linguistic structures, and adduces the need for interpretation and contextual placement if interpretative activities are to have any sense of closure, an issue underlined by Lacan in relation to the subject: that each individual his context specific – 'his history is unified by the law, by his symbolic universe, which is not the same for everyone'.[18] In other words, it is through the relationship of text and context that meaning is to be found. So, if we are to analyse the change in role of the Catholic Church as a system or organisation, then these theorists will prove invaluable in terms of outlining the processes of transformation which are, in the Ireland of the third millennium, possibly the only form of constant that exists. Culture, which is now unmediated by the Church, is a seminal agent of such change.

17   Jacques Derrida, *Mémoires: For Paul de Man*, trans. Cecile Lindsay, Jonathan Culler and Eduardo Cadava (New York: Columbia University Press, 1989), 14–15.
18   Lacan, *Freud's Papers on Technique*, 197.

The value of *Father Ted*, I would suggest, is to place the structure of the Church in a very different context, thereby contributing to the decentring and the deconstruction of the structure. Generally portrayals of priests in Irish film, television and writing have been reverential, positive and serious. Indeed, in January 1962, the first of a series of documentaries was published by RTÉ, a series that would run for the next thirty-four years and produce over 400 programmes:

> *Radharc* is the title of a series of documentaries broadcast by RTÉ between 1962 and 1996. The first programme was aired on January 12th 1962, just 12 days after the new Irish television service was launched. Over the following 34 years, more than 400 programmes were televised. We have made 12 Radharc programmes available to view in this exhibition from RTÉ Archives. The word 'Radharc' (pronounced 'rye-ark') is the Gaelic for 'view', 'vision' or 'panorama'.[19]

What is especially interesting, in the context of this discussion, is that this programme was produced, directed and generally presented by priests, so *de facto*, it was commenting on current affairs and other issues from a very Catholic standpoint. Clearly, the centre that was Catholic hegemony in Ireland was reinforced by people watching priests act as reporters on television.

In Derridean terms, the transformative agency of *Father Ted* was that it altered this 'view' of priests from the serious to the satirical, which would be the first stage of a deconstructive reversal. Satire is very much an interrogative discourse in its mode of operation. As it pokes fun at objects, people and structures, it implicitly questions the standards and codes through which these objects, people and structures were accorded value in the first place. Rather than seeing the Church as an organisation that in some way transcends the norms of system, bureaucracy, hierarchy and the normal structures of society, this programme underlines just how much the Church is part of such structures. The visual image of a priest kicking his bishop 'up the arse', while another priest takes a photograph of this act, is an iconic metaphor of the change in the attitude of people to the Church as structure; it also shows the powerful transformative role that

19   RTÉ Archives <http://www.rte.ie/archives/exhibitions/1378-radharc/>.

cultural production – television, film, fiction – can have on deconstruct-ing master signifiers, decentring structures, and thereby paving the way for change in those structures.

At this juncture, I would like to bring two other visual metaphors to the fore in order to create an iconic image chain wherein the cultur-ally validated change in role of the Church as structure can be traced. These images involve another image of an Irish bishop and priest, as well as two broadly similar fictional representations, which, when viewed in conjunction with the Bishop Brennan episode in a secular quadriptych, will demonstrate the power of fiction as a teller of an alternative truth, to deconstruct hegemonic systems of power.[20] The first image is the iconic one of Ted kicking Bishop Brennan up the arse, while the grinning Dougal takes a photograph of this event. The second is also an image from televi-sion, involving a camera, albeit of a different order, a bishop and a priest.

On recalling the visit of Pope John Paul II to Galway for the youth mass in 1979, one of the images that stays in the mind is that of Father Michael Cleary and Bishop Eamon Casey warming up the crowd by leading them in the hymn 'Bind us Together'. In a way, this scene was the apotheosis of Catholic power in recent Ireland – the pope was drawing huge crowds, the youth mass was thronged with people, and two of the most popular clerics in Ireland, both men seen as being very much in touch with younger people, as well as being telegenic, were the masters of ceremonies. The future for the Church in Ireland seemed bright indeed. With the wisdom of hindsight, it is all too easy to unpack the personal lives of these men, and see them as synecdoches of what was wrong with the Church in Ireland, but that is not the aim of this chapter. Instead I want to juxtapose the different images of bishops and priests – Father Ted and Father Cleary; Bishop Brennan and Bishop Casey – fictional and factual, and then turn to a different set of signifying images.

In 2000, the film *American Beauty* appeared to widespread acclama-tion. The film, an intelligent probing of mid-life crises among middle-class

20   A quadriptych is a painting, typically an altarpiece, consisting of four leaves or panels joined by hinges or folds. They often feature mirroring images, which are then looked at together.

Americans, achieved both popular and critical acclaim. One of the central images of that film is the obsession of the central character, Lester Burnham, with a young friend of his daughter, Angela Hayes, a cheerleader. This obsession begins with Lester watching Angela go through her cheerleader routine, and obsessing about one image, namely that of Angela flipping up her skirt to reveal her underwear. This is an image which haunts Lester's daydreams, and also fuel his masturbatory fantasies. Indeed, Lester, in his voiceover, tells us that his early morning masturbation in the shower is the best part of his day: 'Look at me, jerking off in the shower ... This will be the high point of my day; it's all downhill from here.'[21] I call this to mind because nearly 100 years earlier, another narrative has a similar scene.

In the 'Nausicaa' episode of *Ulysses*, Gertie McDowell is being watched by Leopold Bloom, and as she leans back to watch fireworks, she catches her knee in her hand, revealing to Bloom's gaze her:

> nainsook knickers, the fabric that caresses the skin, better than those other pettiwidth, the green, four and eleven, on account of being white and she let him and she saw that he saw and then it went so high it went out of sight a moment and she was trembling in every limb from being bent so far back that he had a full view high up above her knee where no-one ever not even on the swing or wading and she wasn't ashamed and he wasn't either to look in that immodest way like that because he couldn't resist the sight of the wondrous revealment half offered like those skirtdancers behaving so immodest before gentlemen looking and he kept on looking, looking. She would fain have cried to him chokingly, held out her snowy slender arms to him to come, to feel his lips laid on her white brow, the cry of a young girl's love, a little strangled cry, wrung from her, that cry that has rung through the ages. And then a rocket sprang and bang shot blind blank and O! then the Roman candle burst and it was like a sigh of O! and everyone cried O! O! in raptures and it gushed out of it a stream of rain gold hair threads and they shed and ah! they were all greeny dewy stars falling with golden, O so lovely, O, soft, sweet, soft![22]

The similarity between the two men, both engaged in advertising and in their forties, neither of whom has had sex with his wife in years, and

21 Sam Mendes and Alan Ball, *American Beauty* (Universal City, CA: DreamWorks Home Entertainment, 2000).
22 James Joyce, *Ulysses*, ed. Hans Walter Gabler, Wolfhard Steppe and Claus Melchior, first published in 1922 (London: Bodley Head, 1989), 274.

between the two younger women, who enjoy the sexual attention of the gaze is clear. The dissimilarity is also clear. This scene in *Ulysses*, first serialised in *The Little Review*, was deemed to transgress moral good taste, and lead to confiscation, book burning, legal prosecution for obscenity, and banning in 1921.[23] The scene from the film translated into a number of awards including a Golden Globe and an Academy Award for the screenplay written by Alan Ball.

When we place these images together, in a quadriptych, two of bishops and two of sexual behaviour, what is interesting is the altered role of the Church in terms of the mindset of people exposed to those scenes. The shock and horror that followed Eamon Casey's revelations in 1992 was exacerbated by the wave of revelations that followed in terms of child abuse in church-run organisations. However, reaction to the image of Bishop Brennan is, I would argue, fuelled less by anger or hurt, and more by a sense that the Church is now just another organisation among many. The simple fact is that the symbolic order has changed, and our views and expectations of the clergy are very much not what they were twenty or thirty years ago. Indeed, kicking Bishop Brennan up the arse could well be a metaphor for the gradual disrespect for, or to put it more accurately, gradual lack of importance of, the hierarchical structure of the Church in the day-to-day lives of ordinary people. I would contend that books like *Ulysses*, which was banned from entry into Ireland and widely condemned as a dirty book, but which is now seen as a classic of literature, were a central part of this shift in power. Indeed the rise to respectability of *Ulysses* can be seen as an inverse chiasmus of the fall from grace of the Catholic Church: culture as now in the ascendant over religion.

The revelations about the sexual affairs of Eamon Casey and Michael Cleary, and the reluctance of the hierarchy to deal effectively or correctly with the complaints about paedophiles like Brendan Smyth and Ivan Payne, had a striking effect on the perception of the clergy in contemporary Ireland. In terms of church input into social policy and social issues, especially those of a sexual nature, there was untold damage done to the moral authority

---

23   Richard Ellmann, *James Joyce*, first published 1959 (Oxford: Oxford University Press, 1977), 518–19.

of the hierarchy, and while in earlier referenda about abortion and sexual matters, the hierarchy had a strong input, this lessened as the scandals became known. Being preached to on moral issues by an institution whose own morality was now increasingly subject to question was no longer an option for the Irish people. This altered perception of the Church has been a driver of change in Ireland and this is especially true with respect to the role of women and sexuality, as indicated in the *Ulysses* and *American Beauty* examples.

The images of the scenes of voyeurism and exhibitionism that we see from Gertie McDowell and Angela Hayes in *Ulysses* and *American Beauty*, respectively, are separated in time, demonstrating the hugely different symbolic order that exists in the world of today as opposed to that of the fictive time of *Ulysses*, 16 June 1904. In both texts, there is a certain level of desire on the part of both women and men: just as the men watch, so the women are aware and involved – these are not objects of the male scopic drive: they are participants in the scopic drive. Likewise, the two wives in these two narratives, Molly Bloom and Carolyn Burnham, are active participants in the sexual aspects of the narratives. Molly, famously, is having an affair with Blazes Boylan, having arranged that he will come to her home in Eccles Street later on 16 June, while her husband, aware of this, has obligingly left the way clear. Thus the eternal triangle, traditionally that of one man and two women, has been inverted and it is Molly who both has her cake (seed cake in her case) and eats it. Similarly, Carolyn is having a torrid affair with Buddy Kane, the Real Estate king, something of which Lester is also aware. Here, women are seen as free agents in terms of their sexual preferences, and no longer seen as possessions of men. The structures of the societies within which they live have radically altered, and consequently, so have their behaviours and their choices. Indeed, rapid change is a characteristic of contemporary culture, and the pace of change has been rampant in Ireland over the past twenty years. Women, in society, have become more subject than object, and are agents in their own lives as opposed to bearers of children, or cleaners of houses; they are looking at enhancing the quality their own lives, as opposed to being validated by serving tea to others, and refusing to take no for an answer, like Mrs Doyle.

This is the core problem facing the Church in this present context: it still clings to the sense of itself as an unchanging organisation, when in actual fact it has changed radically over the centuries. In almost every progressive field of social change, from the mother and child controversy, through contraception and the various social issues that have come before it, the Church has adopted an anti-progressive policy, one which it justifies by seeing itself as the guardian of immutable standards, frozen in the past. Many of these issues are involved with sexual behaviour, which reinforces the point made earlier that the culture of desire that permeates the contemporary Western world is inimical to the attitudes of the Church.

Again, in terms of postmodernism, the breakdown of grand narratives means the liberation of smaller ones, and the roles of sexual minorities, like gays and lesbians, has become ever more prominent in the wake of what I term the deconstruction of the Church as we know it, culminating in the passing of the same-sex marriage referendum in 2015. Both of these texts privilege female sexuality as developing through different societies. Just as social structures change, so too does the behaviour of the subjects within those structures. Part of the problem of the Church, it seems to me, is an inability to respond to the societal changes and symbolic conditions within which it exists. The issue of structure has been a preoccupation of this chapter, and it is with the Church's own definition of itself as a structure that I propose to conclude.

John Paul II, in his Apostolic Letter *Ordinatio Sacerdotalis* of 1994, made the position of the Church clear in terms of reasons as to why women have not been, and should not be, ordained. He said:

> Christ chose his apostles only from among men ... the exclusion of women from the priesthood is in accordance with God's plan for His Church. Christ's way of acting [only choosing men] did not proceed from sociological or cultural motives peculiar to his time. Rather it is to be seen as the faithful observance of a plan to be ascribed to the wisdom of the Lord of the universe.
>
> I declare ... that this judgement is to be definitively held by the Church's faithful. This tradition [*of excluding women*] has been faithfully maintained by the oriental churches.[24]

---

24   John Paul II, 'Apostolic Letter *Ordinatio Sacerdotalis* of John Paul II to the bishops of the Catholic Church on reserving priestly ordination to men alone' (The Vatican: Libreria Editrice Vaticana, 1994) <https://w2.vatican.va/content /john-paul-ii/en/

The clear point here is that Christ, as son of God, is a transcendental con-sciousness at work in a particular place and time: he is in time, but not of it, and as such, is not trammelled by its socio-cultural and linguistic mores and limitations. So, the pope's reasons for not ordaining women as part of his apostolic structure had less to do with the prevailing socio-economic status of women, which was little better than livestock at the time, and more to do with a transcendental grand plan. The Church, by extrapolation, is above and beyond the systems and structures of particular places and times, existing as a transcendent structure.

This is fine if one is willing to accept the discourse of the Church at face value, but when deconstructive theory is brought to bear, problems arise. If this specific choice of Christ is not to be explained by his contem-porary symbolic order, why have other such choices been explained dif-ferently, and have not been subsumed into church dogma? Christ chose to be a carpenter, he chose his apostles from a number of trades such as fishermen, tax collectors etc. Why are contemporary priests not asked to undergo training in carpentry, or to receive certificates of mastery in dif-ferent types of fishing? Christ went into a temple twice in his life that we know of according to Scripture: once to argue with the learned doctors, and once to purge the temple of money changers and hucksters. How odd, then, that the Vatican can give sanctuary to Archbishop Marcinkus, who stands accused of fraud and is liable to arrest if he leaves the precincts of the Vatican. All of the apostles were Jews; where does that leave a series of Italian popes, a Polish pope and a German pope? Why are those decisions not seen as beyond the prevailing sociology of Christ's place and time? I would argue that the reason that those questions were not asked before was precisely because the bishops were those *points de capiton* of this discourse, those master signifiers who controlled the play of meaning. Iconically, the kicking of Bishop Brennan up the arse is a ludic demonstration of the displacement of those master signifiers, and concomitantly a sign that the Church has lost its sense of being a transcendent organisation. Instead it is now just another structure in a crowded marketplace.

———————

apost_letters/1994/documents/hf_jp-ii_apl_19940522_ ordinatio-sacerdotalis. html>.

Indeed, further critique would reinforce this point. How can the Church claim to act outside of time, in a transcendent manner, when it avails itself of every possible safeguard of contemporary culture to defend itself against accusations? In a deal done with former minister Michael Woods, the Church has deflected payment liabilities to victims of institutional abuse onto the taxpayer. It has also taken legal action to defend itself against victims, and had Bishop Laws say one of the requiem masses for Pope John Paul II, while he himself was under a cloud in terms of his inaction in the face of rampant child abuse in his American diocese.

Yet, despite all of this, there is a glaring need for a form of the transcendent in contemporary secular Ireland. In many instances, this desire for something in which to believe has become displaced after the fall from grace of the Church. We see it in the fetishisation of sport and spectacle, as the almost countrywide investment into the championships of the GAA in both hurling and football provides a communal outlet for people to express a sense of something beyond themselves. It has been seen in the crowds who flocked to the relics of St Thérèse of Lisieux in 2001; it can be seen in the popularity of alternative forms of spirituality and in the outpouring of genuine emotion that greeted the passing away of Pope John Paul in 2005. Ironically, the grief, the communal sharing of sorrow and the widespread media coverage called to mind an event some eight years earlier, namely the death of Diana, Princess of Wales, in 1997. Here, too, there was a similar outpouring of grief, a binding of people around a departed icon – in a way the epitome of religious desire. Interestingly, however, in the aftermath of her death, things have progressed very much as normal: her name has gradually been forgotten and Prince Charles finally married the third person in his marriage to Diana, namely Camilla Parker-Bowles.

I would suggest that the same is true of the religious fervour which gripped Ireland and, indeed, the Catholic world, in the aftermath of the death of Pope John Paul. The emotional desire for religious experience, for that sense of communal belief, for an identity between the immanent and the transcendent, is very much part of being human, and in Ireland the Catholic religion has for a long time filled this void. Now, however, that the sense of the Church as transcendental structure has been deconstructed, and that it is seen as just another organisation striving to protect its own patch and its own members, people have moved on. To attempt to preach morals and ethics, while at the same time using every legal and political means to defend the organisation against legitimate charges from victims of abuse, has really just placed the Church as one more set of systems – it is the metaphorical equivalent of kicking Bishop Brennan up the arse. He is no longer seen as a religious icon, not to be touched by the venality of human failings: he is just one more abusive boss, who has instilled fear and resentment among his staff, and suffers the consequences accordingly. This, of course, is a metaphorical equivalent of the sense of disappointment felt by Catholics when two of the more charismatic figures within the Church, Eamon Casey, the bishop who scourged governments about the third world, who reputedly drove too fast and drank too much, but who was seen as a decent man, and Michael Cleary, the original singing priest, were both found to be involved in sexual relationships. In the wake of later scandals, these were relatively minor offences among, after all, consenting adults. And indeed, the Church has had a long history of sacerdotal sexual connections: it is not for nothing that there are Irish surnames such as Mac an Sagairt (McEntaggert); Mac an Easpaig (McEnespy) and Mac an Papa (Pope).

However, what is significant here is the differentiating of the status of the Church as transcendent system and as an immanent one. To preach about the redress of poverty or about sexually correct behaviour, as both Casey and Cleary did, on the one hand, and to be found violating those very precepts themselves on the other, made it clear that the Church's warrant to be seen as a transcendental system was in no way sustainable. The position of women in this structure has also been significant, though interestingly, the Church, as already noted, as the one remaining state institution which generically discriminates against women (with the exception of certain clubs), has rarely come under sustained attack from the feminist movement. Now this could be because women as a group have taken on board the pope's transcendental justification for the men-only rule on ordination. However, I think that this state of affairs is a further index of the increasing sense of irrelevance with which the Church is viewed by women – they are just not interested in this last bastion of patriarchy.

Instead, feminists have concentrated on issues of sexual liberation, stressing the freedom of women to control their own procreative processes,

and with the increasing availability of contraception of all types, the control
of the Church over sexual matters has waned completely. Thus, in terms
of our quadriptych, the difference between those 'skirtdancers' separated
by over 100 years, Gertie McDowall and Angela Hayes, is that the latter,
while still a virgin, is so by choice and is quite happy to have sex with Lester
towards the end of the film with no sense of guilt whatsoever. The path-
ways of desire are now open to exploration by both sexes, and any form
of external control by the Church has just lost all validity. People, in this
secular age, are now inclined to voice their desire, and the concomitant
guilt is no longer the price that such desire must pay.

In this way, they are voicing the presence of a different structure, a
new symbolic order, a dissemination of control, and, in short, are joining
Father Ted and Dougal in symbolically kicking Bishop Brennan up the
arse. Thus through two sets of visual images, one dealing with power figures and the other with sexual desire, the alteration in the grand narrative
of the Catholic Church in Ireland is mapped out. The first images, one set
dealing with a bishop in his pomp, accompanied by his priest, addressing
the multitudes in front of the pope, the other of a bishop being kicked up
the arse by one of his priests, delineates the deconstruction of the central
position of the Catholic Church in Ireland. The second set, of two young
women allowing themselves to be the object of the male scopic drive, but
also to a degree controlling that gaze, is another index of the primacy of
desire, both sexual and other, and of a form of liberation of desire from
the repressive regime of traditional Irish Catholic doctrine. The change in
female attitudes to sexual desire is an index of that the symbolic order of
Ireland has changed and is changing, a process which has and will continue
to cause reverberations within the Church.

In the wake of the revelations in October 2005, of the report on child
abuse in the Diocese of Ferns,[25] with strong blame being placed on the
bishop of the diocese for not taking the required action, it would seem as
if the broader community is engaged in a parallel process of deconstructing

25   *The Ferns Report* (2005) Report of Investigation into Catholic Diocese of Ferns
     <http://www.bishopaccountability.org/ferns/>.

the power of the Church and its pretensions to being an unchanging vehicle of moral certitude. In this context it is important to note that deconstruction, contrary to popular belief, does not equate with destruction; instead it suggests a dismantling of the traditional binary oppositions and the creation of a new structure wherein the power relations are more equally defined. In our context, this deconstruction has been enacted through culture, in terms of the power of the bishops being kicked up the arse, to use a colloquialism, and the desire of women being recognised as equal to that of men. If the Church is to survive within the new symbolic order of a postmodern, postcolonial, secular Ireland that has more in common with either Boston or Berlin than Rome, it will need to take these cultural lessons seriously.

JASON KING

9   Irish Multicultural Fiction: Metaphors of Miscegenation and Interracial Romance

The image of blackened hands digging into the Irish earth constitutes a core motif in contemporary Irish literature. One of its most prominent figures is that of the 'farmer-poet' whose agricultural labour is imagined to be a metaphor for creative expression. Whether it be the 'frosty fingers' of Patrick Kavanagh's 'farmer-poet' Art McCooey (1939) that work the 'stony grey soil' of County Monaghan, or Seamus Heaney's recurrent image of 'cold', 'dead', 'fingers' in *Death of a Naturalist* (1966), each of them employs the metaphor of digging as a synecdoche for the cultural conditioning of the Irish writer who grounds his or her creative imagination in an experience of tactile contact with the Irish soil. More recently, the Latvian migrant and author of *The Mushroom Covenant* Laima Muktupavela has written about how her Irish employer 'forbade' her to wear gloves until 'the mushrooms quickly turned her fingers black'.[1] This chapter considers whether Muktupavela's blackened fingers can be incorporated into the Irish literary tradition of Kavanagh and Heaney, and the extent to which Irish culture is either receptive or racialised to the exclusion of immigrant voices like her own.

Broadly speaking, my intention is to examine the emergence of what I will define as Irish multicultural literature, and the narrative strategies employed by Irish and immigrant authors who seek to broaden and contest cultural definitions of Irishness by emphasising its openness and hospitality or ingrained hostility to newcomers within the Irish host society. More specifically, I want to argue that Irish and immigrant writers such as Dermot

---

[1]   Dan Bilefsky, 'Migration's Flip Side: All roads lead out', *International Herald Tribune*, 6 December 2005.

Bolger, Clare Boylan, Bisi Adigun, Roddy Doyle and Cauvery Madhavan tend to imagine a positive ideal of multiculturalism through metaphors of miscegenation and interracial romance. They evoke feelings of cross-cultural affection to symbolise Ireland's embrace of diversity, an affecting Irishness that equates the conciliation of cultural difference with the resolution of a romantic plotline. Their interracial romantic plot lines thus often centre on the self-discovery of the protagonist of his or her commonality of experience with the figure of the Other, either immigrant or Irish, across the cultural, geo-political, or racial divide between Ireland and immigrant countries of origin. In the words of Roddy Doyle, the premise of Irish multicultural fiction is that 'someone born in Ireland meets someone who has come to live here'.[2] Their encounter brings together Irish nationals and newcomers into a single story line and imaginative zone of contact. Elsewhere I have noted that, in the context of Irish theatre, the portrayal of interracial romance seems less indicative of the reconciliation rather than the failure to resolve issues of cultural difference.[3] Most of the works I examine here develop an interracial romantic plotline as a symbolic shorthand for the resolution of cultural conflict, but their achievement of romantic fulfilment is based less, I will argue, on the accommodation rather than the elision of cultural differences that they purport to reconcile.

By contrast, it is the refusal of cultural affinity, rejection of the romantic plotline, and identification of the Irish as the beneficiaries of global inequality that defines a subversive counter-current of Irish multicultural fiction, especially in Laima Muktupavela's chapter from *The Mushroom Covenant* entitled 'Black Balts Among Celts: A Tale of Itinerant Latvian Workers in Ireland.' Although she employs the iconic motif of blackened hands digging into the Irish earth, it is not to write herself into an Irish literary tradition but rather to emphasise the exploitation and lack of empathy that immigrants experience in Ireland. Together these works call into question whether Irish intercultural encounters should be imagined as reciprocal or

---

2   Roddy Doyle, *The Deportees* (London: Jonathan Cape, 2007), xiii.
3   Jason King, 'Interculturalism and Irish Theatre: The Portrayal of Immigrants on the Irish Stage', *Irish Review* 33 (Spring 2005), 23–39: 33.

inequitable forms of exchange, and whether Ireland itself is an open and receptive or closed and racialised society for the immigrants who live there.

The interracial romantic plotline appears a thematic vestige of the nine-teenth-century national tale's romance of reconciliation between English and Irish protagonists whose betrothal allegorically consecrates the Act of Union,[4] but its symbolic resolution of cultural rather than political conflict reflects more recent Irish social concerns. Before the 1990s, immigrants rarely appear as character types, let alone romantic partners, in the vast majority of works of Irish fiction. The exception, of course, is Leopold Bloom, whose cross-cultural heritage and intimate familiarity with the immigrant experience as a second generation Hungarian-Irish Jew posi-tions him as an intermediary between the mainstream and the margins of Irish culture. As a 'foreigner' with 'dark eyes' in Gerty MacDowell's fantasy who captivates Molly because he is 'so foreign from the others', Bloom is imagined a potential marital partner and figure of cross-cultural attraction, a prototype for the protagonist in an Irish interracial romance.[5] Indeed, whether or not he is ultimately restored in Molly's affections, *Ulysses* con-tains the lineaments of such an interracial romantic plotline insofar as it links the resolution of marital tension with the conciliation of cultural difference as the chief obstacles that Bloom has to overcome. Although often perceived as a foreigner, he epitomises an ideal of acculturation and the accommodation of difference in his social interactions and family life.[6]

Another early fictional representation of the figure of the immigrant in Irish culture occurs in James Plunkett's short story 'A Walk Through the Summer' (*The Trusting and the Maimed*, 1959). It is set in a mid-1950s suburban Dublin home and narrated mainly from the perspective of Casey,

---

4 Miranda Burgess, 'The national tale and allied genres', *Cambridge Companion to the Irish Novel*, ed. John Wilson Foster (Cambridge: Cambridge University Press, 2006), 39–59.

5 James Joyce, *Ulysses* (London: Penguin, 1992), 465, 496.

6 See Jason King, 'Commemorating *Ulysses*, the Bloomsday Centenary, and the Irish Citizenship Referendum', *Memory Ireland: James Joyce and Cultural Memory*, ed. Oonagh Frawley and Katharine O'Callaghan (Syracuse, NY: Syracuse University Press, 2014), 172–86.

a bohemian houseguest who is conducting an illicit affair with Barbara, his married host. The household is also occupied by a Polish refugee, Sara, who 'had come from a world of devastated homes, a chaos of maimed people and orphaned children, so remote from the untouched safety of Dublin that few who met her realized it had had any real existence.'[7] As John Brannigan notes, Plunkett represents the suburban gathering as a metaphor to 'explore the social dynamics of a triangular relationship between the "new" Ireland, typified by the cosmopolitan middle class, the "old" Ireland, defined by the twin poles of Catholicism and nationalism, and the figure of the refugee, who is treated with either condescension or contempt'.[8] More specifically, Sara is treated with a mixture of hospitality and hostility by these representatives of the 'new' and 'old' Irish: 'with kindness' by the middle-class household into which she is invited as 'almost, but not quite one of the family', but also with contempt by their family friend, an impoverished Irish blind man who stigmatises her as 'a foreign Catholic[,] brought up in indifference' and not fully appreciative of 'the great faith of the Irish and ... all they suffered'.[9] Her perceived indifference to the magnitude of Irish suffering 'for the faith' ironically incurs the blind man's enmity towards her because of his myopic belief that 'foreign Catholics' are 'soft'.[10] Her dignified assertion that 'I think we suffered' enjoins the reader to supply that sense of cross cultural understanding that is so utterly lacking in her Irish interlocutor.

More significantly, narrative resolution is realised in Plunkett's short story through the abandonment rather than achievement of romantic fulfilment. The narrative comes to a crisis when Casey decides to end his affair and consoles himself that Barbara would find 'plenty of distractions' to alleviate her 'suffering'.[11] Once again, 'suffering' becomes a register of cultural disjunction between Irish insularity and Polish calamity. Brannigan

7   James Plunkett, *The Trusting and the Maimed* (London: Hutchison, 1959), 35.
8   John Brannigan, 'Race, Cosmopolitanism, and Modernity: Irish Writing and Culture in the Late Nineteen Fifties', *Irish University Review* 34.2 (2004), 332–50: 344.
9   Plunkett, *The Trusting and the Maimed*, 40, 53.
10   Plunkett, *The Trusting and the Maimed*, 61–2.
11   Plunkett, *The Trusting and the Maimed*, 68.

notes 'the implication, subtly suggested but surprisingly barbed, is that the liberal tolerance and graciousness of Barbara and [her husband] John, their apparent generosity towards Sara, their polite forbearance of the blind man, and even Barbara's supposedly frivolous affair with Casey, are all the superficial and self-serving distractions of a bored and indifferent suburban middle class'.[12] As the affair unravels, Sara herself becomes an unwitting 'distraction' for Casey's lascivious friend Ellis: 'Out of some nightmare background of suffering, at some awakened memory of a family scattered and murdered, Sara had wept in front of Ellis. He had been touched to the extent that he desired to seduce her.'[13] Casey's indifference and Ellis's callous desire for Sara reduce her to an afterthought in the resolution of the narrative's romantic plotline. Its suppression further circumscribes her role as a marginal rather than integral member of the household and precludes the possibility of reciprocal cultural exchange. Ultimately, Sara is more a static than a sympathetic figure: not quite part of the family, nor in a position to start her own.

The romantic plotline remains similarly unrealised in Dermot Bolger's play about the departure and arrival of Irish and Polish unwed mothers in Ballymun entitled 'The Townlands of Brazil' (2007). It is a site specific work that was commissioned to mark the regeneration of the area and the opening of the Axis Arts Centre. As Peter Crawley notes, the play pairs the story of 'a young unmarried Irish girl [in 1963] who conceives a child and chooses emigration over the looming threat of the Magdalen laundry' with the reversed journey of a young Polish woman who arrives in Ballymun in the present. 'In its echoes between the parallel stories of Irish and Polish exile … [the play] offers something of a dramatic palimpsest, in which the new city is inscribed in the old one, and the changing face of the country emerges.'[14] This inscription of the immigrant into the historical narrative of Irish emigration Ronit Lentin describes as 'return of the national

12 Brannigan, 'Race, Cosmopolitanism, and Modernity', 347.
13 Plunkett, *The Trusting and the Maimed*, 68.
14 Peter Crawley, 'Searching for Home from Home', *Irish Times*, 17 November 2006.

repressed':[15] it is also a narrative conceit that provides the underlying premise for a number of works of contemporary Irish theatre.[16] In a similar
vein, Bolger's play dramatises the plight of the unwed Polish immigrant
and Irish emigrant mother as two sides of the same story. Whatever their
commonalities of experience, however, their paths never cross nor bring
Irish nationals and newcomers into contact with one another, as in the
interracial romantic plotline. Indeed, as unwed mothers, they represent
the antithesis of romantic fulfilment, and their offspring symbolise failed
relationships rather than an ideal of reconciliation.

Before 'The Townlands of Brazil', Bolger had also explored the shared
historical experience of Irish and immigrant industrial labourers in his novel
The Journey Home (1990). Its protagonist Shay appears to represent a new
generation of emigrants who leave Ireland in the 1980s not just because of
unemployment but also in search of the more culturally expansive 'world
they had grown up with in their minds: the American films, the British
programmes, the Dutch football they watched on satellite channels.' 'For
most' of them, Bolger writes, 'the fields their fathers worked would have
been exile'.[17] That Shay makes common cause with the Turkish 'political
refugees'[18] and Gastarbeiter or guest workers he encounters as fellow travellers in the cities and factories of Holland and Germany is thus indicative
not only of his openness to other cultures but of the insularity of the Irish
cultural milieu that he has left behind. His expression of labour solidarity
with a group of Turkish employees during a strike in Germany for better
working conditions and equal pay leads them to transform their factory

15   Ronit Lentin, 'Anti-racist responses to the racialisation of Irishness: Disavowed
      multiculturalism and its discontents', *Racism and Anti-Racism in Ireland*, ed. Ronit
      Lentin and Robbie McVeigh (Belfast: Beyond the Pale, 2002), 223.
16   See Jason King, 'Black Saint Patrick: Irish Interculturalism in Theoretical Perspective
      and Theatre Practice', *Global Ireland*, ed. Ondrej Pilný and Clare Wallace (Prague:
      Litteraria Pragensia, 2005), 38–51; Jason King, 'Beyond Ryanga: The Image of Africa
      in Contemporary Irish Theatre', *Echoes Down the Corridor: Irish Theatre Past, Present,
      and Futures*, ed. Riana O'Dwyer and Patrick Lonergan (Dublin: Carysfort Press,
      2007), 153–68.
17   Dermot Bolger, *The Journey Home* (Dublin: Viking, 1990), 107.
18   Bolger, *The Journey Home*, 329.

floor into a carnivalesque space of cultural intermixture. 'It was really great crack actually. Before then none of us has really mixed much' Shay recalls.[19]

When their revelries are disrupted by a party of strike breakers, however, what he finds particularly devastating is not the physical assault that he suffers but that the perpetrators are 'pure, unmistakeable bog Irish'.[20] Their refusal of affinity with their fellow Turkish migrant workers identifies the antagonists in the novel with the enemies of cultural diversity. Shay's experience abroad thus ironically confirms his belief that Ireland is a fundamentally inhospitable country which leads him to repudiate his Irish identity altogether, and to withdraw into an ever more interiorised sense of self: his 'own home place which no longer exists except in [his] head'.[21] Ultimately, the novel's narrator Hano similarly renounces his national identity and derives his only sense of cultural belonging from his condition of displacement, as a self-professed 'internal exile' and fellow traveller with 'tramps, Gypsies, the enemies of the community who stay put'. In place of Ireland, 'the only nation I give allegiance to', he declares, is his dispossessed family.[22] Conor McCarthy argues that there is a deeply conservative aesthetic ideology at work in Bolger's treatment of 'such themes as emigration ... [and] the deterritorialization of identity' which is predicated upon 'an implied narrative of victimhood as simplistic as any ... of national struggle'.[23] Be this as it may, the novel's renunciation of Irish national identity in favour of itinerancy and internal exile demarcates one extreme position of cultural self-definition that immigrant communities have to grapple and negotiate with in their own narratives of identity formation.

Dermot Bolger's novel *The Journey Home* can be most usefully regarded, I would suggest, as a narrative of the interregnum, written at the very moment of Ireland's transformation from an emigrant sending to an immigrant receiving society. Since its publication in 1990, cross-cultural

19   Bolger, *The Journey Home*, 273.
20   Bolger, *The Journey Home*, 274.
21   Bolger, *The Journey Home*, 276.
22   Bolger, *The Journey Home*, 390, 391.
23   Conor McCarthy, *Modernisation: Crisis and Culture in Ireland, 1969–1992* (Dublin: Four Courts Press, 2000), 151–2, 164.

encounters between Irish and immigrant characters have become much more common in Irish fiction. The interracial romantic plotline is parodied, for example, in Clare Boylan's novel *Black Baby* (1988), which invokes the memory of Ireland's missionary history in a seemingly magical realist fashion to imagine the 'homecoming' of an African black baby to Ireland as a metaphor for the 'return of the national repressed'. The frontispiece for the novel is from the *Epistle of Paul to the Hebrews*: 'Be not forgetful to entertain strangers: for thereby some have entertained angels unawares.' Thus, Boylan's protagonist is an elderly Irish woman named Alice who, when confronted with an adult black woman, Dinah, on her door step in Dublin, assumes that she must be the now fully grown African black baby whom she symbolically adopted in her youth. Like 'all the children [she] bought a black baby', as 'few could resist this early placation of maternity', she recalls, and now, finally, her 'black baby' 'had come home'.[24] The novel's fantastic plotline is further complicated by an unstable narrative perspective that is largely filtered through Alice's increasingly doddering form of consciousness.

Ultimately, the character of the black baby is revealed to be an impostor from Brixton who is of African descent, but in the course of the narrative she genuinely befriends Alice as well as a number of other socially marginalised Irish figures, like her impotent lover Figgis, across cultural, generational and racial lines. 'I always wanted to sleep with a black woman', Figgis declares,[25] but proves unable to consummate their relationship. Boylan's portrayal of thwarted miscegenation parodies the interracial romantic plotline as well as the idea that Ireland's 'black babies' – the symbolic progeny of missionary encounters with the peoples of Africa – are immaculately conceived from a collective spirit of missionary zeal. As the iconic offspring of Ireland's relationship with African cultures, Boylan's black baby incarnates the metaphor of miscegenation that is grounded in the Irish missions' appeal for support through a figurative exercise in interracial adoption. If she represents the 'return of the national repressed', however, Boylan's immigrant is also revealed to have a lot in common with Alice and Figgis who exist at very

24   Clare Boylan, *Black Baby* (London: Hamish Hamilton, 1988), 49.
25   Boylan, *Black Baby*, 46.

different removes from the mainstream of Irish society. Their shared experience of marginalisation as black and elderly women and an unemployed alcoholic becomes a vehicle for their reciprocal intercultural exchange.

This ideal of cultural reciprocity is also figured through the metaphor of interracial romance in Cauvery Madhavan's novel *Paddy Indian* (2001). As William Flanagan notes, Madhavan's novel 'tells the story of a surgeon from India who emigrates to Ireland and becomes involved with the chief surgeon's daughter'.[26] Their 'cross-cultural relationship'[27] appears almost entirely devoid of 'friction between the [Indian] newcomer ... and the native-born Irish' woman.[28] Instead, it is her recreational drug use rather than cultural incompatibility that proves to be the most insurmountable blocking agent that threatens to undermine their romance. It is true that Madhavan's Indian protagonist Sunil does complain that 'we knew much more about the Irish before we came to Ireland than they know about us Indians', and her Indian characters do grapple 'with the incongruity of growing up with westernised aspirations and Indian values',[29] but by and large these are revealed in the course of the narrative to be complementary cultural norms.

Ironically, the spectre of interracial conflict that *Paddy Indian* represses appears more evident in the life of its author. As William Flanagan observes, 'Cauvery herself had immigrated [to Ireland from Madras] in 1987 with her surgeon husband, raising questions about the link between biography and fictional storytelling' that he posed when he interviewed the couple.[30] More specifically, Flanagan queried the extent to which they, as 'people of colour' in Ireland, were 'perceived and accepted by other members of [Irish] society'. By and large they describe their experiences to have been overwhelmingly positive, but Madhavan's husband Prakash, the role model for her aspiring Indian surgeon in *Paddy Indian*, expresses doubts about

---

26 William Flanagan, *Ireland Now: Tales from the Global Island* (Notre Dame, IN: University of Notre Dame Press, 2007), 231.
27 Cauvery Madhavan, *Paddy Indian* (London: Black Amber Books, 2001), 199.
28 Flanagan, *Ireland Now*, 231.
29 Madhavan, *Paddy Indian*, 36, 180.
30 Flanagan, *Ireland Now*, 230.

whether the Irish medical system – and, by extension, Irish society as a whole – is as meritocratic and colour blind as the novel implies. In his own words: 'the truth is for me to have got [a] job [in a hospital consultancy position] is the exception rather than the rule'.[31] As a rule, occupational mobility is more limited for immigrants and visible minorities in Ireland, he suggests: 'the widespread perception of discrimination [against their] promotion' in the work place would seem to be well founded. 'It's blatantly obvious to me what they are trying to tell a black person', Prakash adds: such discrimination 'hasn't happened to me, but I can see it happening all around me'.[32] Thus, whereas Madhavan's fictional protagonist encounters no significant obstacles to hinder his advancement in the Irish medical system, his actual prototype, her husband, offers a much less reassuring view. If Madhavan's novel is premised on the positive experiences 'of newly arrived immigrants like herself becoming Indo-Irish or Paddy Indians'[33] in a largely welcoming Irish society, then it also appears compensatory for their anxieties about discrimination and exclusion. The resolution of the interracial romantic plotline in *Paddy Indian* provides an anodyne for these apprehensions that appear repressed in the text.

A similarly light-hearted approach to the portrayal of cultural difference can be discerned in Roddy Doyle's collection of short stories entitled *The Deportees* (2007), many of which first appeared in the Irish immigrant newspaper *Metro Éireann*. Like Cauvery Madhavan, Doyle signifies an ideal of Irish openness to other cultures through the metaphor of interracial romance. For example, in 'Guess Who Is Coming for the Dinner', 'The Deportees' and 'I Understand', Doyle's African protagonists Ben, Gilbert and Tom, all of whom are asylum seekers from Nigeria, find some measure of social acceptance in the arms of Irish women, whereas in '57% Irish' the Irish protagonist Ray Brady signals the host society's commitment to cultural diversity through the consummation of his relationship with his Russian girlfriend Darya. 'Black Hoodie' begins with an Irish adolescent's assertion that 'my girlfriend is Nigerian'; and in 'Home to Harlem' the

31   Flanagan, *Ireland Now*, 235.
32   Flanagan, *Ireland Now*, 236.
33   Flanagan, *Ireland Now*, 241.

black Irish character Declan feels enamoured with America after 'hooking up' with his love interest Kim.[34] In 'The Pram' the romantic storyline is disrupted when a Polish nanny's assignation with a Lithuanian man is exposed by the children she tends and then frightens with a disturbing Gothic tale to exact her revenge. Her thwarted liaison appears emblematic of failed acculturation. In each of these stories, Doyle employs the narrative device of interracial romance to signify that 'contact is the key' to resolving issues of cultural difference and 'ending racism in Ireland',[35] which Doyle believes is an incidental rather than a structural feature of Irish society. The repeated resolution of cultural conflict through romantic fulfilment symbolises Irish acceptance of immigrants whose presence constitutes no underlying threat to the nation's normative self-image. And yet, in each of Doyle's short stories reconciliation is achieved through the elision rather than accommodation of cultural difference. Both the gestural short story form and Doyle's own signature style of highly idiomatic urban realism convey surface impressions of intercultural contact between Dublin's working-class and immigrant communities that learn to empathise with one another as fellow submerged population groups, but their mutual identification is registered through the medium of popular culture that inflects Doyle's style to such an extent that it flattens out all cultural differences between them. Declan Kiberd and Luke Gibbons both interpret Jimmy Rabbitte's famous contention in *The Commitments* 'that the Irish were the blacks of Europe' as evidence of wider imaginative bonds of sympathy the Irish feel for other disempowered and impoverished groups.[36] As a sequel to *The Commitments*, Doyle's short story 'The Deportees' presses Jimmy Rabbitte back into service to demonstrate that African immigrants are the

---

34 Doyle, *The Deportees*, 130, 192.
35 Maureen T. Reddy, 'Reading and Writing Race in Ireland: Roddy Doyle in *Metro Eireann*', *Irish University Review* 35.2 (2005), 374–88: 382.
36 Declan Kiberd, 'Strangers in their Own Country', *Multi-Culturalism: The View from the Two Irelands* (Cork: Cork University Press, 2001), 48; Luke Gibbons, 'The Global Cure: History, Therapy, and the Celtic Tiger', *Reinventing Ireland: Culture, Society, and the Global Economy*, ed. Michael Cronin, Luke Gibbons and Peadar Kirby (London: Pluto Press, 2002), 92–4.

true Northsiders of Dublin. Kiberd likens these imaginative identifications between Africa and Ireland to the same spirit of interracial solidarity that made the Irish 'the largest contributors to Third World relief in
Live Aid'.[37] In Doyle's short story 'Guess Who's Coming for the Dinner',
his protagonist Larry Linane impresses this fact upon his African guest in
order to illustrate that 'the Irish are warm friendly people',[38] a self-image
that is rarely challenged in the text.

Thus, it is through the medium of interracial romance and popular
culture – soul music, Live Aid, the multicultural medley of styles performed
by the rock band the Deportees – that the Irish express their affinity with
other peoples and, more importantly, that immigrants become integrated
into Irish society. For example, in 'New Boy' and 'I Understand', African
immigrants adjust to life in Dublin and make friends through their gradual
acquisition of Dublin slang and working-class attitudes of irreverence to
authority, a kind of assimilation through slagging. Intercultural contact also
occurs in Doyle's fiction in conspicuously modern and urban settings: a
Liffey barge, a multi-ethnic classroom, an immigrant hostel, Henry Street
shops and department stores, Temple Bar. Larry Linnane's positive self-
image is reinforced every time he drives around the Artane roundabout
which makes him feel 'modern, successful, Irish'; while Jimmy Rabbitte is
energised by the cosmopolitan ambience of the Forum super-pub, with
its 'Portuguese looking barman, Spanish looking lounge-girl, Chinese
looking girl on the stool beside him, good looking pint settling in front
of him, REM's new album on the sound system … African locals chat-
ting and laughing.'[39] These modern settings are imagined as multicultural
spaces that appear devoid of either ethnic friction or local association. Their
incompatibility with the more localised working-class environs that Doyle
is more renowned for, along with the incongruity of African immigrants
speaking Dublin slang, provide his short stories with much of their comic
impetus. It would be pointless to expect a more nuanced and sophisticated
representation of cultural contact than Doyle's use of genre and style can

37   Kiberd, 'Strangers in their Own Country', 55.
38   Doyle, *The Deportees*, 15.
39   Doyle, *The Deportees*, 3, 39.

deliver. His short stories attest to the redemptive power of popular culture to transcend and negate cultural difference while exposing its limits as a medium for intercultural exchange.

Roddy Doyle and Bisi Adigun's new version of *The Playboy of the Western World* resembles Doyle's short stories in its development of an interracial romantic plotline between Christopher Malomo and Pegeen and saturation of the script with popular cultural references.[40] Its transformation of Synge's protagonist, however, from an archetypal figure of the itinerant storyteller into a Nigerian asylum seeker provides a more substantive premise for intercultural contact than Doyle's short stories because it is anchored in the recuperation of collective memory. Adigun and Doyle's new version of *The Playboy* is set in a 'modern suburban pub on the west side of Dublin'[41] like The Forum super-pub in 'The Deportees', where Christopher Malomo ingratiates himself into the family of a Dublin crime lord through his physical prowess and prodigious feats of storytelling. Although thoroughly adapted to a contemporary Dublin setting, the plotline of the play closely adheres to Synge's script and thereby inscribes the figure of the immigrant into a long lineage of itinerant storytellers and seanachies who similarly find hospitality by regaling their hosts such as, in Pegeen Mike's words, 'Owen Roe O'Sullivan or the poets of the Dingle Bay ... fine fiery fellows'[42] whom refugees are imagined to resemble. By equating asylum seekers with these archetypal figures, Adigun and Doyle represent them to be the most recent incarnation of the seanachie whose claim to hospitality is deeply rooted in Irish cultural memory.

The production of their new version of *The Playboy of the Western World* was a commercial success but garnished mixed reviews. On the

---

40 See Jason King, 'Contemporary Irish Theatre, the New *Playboy* Controversy, and the Economic Crisis', *Irish Studies Review* 24 (2016), 67–78.

41 Bisi Adigun and Roddy Doyle, *The Playboy of the Western World: In A New Version By Bisi Adigun and Roddy Doyle. Theatre as Resource: Guidance Notes*, ed. Aoife Lucey, Helen Blackhurst and Phil Kingston (Dublin: Abbey Theatre, 2007), 24 <http://www.abbeytheatre.ie/pdfs/ Playboy-notes.pdf>.

42 John Millington Synge, 'The Playboy of the Western World' [1907], *Irish Writing in the Twentieth Century: A Reader*, ed. David Pierse (Cork: Cork University Press, 2000), 176.

one hand, Luke Gibbons lauded their adaptation of Synge in *The Irish Times* as a 'dress rehearsal [for] a future multi-ethnic Ireland, a western world renewed through contact with other wider worlds'.[43] On the other hand, Peter Crawley, Karen Fricker and Susan Conley found fault with both the language and the politics of the play, which they felt were insufficiently evocative of either Synge's poetic lyricism or the reality of racism in modern Ireland. In particular, they objected to its seemingly naïve portrayal 'of mixed race romance' as a plot device that appears devoid of 'dramatic racial tension'.[44] According to Karen Fricker, Adigun and Doyle do not place sufficient emphasis on their protagonist's African ethnicity to such an extent that 'once his provenance is established, his blackness is pretty much ignored, even when Christy and Pegeen present themselves as a couple'.[45] As in *Paddy Indian* and *The Deportees*, the play's interracial romantic plotline serves the same allegorical function to symbolise Irish attitudes of openness and acceptance of immigrants, a positively receptive ideal that is personified by Pegeen. Thus, Christopher Malomo perceives her as a welcoming figure who 'told me I would find peace and happiness here'.[46] Negative criticism of this plot device of interracial attraction as appearing devoid of 'racial tension' could just as readily be levelled against most of the works of Irish multicultural fiction discussed here.

The play's treatment of celebrity culture and colourful criminality has also generated controversy. The ultimate transformation of Christopher Malomo from Synge's 'likely gaffer in the end of all'[47] into a 'hard man'[48] could certainly be interpreted as trivialising the original Playboy as a popular cultural stereotype. But the pervasive influence of popular culture does not negate cultural difference in the new play, as it does in Doyle's short stories,

43 Luke Gibbons, 'Finding Integration through engaging with our past', *Irish Times*, 29 October 2007.
44 Susan Conley, 'The Playboy of the Western World: A New Version by Bisi Adigun and Roddy Doyle', *Irish Theatre Magazine*, 5 October 2007.
45 Karen Fricker, 'The Playboy of the Western World: A New Version by Bisi Adigun and Roddy Doyle', *Variety*, 9 October 2007.
46 Adigun and Doyle, *The Playboy of the Western World*, 54.
47 Synge, 'The Playboy of the Western World', 194.
48 Adigun and Doyle, *The Playboy of the Western World*, 10.

because it is counterbalanced by the archetypal significance of the figure
of the itinerant storyteller. Whether he be a seanachie, Synge's 'fine, fiery,
fellow', an asylum seeker or a hard man, the archetype itself is deeply rooted
in Irish culture and its recuperation by immigrants provides the dramatic
impetus for Adigun and Doyle's play. They both declare that 'every asylum
seeker has a story to tell';[49] and Christopher Malomo's account of a refugee's
journey to Ireland resonates with Synge's own description of tramping as
a 'lonesome thing to be passing small towns with lights shining sideways
when the night is down, or going in strange places'.[50] Christopher Malomo
similarly recounts to Pegeen that the refugee's journey 'can be a lonely and
terrible experience ... Crossing the desert, for days, burnt, scorched, dehy-
drated and famished ... And in this city, where everybody stares at me ... I
do not exist. I have become simply a feeling. Sheer and utter loneliness'.[51]
He reimagines the plight of the asylum seeker through the lens of Synge's
vagabonds, as another manifestation of 'the return of the national repressed'.
Like Synge's original playboy, Christopher Malomo is able to gain acceptance and find hospitality in a new community through his imaginative acts
of storytelling and capacity for reinvention. Ultimately, it is the power of
self-invention through storytelling that both versions of the play affirm,
whether it be to revive the national character or incorporate the immigrant
into Irish culture. The 'great gap'[52] or 'huge difference'[53] between 'a gallous
story and a dirty deed' exposes communal hypocrisy in the old version
and cultural insularity in the new version of *The Playboy*: but in both, the
protagonist's eventual triumph over communal adversity encourages the
audience to reimagine its sense of Irishness in his own image.

By contrast, a much more negative view of the Irish host society
as intrinsically racialised and hostile to immigrants is expressed in the
Latvian Laima Muktupavela's short story 'Black Balts Among Celts.' As
I have noted, Muktupavela eschews the interracial romantic plotline and

49 Adigun and Doyle, *The Playboy of the Western World*, 28, 32.
50 Synge, 'The Playboy of the Western World', 182.
51 Adigun and Doyle, *The Playboy of the Western World*, 62.
52 Synge, 'The Playboy of the Western World', 193.
53 Adigun and Doyle, *The Playboy of the Western World*, 12.

denies any possibility of reconciliation between her Irish and immigrant characters. Rather, her novel *The Mushroom Covenant*, from which only the chapter 'Black Balts Among Celts' has as of yet been translated into English, documents her experiences as an itinerant agricultural labourer in County Monaghan where she worked picking mushrooms from dawn to dusk. After her return from Ireland her novel was published in Latvia and became a national best-seller. The publication of *The Mushroom Covenant* is highly significant, in my view, because it represents one of the first narrative accounts of Celtic Tiger Ireland that has been written from an immigrant rather than an Irish perspective. Unlike Roddy Doyle, Laima Muktupavela can hardly be accused of ventriloquising the voice of the Other.[54] Rather, she speaks for herself as an immigrant in Ireland in a language that is entirely unmediated by the conventions of Irish literary tradition or the expectations of an Irish readership. *The Mushroom Covenant* thus offers one of the first glimpses of multicultural Ireland as it is imagined from below, from an immigrant rather than an Irish perspective of 'what Ireland looks like', in Maureen Reddy's phrase, 'in the imagination of Ireland's others'.[55] The view, suffice it to say, is of an unremittingly bleak and inhospitable place.

More precisely, Ireland is imagined in *The Mushroom Covenant* within a historical continuum of oppressive, authoritarian, and racialised regimes to be a beneficiary of the polarising effects of globalisation that have divested Latvian workers of any sense of agency. Her observations about Latvian disempowerment do not lead Muktupavela to identify her experiences, however, with Irish historical memory, but rather to associate Ireland itself with German and Soviet authoritarian labour regimes that appear replicated on Irish mushroom farms. For example, she explicitly equates Irish and Soviet means of cultural deracination through the imposition of forced labour on a docile Latvian population. Thus, the only definitive cultural reference to Ireland in the narrative is to 'Tara, home of the Gods ... the ancient gods of Eire'[56] which is in the immediate vicinity of the mushroom farm where

---

54   Reddy, 'Reading and Writing Race', 386.
55   Reddy, 'Reading and Writing Race', 387.
56   Laima Muktupavela, 'Black Balts Among Celts: A Tale of Itinerant Latvian Workers in Ireland', *The Mushroom Covenant*, *DESCANT* 124, 35.1 (Spring 2004), 197.

the Latvians work; but their intended excursion to Tara on their day off is pre-empted by the need to pick mushrooms before the arrival of an early frost. For Muktupavela, the peremptory cancellation of her day off by her employers, who are identified simply as 'The Owner' and 'Mushroom Boss', reminds her of 'the Soviet period' during which the Latvian cultural fes-tivity of 'Midsummer's Eve' was consciously eradicated by Soviet policies of enforced modernisation: 'in order to [take] steps towards a better life', Muktupavela remarks, 'you have to lay the traditions of your ancestors aside'. Latvian cultural values appear equally inimical to both Irish and Soviet labour regimes, which would seem largely undifferentiated in the Latvian migrant's imagination. For Muktupavela, the shortest way to Tara is via 'the *kolkhozs*, or collective farms'[57] that become a metaphor for the place of the immigrant in modern Ireland.

Thus, Muktupavela associates the Irish with the imposition of ruth-less labour discipline that is intended both to dehumanise and racialise the migrant worker as part of a global underclass that is 'subservient', in her own words, 'looking up from below'.[58] She identifies Latvian workers in Ireland, for example, with American 'black slaves … standing in line, holding their bundles of worldly goods' whose 'eyes … have the same abject expression' of the Latvians, 'as if looking from below'. Similarly, when in the Garda immigration office, Muktupavela notes that they 'stand like photographs in the Latvian newspaper *Cīņa* [the *Struggle*] of many years ago, when it was the Soviet style to photograph the working people' in this same posture of 'looking from below, subservient'.[59] Finally, she extends her historical imagination of migrant labour impressments to the figures of the Jewish woman and Roman slave, both of whom she identifies with in 'being regarded as a stranger, odd, unacceptable, different, [unable to] speak or even understand the language'. 'And in the Irish Garda [station] I stand exactly as the Jewish woman', she declares, 'marked with the Star of David, or the Roman galley slave waiting to be branded – with the sign

57   Muktupavela, 'Black Balts', 201.
58   Muktupavela, 'Black Balts', 198.
59   Muktupavela, 'Black Balts', 201.

of the Green Card on my forehead'.[60] For Muktupavela, it is Roman and American slavery as well as the Nazi and Soviet invasions of her native Latvia that provide the objective historical correlatives for her experiences as an agricultural worker in Ireland, rather than any cognisance of cultural affinity with such figures as the emigrant, the navvy, the traveller or the wandering storyteller who remain transfixed in Irish historical memory.

Muktupavela's tale of itinerant Latvian workers in Ireland might seem hyperbolic and even obscene in its apparently indiscriminate register of suffering that is attributed to the Irish who are imaginatively identified with the totalitarian regimes that have shaped modern Latvian history. We should be cautious about dismissing her impressions, however. The more challenging and rewarding task, in my view, would be to trace and contextualise Muktupavela's Irish impressions in relation to Latvian literary conventions and narrative genres that have helped to shape and form them. For example, in her study of *Narrative and Memory in post-Soviet Latvia*, Vieda Skultans notes the significance of such 'recurring narrative themes' in Latvian popular culture as 'the reward for relentless hard work, stoical acceptance of pain ... [and the] engulfment of ... individual destiny ... by the brute force of historical events',[61] all of which appear to shape Muktupavela's own perceptions of Ireland in *The Mushroom Covenant*. Skultans also emphasises the importance of the idea of 'love of work'[62] in the Latvian self-image, whereas Muktupavela's abjuration of such Latvian proverbs as '*all work is good work* (*is work to be honoured*); and *black work, white bread*'[63] becomes a touchstone of the cultural incommensurability between Latvian and Irish values.

In conclusion, Irish multicultural fiction has entered the mainstream in the works of highly acclaimed writers like Roddy Doyle and Hugo Hamilton, whose *The Speckled People: A Memoir of a Half-Irish Childhood* (2003) reminisces about a cross-cultural romance from the perspective of

---

60   Muktupavela, 'Black Balts', 202.
61   Vieda Skultans, *The Testimony of Lives: Narrative and Memory in post-Soviet Latvia* (London: Routledge, 1998), 7.
62   Skultans, *The Testimony of Lives*, 128.
63   Muktupavela, 'Black Balts', 203.

its offspring, although there is insufficient space to examine it here.[64] A St Patrick's Day editorial in *The Irish Times* in 2007 declared that 'we are all the speckled people today'.[65] 'Confident, wealthy, forward-looking, internationalist, we can afford to define our identity in terms that celebrate our overlapping multiplicity of allegiances and diversity.' Its emphasis on a more generous and inclusive attitude to cultural diversity is symptomatic of the redefinition of Irish national identity in the era of the Celtic Tiger: one that is often symbolised in Irish multicultural fiction by the resolution of the interracial romantic plotline as a metaphor for cultural reconciliation. And yet, these works often elide issues of cultural difference and the often profound socio-economic disparities between immigrants and members of the Irish host society that Muktupavela calls attention to in *The Mushroom Covenant*. Although her blackened fingers have dug into the very same 'stony grey soil' that proved such a fertile ground for the creative imagination of numerous Irish writers, her impressions of Ireland seem much more negative in tone than most of her Irish literary predecessors. Her fiction thus provides a corrective for Madhavan, Doyle and Adigun's more positive vision of Irish multiculturalism in her very refusal to countenance the possibility of meaningful or reciprocal cultural exchange. Paradoxically, the spirit of collaboration between established Irish and emerging immigrant writers like Roddy Doyle and Bisi Adigun epitomises the very ideal of reciprocal cultural exchange that they purport to represent but are perceived to circumvent through their adherence to romantic convention, whereas Muktupavela's unequivocal repudiation of Irish society appears too sweeping in its delineation of cultural difference that most of the works examined here seek to reconcile. The tension between them defines the parameters of Irish multicultural fiction and conceptions of Ireland as an open and welcoming or closed and racialised host society.

---

64 See Jason King, 'Irish multicultural epiphanies: modernity and the recuperation of migrant memory in the writing of Hugo Hamilton', *Literary Visions of Multicultural Ireland*, ed. Pilar Villar-Argáiz (Manchester: Manchester University Press, 2013), 176–87.

65 'The Rebranding of Ourselves', *Irish Times*, 17 March 2007.

10   Advertising, Media and Irish Identity:
       Reflections on the Celtic Tiger Period

> The more anxious, confused, uncertain, and bewildered modern society
> gets, the stronger will be the role played by advertising.[1]

Introduction

Given that advertising 'concentrates at those points where the individual and society meet',[2] it is perhaps little wonder that it has long been a
subject of considerable interest, for both academics and the public alike.
Advertising is colourful, topical and often brilliantly creative; yet it is also
commonly viewed as manipulative, mendacious and morally corrupting.
(Indeed, studies of advertising remain decidedly at the margins of media
studies, as if its blatant commercialism makes it an unworthy subject.) In
this chapter, I consider the relationship between advertising, media and
Irish identity, using the period up to and including the so-called 'Celtic
Tiger' as a case study.

Media culture provides the materials out of which 'we forge our identities'[3] – or as John Thompson puts it, mediated symbolic materials are

---

1   Varda Leymore, *Hidden Myth: Structure and Symbol in Advertising* (New York: Basic
     Books, 1975), x.
2   Peter Corrigan, *The Sociology of Consumption: An Introduction* (London: Sage, 1997).
3   Douglas Kellner, 'Cultural Studies, Multiculturalism and Media Culture', in Gail
     Dines and Jean Humez, *Gender, Race and Class in Media* (London and New York:
     Sage, 2003), 9.

central to the construction of 'a narrative of self-identity'.[4] However, this identity-building role is not restricted to individuals. In fact, prior to the 'invention' of the individual, the mass circulation of media representations played a crucial role in the emergence of nation-states and have since played an important role in fostering national identity. Benedict Anderson's much quoted description of nations as 'imagined communities' points to the fact that although the vast majority of people comprising a nation will never actually meet, their consumption of the same kinds of media can neverthe-less engender a sense of shared interests and common culture.[5] In much the same vein, Judith Williamson claimed in her seminal book *Decoding Advertisements*, that advertisements were amongst 'the most important cultural factors moulding and reflecting our life today' – a view that is still widely held.[6] For example, in an article in the *New Statesman* in 2000, Ziauddin Sardar proclaimed that 'advertising has not just become news, it has, in fact, become everything. Advertising is now the eminent domain of our existence, dissolving all categories and boundaries within its imagina-tive grasp'.[7] While Sardar perhaps overstates its pervasiveness and power, advertising undoubtedly functions as an important symbolic resource for identity construction and serves as 'a key index of the normal'[8] – a point which applies to media more generally:

> Through the media-driven streams of discourse surrounding us daily, rooted in our lifeworld, we shape our conceptions of reality and spin out the collective 'common sense' which underpins everyday life. This forms the basic tissue of the prevailing sense of communality in every part of Ireland. This may be the electronic media's most powerful and important effect.[9]

4   John Thompson, *The Media and Modernity* (Cambridge: Polity Press, 1995).
5   Benedict Anderson, *Imagined Communities* (London: Verso Books, 1983).
6   Judith Williamson, *Decoding Advertisements: Ideology and Meaning in Advertising* (London: Boyars, 1978).
7   Ziauddin Sardar, 'Ad Infinitum', *New Statesman*, 31 July 2000.
8   Anne Cronin, 'Currencies of Commercial Exchange: Advertising Agencies and the Commercial Imperative', *Journal of Consumer Culture* 4.3 (2004), 126.
9   Farrell Corcoran, *RTÉ and the Globalisation of Irish Television* (Bristol: Intellect Books, 2004).

In this chapter, I examine advertising and media in the period up to and including the Celtic Tiger to develop a picture of the 'common sense' Corcoran describes. In particular, I consider how advertising of that period reflected the prevailing view that Irish identity had pluralised, and that Irishness was increasingly uncertain and contested. Writing in 2002, Debbie Ging argued that the definition of Irishness 'has never been more contentious'.[10] Globalisation and large-scale immigration in particular were seen to have unhinged cultural and constitutional understandings of Irish identity and opened up new ways of being Irish. Yet, at the same time, representations of Ireland and Irishness in the global context – in advertising, tourism, film, and other branches of the media and cultural industries – continued to draw from a stock of particularisms (as they do now). For this reason, it is perhaps useful to think of Irishness as a regime of representations.

Although Irishness is merely one of innumerable points of connection between advertising (as a commercial activity) and advertisements (as socially meaningful texts), I suggest that it provides a particularly good analytical pivot or lens through which to frame these relations, especially because it enables us to bring some recent renegotiations of Irish culture and identity into dialogue with advertising and marketing discourses.

Irishness and the Celtic Tiger

According to Colin Graham, the idea of Ireland is 'deconstructive' in the sense that it is continually unravelling and reforming, producing what he calls 'a promiscuity of Irelands'.[11] In much the same way, definitions of

10   Debbie Ging, 'Screening the Green: Cinema under the Celtic Tiger', in Peadar Kirby, Luke Gibbons and Michael Cronin (eds), *Reinventing Ireland: Culture, Society and the Global Economy* (London: Pluto Press, 2002), 191.
11   Colin Graham, *Deconstructing Ireland: Identity, Theory and Culture* (Edinburgh: Edinburgh University Press, 2001), 3.

Irishness appear increasingly unstable. As with other varieties of nationness, Irishness has been constructed across a variety of cultural forms, including advertising, art, film, novels, travel brochures, plays and documentaries. Importantly, it has also to a great extent been constructed *outside* of Ireland. As is well known, Irishness was historically imagined as a primitive subconscious or visceral sense couched in rural mythology.[12] Johnson, for example, argues that orthodox nationalist historiography locates the root of collective Irish cultural consciousness in the west of the island, which was constructed as a repository of Gaelic language and values and which in turn provided the cultural matrix used to define a *de facto* Catholic 'Irish-Ireland' in contrast to Britain.[13] However, since the 1990s, economic turnaround (and more recently severe downturn), Europeanisation, globalisation and ethnic diversity have challenged the myths underpinning ethnicity and nationalism in Ireland.[14] Crowley, Gilmartin and Kitchin indicate that Ireland's colonial history, the legacy of Protestant settlers and unionism, and the presence of a considerable Traveller population, all ensure that Irishness within Ireland remains contested and uncertain.[15] In parallel, some commentators, such as Mac Éinrí, argue that legislative changes like the 1998 Belfast Agreement – which putatively decoupled the territorial state and nation – may also have inadvertently recoded Irishness 'in terms of bodies, not territories' and may have reinforced the notion of 'Irishness of the mind'.[16] In a similar vein, Fanning and Mutwarasibo

12   Mark Hederman and Richard Kearney, 'A Sense of Nation', in Mark Hederman and Richard Kearney, *The Crane Bag Book of Irish Studies (1977–1981)* (Dublin: Blackwater Press).

13   Randal Johnson, 'Editor's Introduction: Pierre Bourdieu on Art, Literature and Culture', in Pierre Bourdieu, *The Field of Cultural Production* (Cambridge: Polity, 1993).

14   Marian Cadogan, 'Fixity and Whiteness in the Ethnicity Question of Irish Census 2006', *Translocations: The Irish Migration, Race and Social Transformation Review* 3.1 (2008), 5.

15   Una Crowley, Mary Gilmartin and Rob Kitchin, 'Vote Yes for "Common Sense Citizenship": Immigration and the Paradoxes at the Heart of Ireland's "Céad Míle Fáilte"', *NIRSA Working Papers* no. 30 (2006), 1–35.

16   Piaras Mac Éinrí, 'If I wanted to go there I wouldn't start from here: Re-imagining a multi-ethnic nation', in Debbie Ging, Michael Cronin and Peadar Kirby, *Transforming*

insist that constitutional definitions of Irishness have narrowed at a time when the composition of Irish society has broadened significantly through immigration.[17]

Unsurprisingly, globalisation features heavily in accounts of trans-formations in Irish identity from the 1990s onwards. Tom Inglis claims that there has been 'an explosion in varieties of Irishness' and that global flows of ideas and people are creating 'new ways of being Irish.'[18] While some celebrate the ambiguity of the Celtic Tiger period as a resource for cultural accommodation, others noted the sense of uprooting and dis-orientation popularly felt. With prosperity came a relaxation of social values and a frank materialism that worried the older generation still in the thrall of tradition.[19] Likewise, in his depiction of organic Irish soci-ety held under siege by insidious global forces, O'Connell renounced 'a new Irish psyche' owing to 'rampant consumerism and individualism.'[20] That advertising featured among the key targets of critics like O'Connell during the heyday of the Celtic Tiger should hardly surprise us. The ori-gins of modern advertising lie in the roots of mass consumer society, and fears about unstoppable 'homogenisation' have always been central to critiques of marketing and advertising – as Norris suggests (writing about America):

> If [automobile magnate Henry] Ford represented the triumph of mass production to his admirers, he represented the terror of uniformity and conformity to his critics. Moreover, the toll that mass production extracted from workers was matched to the loss from the uniformity of mass production. All too often, the price of decreasing

Ireland: Challenges, Critiques, Resources (Manchester: Manchester University Press, 2009).

17 Bryan Fanning and Fidele Mutwarasibo, 'Nationals/non-nationals: Immigration, Citizenship and Politics in the Republic of Ireland', *Ethnic and Racial Studies* 30.3 (2007), 439.

18 Tom Inglis, *Global Ireland: Same Difference* (New York and London: Routledge, 2008).

19 G. Paschal Zachary, 'Letter from Ireland', *Washington Quarterly* 22.4 (1999), 131.

20 Michael O'Connell, *Changed Utterly: Ireland and the New Irish Psyche* (Dublin: Liffey Press, 2001).

costs associated with mass marketing was a frightening loss of the rich mosaic of American culture.[21]

Likewise, in many accounts, advertising is implicitly understood as an agent of globalisation. For example, Twitchell wryly suggests that 'if ever there is to be a global village, it will be because the town crier works in advertising'.[22] Again, the close connection between globalisation and advertising was identified by many cultural critics during the Celtic Tiger period. Writing in 2000, Vincent Buckley described Ireland as 'a nothing – a no-thing – an interesting nothing, to be sure, composed of colourful parts, a nothing-mosaic. It is advertising prose and muzak'.[23] In the same year, Helen Kelly-Holmes stated glumly:

> It can be argued that [...] advertising and commercial texts have now somewhat depressingly, but perhaps predictably, come to compose the new prescribed texts of 'Irishness' and may eventually become the foundational texts, forming the givens and providing the pathways through which new texts of 'Irishness' will in turn be read and written.[24]

Writing two years later, Debbie Ging similarly pointed to the prevalence of 'easy, globally-digestible' forms of Irishness in the media generally.[25] In particular, she observed that the putative complexity of Irish identity on the ground was yet to be reflected in cinematic representations:

> It could also be argued that the increased movement of people around the world and the renegotiation of questions of citizenship which surround both indigenous (for example, Traveller) and immigrant groups, Irish identity is becoming increasingly complex and difficult to define. Yet in spite of this, on-screen characters are

21 James Norris, *Advertising and the Transformation of American Society, 1865–1920* (New York: Greenwood, 1990).
22 James B. Twitchell, *Adcult USA* (New York: Columbia University Press, 1996).
23 Lance Pettitt, *Screening Ireland* (Manchester: Manchester City Press, 2000).
24 Helen Kelly-Holmes, 'Strong Words Softly Spoken: Advertising and the Intertextual Construction of "Irishness"', in Ulrike Hanna Meinhof and Jonathan Smith, *Intertextuality and the Media: From Genre to Everyday Life* (Manchester: Manchester University Press, 2000), 39.
25 Ging, 'Screening the Green', 186.

becoming increasingly stereotypical and bland. They tend to be simple, fun-loving yokels [...] or breezy, prosperous urbanites [...] while locations are divided between the rural idyll of the west and the hip cultural capital that is Dublin.[26]

However, not all commentators on Irish identity during the Celtic Tiger period were as troubled by the prospect of cultural dilution, homogenisation or globalisation. Some astute commentators noted that firstly, traditional monolithic Irish culture is itself a cultural construction and that Irishness has always been a globalised identity;[27] and secondly, that globalisation does not merely (or even necessarily) erode tradition but rather *co-opts* it and often *reinvigorates* it. For example, Luke Gibbons observed that it is often Ireland's integration 'into the new international order which activates some of the most conservative forces in Irish society'.[28]

In the international context, scholars similarly drew attention to both the functionality and increasing malleability of Irishness. Natasha Casey pointed out that Irishness appeared to exist 'in a myriad of forms' and suggested that it continued 'to adapt, accommodate, and appeal to remarkably diverse audiences'.[29] Likewise, Diane Negra argued that Irishness had 'achieved greater and more complex representability' and had become a kind of 'everything and nothing' identity currency.[30] In the advertising and branding space, however, practitioners were much more optimistic about the creative possibilities presented by transformations in Irish culture and identity. For example, in his book *The Importance of Being Branded*, the well-known Irish advertising practitioner John Fanning – who was

---

26   Ging, 'Screening the Green', 186.
27   Honor Fagan, 'Globalised Ireland, or, Contemporary Transformations of National Identity?', in Colin Coulter and Steve Coleman (eds), *The End of Irish History? Critical Reflections on the Celtic Tiger* (Manchester: Manchester University Press, 2003).
28   Luke Gibbons, *Transformations in Irish Culture* (Cork: Cork University Press, 1996).
29   Natasha Casey, 'The Best Kept Secret in Retail: Selling Irishness in Contemporary America', in Diane Negra, *The Irish in Us: Irishness, Performativity, and Popular Culture* (Durham and London: Duke University Press, 2006), 84.
30   Diane Negra, 'Irishness, Innocence, and American Identity Politics before and after September 11', in Diane Negra, *The Irish in Us: Irishness, Performativity, and Popular Culture* (Durham and London: Duke University Press, 2006), 11.

formerly chairman of the McConnell's advertising agency in Dublin and is sometimes described as the 'grandfather of Irish advertising'[31] – suggested that the new Ireland of the period was ripe for commercial exploitation.[32] Throughout his book, John Fanning argues cogently for the importance of local branding. He insists that marketers must be 'alert to sociological change' but should be slow to relinquish cultural bearings. In particular, he stresses that local brands not only reflect but also 'form part of the character of a society'. In rather an anthropological vein, he insists that local brands 'are part of the sights and sounds and smells that give a place its character.'[33] For Fanning, there is no contradiction between asserting national difference and competing as strongly as possible in the global economy. Yet he concedes that the logistics of advertising production make it culturally reductivist; the need for consensus on the 'core branding proposition', consistency of communication and single-mindedness (as well as long term planning, time and budget constraints) drive simplification and fixity into the process. Hence, while acutely aware that national identity is constructed and dynamic rather than fixed and static, Fanning recognises the benefits of maintaining a distinct Irish identity and regards the national brand as an invaluable asset. Towards the end of his book Fanning argues that identifying 'cultural contradictions' (such as 'cash rich, time poor') will be key to the branding exercise going forwards. He suggests that twenty-first-century Ireland is especially rich in such contradictions and he identifies six which are particularly worthy of attention.[34] In the following section, I examine how Irish media and advertising have always negotiated different varieties of Irish identity and I consider some examples of this (in advertising) during the Celtic Tiger period.

---

31   C. O'Mahony, 'Fanning Still Fits the Bill', *Sunday Business Post Online*, 3 October 2004.

32   John Fanning, *The Importance of Being Branded* (Dublin: The Liffey Press, 2006).

33   Fanning, *The Importance of Being Branded*, 229.

34   These are: 'freedom vs constraint', 'individualism vs community', 'globalisation vs dinnseanchas', 'affluence vs affluenza', 'control vs chaos', and 'conformity vs creativity'.

Media, Advertising and the Celtic Tiger

Kelly and Rolston suggest that, historically, Irish media have had to tread a fine line between seeking 'to represent the existing socio-cultural worlds' within Irish society and 'reproducing a particular version of cultural and national identity'.[35] The particular version of cultural and national identity alluded to was, and to a large extent still is, informed by the tenets of cultural nationalism. In his study of Irish broadcasting, for example, Maurice Gorham claimed that in its formative years the State 'foresaw broadcasting as promoting the spread of the national language and of the phonetic teaching of modern languages, the elementary principles of hygiene, of gardening, fruit-growing, bee-keeping, poultry-keeping and the like; and this it considered vastly more important than its use for entertainment, however desirable'.[36] Luke Gibbons observes that in the Irish case, radio became very early on 'the organ of an official Catholic, Gaelic-inflected culture', dedicating considerable time to covering such items as Gaelic games, Irish music and language, feast days and the 1932 Eucharistic Congress.[37] Later, television – the 'national billboard'[38] – was also co-opted for the promotion of 'ideal' national values and practices, as is pointed out by Carey. 'Television completed and perfected the national system, finished what the printing press, telegraph, telephone, wire services, and national magazine began.'[39] For example, O'Connor points to the significance of *The Riordans*, which was the first rural serial broadcast on Irish television and which was originally designed to encourage farmers to adopt 'modern'

---

35 Mary Kelly and Bill Rolston, 'Broadcasting in Ireland: Issues of National Identity and Censorship', in Patrick Clancy, Sheelagh Drudy, Kathleen Lynch and Liam O'Dowd (eds), *Irish Society: Sociological Perspectives* (Dublin: IPA, 1995), 563.
36 Maurice Gorham, *Forty Years of Broadcasting* (Dublin: RTÉ, 1967).
37 Quoted in Pettitt, *Screening Ireland*, 144.
38 Todd Gitlin, *Inside Primetime* (London: Routledge, 1994).
39 James W. Carey, '"Globalization Isn't New; Anti-Globalization Isn't Either": September 11 and the History of Nations', *Prometheus* 20.3 (2002), 289–93.

farming practices.[40] These examples support Morash's suggestion that the idea of the Irish nation has always been inseparable from the media used to represent (and construct) it, and therefore that Ireland can be conceived as 'the nodal point of successive and overlapping forms of media'.[41]

Although sometimes overlooked, it is important to note that the media in Ireland have also historically played a role in challenging prevailing norms and values and in disseminating alternative ideas.[42] In this vein, Cleary describes changes in 'the technology of subject production' in Ireland since the 1960s, which in his view have been as 'dramatic and far-reaching as that inaugurated in the nineteenth-century Devotional Revolution consolidated after the Famine'.[43] Much of this, he suggests, is owing to the mediatisation of Irish culture:

> Since 1958, when the Irish political elite finally abandoned economic autarky, the southern Irish state's single major project has been to integrate the country into the European Union and global capitalism. The same period witnessed the introduction of new communications technologies, especially television, which brought the country into closer contact with the wider international political scene and, more importantly, into contact with British and North-American consumer society.[44]

Like Cleary, Lance Pettitt highlights that media development in Ireland was always heavily dependent on innovations and practices elsewhere (especially Anglo-American models), yet he points out that these were always adapted to Irish circumstances. As a consequence, he suggests that early media forms like the picture house, wireless and television set, were representative of Ireland's particular modernity, which he describes as 'a complex collision of a global Anglo-American culture with a local, native culture that was

40   Barbara O'Connor, 'Nationality', in Daniele Albertazzi and Paul Cobley, *Media: An Introduction*, 3rd edn (London: Pearson, 2010), 508.
41   Chris Morash, *A History of the Media in Ireland* (Cambridge: Cambridge University Press, 2010).
42   See Morash, *A History of the Media*.
43   Joe Cleary, *Outrageous Fortune: Culture and Capital in Modern Ireland* (Dublin: Field Day Publications, 2006), 72.
44   Pettitt, *Screening Ireland*, 23–4.

itself already bifurcated politically, demographically and culturally'.[45] In his *Screening Ireland*, Pettitt explores the ideological role of Irish national cinema 'in fabricating a collective screen fiction'.[46] Pettitt's particular interest is in the dissident, subversive and iconoclastic; in short, cinema's potential to scrutinise and demythologise the nation and disrupt cosy narratives of belonging. Yet he also draws attention to the ways in which cinema often endorses the culturally hegemonic and panders to global stereotypes of Irish identity; documentary films like *Man of Aran* and early Hollywood productions like *The Quiet Man* are far and away the most popular screen representations of Ireland and Irish national archetypes. Beyond touristic nostalgia, this also highlights the marketing logic which generally attends the cultivation of national identities as distinctive kinds of 'otherness'.[47] Indeed, Pettitt notes that upon its release, *The Quiet Man* 'became an international advert for Ireland just months before the state's new tourism agency, Bord Fáilte, came into existence in July'.[48]

If advertising formed a backdrop to other more direct means of nation-building in the State's formative years, its potential in this respect was duly noted. For example, King argues that advertising for Aer Lingus in the 1950s – the era in which 'nothing' supposedly happened – played a pivotal role in the construction of Irish identity, especially overseas.[49] Oram suggests that while Ireland was a deeply conservative nation for much of the last century owing to close Church–State ties, advertising was one of the few cultural domains in which outside influence registered.[50] Moreover, the emergence of an identifiable advertising 'industry' in Ireland was largely due to developments in the United States and Britain, and the tendency of British advertisers to export campaigns to Ireland. Indeed, advertising

45   Pettitt, *Screening Ireland*, 23–4.

46   Pettitt, *Screening Ireland*, 30.

47   See Kristin Kuutma, 'Changing Codified Symbols of Identity', *FF Network* 31 (December 2006), 10.

48   Pettitt, *Screening Ireland*, 64.

49   Linda King, 'Advertising Ireland: Irish Graphic Design in the 1950s under the Patronage of Aer Lingus', *Circa* 92 (Summer 2000), 16.

50   Hugh Oram, *The Advertising Book: The History of Advertising in Ireland* (Dublin: MO Books, 1986).

in Ireland prior to the First World War was almost entirely produced by English agencies for brands such as Bisto, Pears and Bovril. In turn, advertising practices and traditions were mainly imported from foreign agencies, with the indigenous industry failing to develop what might be regarded as 'a nationally distinctive advertising philosophy' comparable to the 'image' and 'claim' traditions of the United States.[51] The Irish experience was preceded by similar developments elsewhere in Western Europe, as forms of advertising practice (such as cost accountancy systems and television production techniques) spread from core to periphery. In the view of some, such as John Fanning, this historical dependence may have accounted for a lack of confidence in Irish advertising and for the industry's failure to craft a unique identity. As Fanning sees it, conservatism was the defining characteristic of Irish advertising for the first fifty years of the new state: 'It was a tame affair dominated by prosaic announcements from myriad small retailers. They were inevitably copy-led and were full of what could most charitably be described as quaint little verses.'[52] However, the arrival of television changed everything. As Oram puts it, 'in many respects, Irish advertising did not come of age until the start of Telefís Éireann on January 1, 1962'.[53] He further highlights that Ireland's entry into the European Economic Community (EEC) in 1973 coincided with the advent of computerisation in the advertising industry, profoundly shaping all aspects of advertising practice since.

Mirroring much of the commentary (above) about contested Irish identities during the Celtic Tiger period, studies of advertising from this time onwards identify similar themes. Indeed, different studies of the same brand advertising sometimes diverge in their findings and conclusions. For example, Barbara O'Connor describes a Guinness billboard advertisement in the mid-2000s that was used to communicate the brand's sponsorship of

---

51   See Aidan Kelly, Katrina Lawlor and Stephanie O'Donohoe, 'Encoding Advertisements: The Creative Process', *Journal of Marketing Management* 21.5 (2005), 505–28.

52   John Fanning, 'Irish Advertising – Bhfuil Sé or Won't Sé?', *Irish Marketing Review* 16.2 (2003), 7.

53   Oram, *The Advertising Book*, 6.

Irish rugby. In the scene depicted a group of sturdy tree men (reminiscent of the 'Ents' in the *Lord of the Rings*) stand in pack-like formation with the central figure holding a rugby ball, under the caption 'Born of Our Land'. For O'Connor, this advertisement contains a number of signifiers of national identity. The trees, for example, suggest rootedness in the land while the Guinness harp symbol is long synonymous with Irish nationalism. O'Connor further suggests that the caption 'Born of Our Land' functions to construct both the rugby team and Guinness as essential parts of Irish culture in which people should take pride: 'All of these signs coalesce to offer us, the viewer, a sporting (and masculine) and a consumerist sense of national identity.'[54] In a somewhat different vein, O'Brien's insightful analysis of Guinness advertising from the 1920s to the mid-2000s – which draws upon the complex theoretical perspectives of Althusser, Lacan and Lukács, amongst others – suggests that Guinness (or rather its representation in advertising) is an iconic signifier of the *varieties* of Irishness.

> So we have come full circle here, as Guinness is now hailing post-modern, intelligent, cosmopolitan subjects through the aura its product creates. As a synecdoche of Irishness, that image of the harp in 'natural Anthem' has turned out to be a polysemic one. The commodity here is protean, suggesting that it has paralleled all the changes of the Irish economy and psyche over the past 75 years.[55]

On one hand, Irish advertising during the Celtic Tiger was littered with representations of Irish identity that were decidedly quixotic (found, for example, in advertising for brands like Kerrygold, Galtee and Erin), while on the other hand it is possible to identify advertisements in this period which appear to hail the postmodern. Much like O'Brien, Carmen Kuhling examines a series of advertisements from the mid-2000s which she considers illustrative of Ireland's experience of 'liquid modernity'. She suggests that globalisation and accelerated modernisation have produced cultural ambivalence in Ireland, which is evident in the contradictory representations of Irishness in certain advertising texts. One campaign analysed by

54 O'Connor, 'Nationality', 505–6.
55 Eugene O'Brien, *'Kicking Bishop Brennan up the Arse': Negotiating Texts and Contexts in Contemporary Irish Studies* (Oxford: Peter Lang, 2009), 188.

Kuhling is Jameson's 'Beyond the Obvious'. In 'The Harpist', which is perhaps the most well-known television commercial in this series (and which also ran as a print and outdoor advertisement), a dreadlocked, leather-clad, mixed-race man plays 20th Century Boy on a green and gold harp. According to Kuhling, who follows Bakhtin's theory of 'dialogization' – the process by which culture becomes relativised and contested – this commercial 'disrupts the taken-for-granted binary opposition between tradition/modernity, insider/outsider, Irish/non-Irish, white/non-white, and opens up our minds to an idea of Irishness much more fluid, hybrid, and produced in dialogue'.[56] This resonates with Colin Graham's analysis of a television commercial for Smithwick's ale, appropriately titled 'Ireland', produced in the late 1990s.[57] In this commercial, which Graham describes as a postmodern montage, numerous images of Ireland past and present are jumbled-up in a knowing, ironic way: maudlin, Americanised Irishness is juxtaposed with the awkward realities of a newly postmodern, postcolonial and urban Ireland. Graham considers whether 'Ireland' represents a form of culture that is anti-authentic or if it is directed towards establishing an alternative kind of authenticity. In the end he concludes that despite its 'joyous uncovering of myths *as myths*, and signs of reality *as signs*', the commercial merely 'toys with an alternative authenticity, but finally cannot rest on anything but its ironic 'maybe that's just Blarney'.[58]

Graham's analysis points to the limitations of advertising as a vehicle for iconoclasm. It acknowledges the basic reality that cultural difference *sells*. Beyond this, it is also important to point out that the production structure of advertising, notably the constraints of time, budget and convention (e.g. the thirty-second television slot) significantly reduce the possibility of cultural critique, though one can of course identify advertisements which appear to do so (e.g. Paddy Power's parodying of da Vinci's *Last Supper* in

56   Carmen Kuhling, '"Liquid Modernity" in Irish Identity: Irishness in Guinness, Jameson and Ballygowan advertisements', *Advertising and Society Review* 9.3 (2008) <http://muse.jhu.edu/journals/advertising_and_society_review/v009/9.3.kuhling.pdf>.

57   Graham, *Deconstructing Ireland*.

58   Graham, *Deconstructing Ireland*, 150.

a 2005 advertisement, which was hastily removed by the ASAI).[59] This is a point often missed by those intent on exposing stereotypes in advertising. From the perspective of advertising producers, the use of stereotypes rarely signals ideological endorsement but rather pragmatism and expediency. Stereotyping is quick, cost-efficient and generally pleasing to global clients. Contrary to often idealised accounts of cultural production, the bulk of work in advertising and other cultural industries is generally routine, mundane and highly predictable.

However, the persistence of cultural conservatism in much Irish advertising throughout the Celtic Tiger period also lends support to the suggestion that 'the vestiges of the ideal forms of traditional community still haunt and hold sway over people'.[60] Similarly, while Fagan argues that 'the Ireland of today has seen the full effect of the deterritorialisation of culture',[61] she acknowledges that locality remains important (which is also evident in exceptionally high rates of home ownership). Bank of Ireland's award-winning sponsorship of the GAA in the mid-2000s illustrates this point very well. The campaign was designed to capture the intense emotional loyalty and community spirit enshrined in the GAA, particularly in rural areas and parishes. In the advertisements produced (which had a clear rural bias), local identity ostensibly trumped national identity, and was underscored by the replacement of the word 'country' with 'county'

---

59   This advertisement depicted Jesus and his disciples gambling during what is historically envisioned as a most cheerless occasion. Poker chips are stacked neatly in front of Jesus while the apostles are intently playing an assortment of games under a caption that reads 'There's a time for fun and games.' Jesuit sociologist Fr Michael McGreil was among the most vocal critics of this advertisement at the time and his comments received coverage in various national newspapers. McGreil attacked the ad for showing a 'lack of respect of the beliefs of the vast, vast majority of Christians in Ireland, both Catholic and Protestant'. He added that it was an 'example of vulgarity at its worst to misuse a sacred image like this' and that it represented 'the vulgarity of rank materialism'. See D. Quinn, 'It's holy war over Jesus the gambler poster' (*Irish Independent*, Bottom of Form 29 September 2005).

60   Kieran Keohane and Carmen Kuhling, *Collision Culture: Transformations in Everyday Life in Ireland* (Dublin: The Liffey Press, 2004), 69.

61   Fagan, 'Globalised Ireland', 118.

in John F. Kennedy's iconic words 'Ask not what your country can do for you.' Kelly observes that the Bank of Ireland GAA advertisements drama-tised 'the lengths which GAA fans will go to demonstrate support for their county'.[62] He describes two commercials from this series: one that showed two Dublin fans risking arrest to repaint the chimneys of the Poolbeg ESB Power Station in Dublin from red and white to blue and navy (the colours of the Dublin football team) and another in which a young girl chooses to wear an orange communion dress in her class photo (while all her classmates are wearing white) to show her support for the Armagh football team. Similarly, in its more recent sponsorship of the GAA Club Championships, AIB's 'Club is Family' campaign builds on essentially the same idea. These campaigns are useful examples of attempts to situate Irish identities within a climate of confident globalism while at the same time reinscribing the more familiar variant, which is predicated on a com-munitarian anti-globalisation.[63]

Indeed, perhaps the most common variant of Irishness in advertising during the Celtic Tiger period (apart from the quixotic) was a kind of confident, 'rooted cosmopolitanism', which married a global outlook with a local sensibility, while keeping the exotica of Irishness firmly intact. A particularly good example of this is found in a television commercial for Carlsberg lager in 2002, in which three 'ordinary' Irishmen enter an upmar-ket nightclub in an unspecified European city. As they approach the bar, one of the three orders a pint of Carlsberg. 'Sure', the barman replies and begins to pull the pint. He then asks: 'Where are you from?', to which one of the three replies 'Ireland'. 'Ireland', the barman says in a surprised, almost disbelieving tone. 'Do something Irish', he demands. 'Some Irish singing', a man sitting at the bar suggests. 'Exactly. What about Irish dancing?' the

---

62   Aidan Kelly, 'Mediators of Meaning: A Critically Reflexive Study of the Encoding of Irish Advertising' (DIT Dublin: <http://arrow.dit.ie/busdoc/6/>, 2008).

63   Michael Cronin, 'Is it for the Glamour?: Masculinity, Nationhood and Amateurism in Contemporary Projections of the Gaelic Athletic Association', in Wanda Balzano, Anne Mulhall and Moynagh Sullivan (eds), *Irish Postmodernisms and Popular Culture* (New York: Palgrave Macmillan, 2007), 45.

barman suggests. 'Dance or sing', an attractive woman orders, as she leans into the ear of the lead actor.

As two of the three Irishmen begin to squabble over what 'Irish' feat is to be carried out (and by whom), the lead actor, who is noticeably smaller than his two friends, suddenly breaks into garbled Irish. 'An bhfuil cead agam dull amach go dtí an leatheras?' [Can I go out to the toilet?] he says, followed by 'agus madra rua' [and red dog] and 'is maith liom caca milis' [I like cake], as the expression on his face changes from initial hesitancy to growing confidence. Grasping what he is doing, one of the others quickly informs the barman that his friend is reciting 'a poem in our native Irish tongue'. Soon the lead actor is spouting all manner of inane phrases (with the most earnest expression on his face) to a group of captivated onlookers. The commercial closes with the lead actor dancing with another attractive woman who insists that he 'speak more Irish'.

This particular Carlsberg commercial is important for a variety of reasons. Most obviously it reaffirms the qualities of charm and fun-loving sociability popularly associated with Irish people and exemplifies the still prevalent notion of the Irish as 'simple, clever and friendly folk'.[64] Likewise, it reflects the positive currency of Irishness as a globally marketed identity as well as its continually fantasised forms – not to mention the recurrent depiction of Irishness as an 'available' and 'innocent ethnicity'.[65] On the latter point it is noteworthy that the three central characters in the commercial are distinctly non-threatening in their otherness (and average-ness), which is underscored by the small stature of the lead actor. Yet this commercial also plays upon the Celtic Tiger glamour of 'being Irish' for cosmopolitans in global cities.[66] In this respect it conveys a sense of the small holding their own amongst the big. More than that, it signals the newfound confidence of the formerly demure Irish, who now brazenly use their natural wit and intelligence to weasel their way into elite society.

---

64 Michael Clancy, *Brand New Ireland: Tourism, Development and National Identity in the Irish Republic* (Surrey and Vermont: Ashgate, 2009), 98.

65 Diane Negra, 'The New Primitives: Irishness in Recent US Television', *Irish Studies Review* 9.2 (2001), 231.

66 Inglis, *Global Ireland*, 99–100.

As such, the Carlsberg commercial serves as an excellent example of 'how skilled the Irish have become at playing the game', as Tom Inglis puts it.[67]

By far the most interesting aspect of this commercial, however, is the centrality of the Irish language. Once scorned and 'consigned along with Faith and Fatherland to the trash-can of late modernity',[68] the Irish language is now championed as the last vestige of Irish difference in a global world; this despite the fact that few Irish people speak it fluently.[69] Though the irony of this is clearly raised in the commercial, the emphasis placed on the Irish language (albeit in pigeon, nonsensical form) nevertheless works to paint Irish identity as exotic and exclusive. Besides the fact that using Irish is automatically alienating for those incapable of speaking it – such as many of Ireland's immigrant adults – its importance in this commercial in signalling groupness offers a reminder that 'even à la carte Irishness has its rules of belonging'.[70]

Conclusion

The porousness and, in recent times, pluralisation of Irishness has received much scholarly attention, especially since the 1990s, which for Kornprobst marked 'a watershed' in elite representations of Irish identity.[71] While some

---

67   Inglis, *Global Ireland*, 150.
68   Kirby, Gibbons and Cronin, *Reinventing Ireland*, 14.
69   Tom Inglis (131) points out that when Irish people claim to be able to speak Irish, what they generally mean is that they know a few words and phrases, which are rarely if ever used. He also highlights that Irish has survived largely 'because many cosmopolitan city-dwellers have recognised the personal kudos and cultural benefit to themselves of promoting and developing the language by sending their children to all-Irish schools' (133). In the view of Kirby, Gibbons and Cronin, this also reflects a felt need in Irish society 'to source elements of a linguistic and cultural past to situ-ate people in the present, a need that has not disappeared with the radical economic changes in Irish society' (14).
70   Bryan Fanning, *New Guests of the Nation* (Dublin: Irish Academic Press, 2009), 21.
71   Markus Kornprobst, 'Episteme, Nation-builders and National Identity: The Re-construction of Irishness', *Nations and Nationalism* 11.3 (2005), 403–21: 417.

have celebrated the decentring of Irish identity, others have expressed concerns about its increasing commercialisation and commodification. Still others point out that despite sweeping transformations in Irish culture and identity, essentialist ideas linger and in some respects have received a new lease of life under conditions of advanced globalisation. If institutions like RTÉ continue to play a dominant role in the symbolic environment in which Irish people construct their identities and notions of common sense, this is increasingly under threat by the myriad 'new media' platforms now available. This relates to the argument that information and communication technologies are loosening geographical binds and facilitating a diffusion of imagination across national, social and geographical boundaries.

   In this chapter, I reflected on the relationship between advertising, media and evolving Irish identities, in the period up to and including the Celtic Tiger. At the beginning of the twenty-first century, a 'new-yet-essentially-traditional'[72] Irishness was perhaps its dominant form – at least in advertising. This should hardly surprise us. It is commonly accepted nowadays that globalisation is producing a reactionary mobilisation of cultural/national/ethnic identity; that globalisation begets identity as it were. As Inglis argues, 'entry into the global flow of culture has not diminished the impetus to remain authentic and different',[73] nor has it diminished the ontological importance of cultural bearings. Ireland is in many respects a paragon of the postcolonial, tightrope nation; utterly globalised and putatively postmodern (even postnational), yet still deeply dependent on its invented traditions and inherited myths. Hence, at least during the Celtic Tiger, one detected 'consistently recalcitrant tropes'[74] and 'a lingering nostalgia for certainties'[75] in many postmodern versions of Ireland and Irishness. Ireland's advertising industry is positioned at the axis of these competing drives and forces, forever managing sameness and difference. Yet above all, perhaps, the Irish case demonstrates their simultaneity. It highlights that the coexistence of homogenising and heterogenising trends

---

72   Michael Cronin, 'Is it for the Glamour?', 46.
73   Inglis, *Global Ireland*, 144.
74   Graham, *Deconstructing Ireland*, 6.
75   Pettitt, *Screening Ireland*, 216.

is neither paradox nor contradiction;[76] that notions of Ireland as global and notions of Ireland as having an essentialised culture are largely convergent. Martin McLoone arrives at a broadly similar position in his analysis of Neil Jordan's film *The Butcher Boy*, which he considers the perfect articulation of the concatenation of forces shaping Celtic Tiger Ireland: 'Thus the old and the new, the past and the future, coexist uneasily in an unsettled present.'[77]

76   Gage Averill, 'Global Imaginings', in Richard Ohman (ed.), *Making and Selling Culture* (Wesleyan: Wesleyan University Press, 1996).
77   Martin McLoone, *Irish Film: The Emergence of a Contemporary Cinema* (London: British Film Institute, 2000), 223.

11   O'Connell Street as the 'Nation's Main Street':
      The Image of Ireland's Modernity and *Irelantis*

In 1959, Taoiseach Sean Lemass initiated T. K. Whitaker's First Programme
for Economic Expansion, encouraging foreign investment and multina-
tional capital to come to the Republic of Ireland with the understanding
that participating companies would export most of their production.[1] Five
years later, *US News and World Report* said the initiatives were resulting
in '[t]he old picture of Ireland as a backward little island of quaint peasants, periodic famines and mass emigration ... becoming outdated'.[2] The
American magazine characterised Ireland's transformation in terms of progress facilitated by the Marshall Plan's Economic Cooperation Agreement
and it concluded that '[a] dynamic brand of internationalism' was 'replacing
the isolationism that led to Ireland's neutrality in World War II'.[3]

Of interest to this chapter is a nearly standard photographic image
featuring the O'Connell Bridge and Street Lower in central Dublin as seen
from an undisclosed location above the south end of the bridge (Figures
11.1, 11.2, 11.5). It records buses, cars and pedestrians crossing the bridge
and continues north to show the equally wide street flanked by business and retail spanning from the O'Connell Monument past a horizon
visually marked by Nelson's Pillar. During the 1950s, as the Republic of
Ireland continued to sign agreements with the United States to receive

1   Brian Girvin, *Between Two Worlds, Politics and Economy in Independent Ireland*
     (Dublin: Gill and Macmillan, 1989), 193.
2   'Ireland's Changing Face – Story of a New Boom', *U. S. News & World Report* 571.1
     (1964), 84.
3   *U. S. News & World Report.*

economic support,[4] iterations of the image routinely featured in popular, trade and government authored books and journals circulating in Ireland, and from Ireland to the United States and Europe. At the beginning of the decade an example appeared in Adolph Morath's *Portrait of Ireland*, 1951 (Figure 11.1) and at the end, an atypical colour representation graced the cover of the government-sponsored magazine, *Ireland of the Welcomes*, 1960 (Figure 11.2). I contend that during the 1950s and into the 1960s, the image served Ireland as a sign of what *US News and World Report* would celebrate in the 1960s – the nation's achievement of a pleasant urban space vitalised by a combination of transport, commerce and retail signifying its modernity especially for an international audience. In question here is the relationship of the image to two features of 'the old picture' that ostensibly, Ireland was leaving behind its history and pastoralism.

By exploring the meaning and significance of the image I aim to contribute to a vital strand in the scholarship of Ireland's modernity that emphasises how material remains understudied in comparison to text-based representations, a situation that many authors note and are remedying with important new publications.[5] My discussion of published photographs that were widely distributed in and beyond Ireland also engages with the growing body of work devoted to urban history and culture focusing on Dublin.[6] However, whereas much of the new scholarship revisits the 1960s, long considered by historians as the decade when 'a decisive break was made with the Ireland created at the time of Independence',[7] and emphasises architecture and urban space,[8] I stress the period prior to the Lemassian

4   Bernadette Whelan, 'Ireland, the Marshall Plan, and U. S. Cold War Concerns', *Journal of Cold War Studies* 8.1 (2006), 92.
5   For example, Gail Baylis and Sarah Edge, 'The Great Famine: Absence, Memory and Photography', *Cultural Studies* 24.6 (November 2010), 778–800 and Justin Carville, *Photography and Ireland* (London: Reaktion Books, 2011).
6   Such as Yvonne Whelan, *Reinventing Modern Dublin: Streetscape, Iconography and the Politics of Identity* (Dublin: University College Dublin Press, 2003), and Niamh Moore and Yvonne Whelan, *Heritage, Memory and the Politics of Identity: New Perspectives on the Cultural Landscape* (Aldershot: Ashgate, 2007).
7   Erika Hanna, 'Dublin's North Inner City, Preservationism, and Irish Modernity in the 1960s', *The Historical Journal* 53. 1 (2010), 1016.
8   Andrew Kincaid, 'Memory and the City: Urban Renewal and Literary Memories in Contemporary Dublin', *College Literature* 32.2 (Spring 2005), 22.

'reorganization of the city – planning, construction, suburbanization, inner-city renewal along corporate lines'.[9]

55. O'Connell Street, showing the statue of O'Connell the Liberator, and Nelson's Pillar in the background.

Figure 11.1: Adolph Morath, *Portrait of Ireland*, Max Parrish, 1951.

9   Kincaid, 'Memory and the City', 22–3.

In addition, I relate the photographic images of O'Connell Bridge and Street to a contemporary work of art. Interpretations of *Irelantis*, 1994– 1999, Sean Hillen's series of twenty-eight small collages of landscapes and seascapes, emphasise its postmodern, satirical treatment of Irish popular culture and myth,[10] thus rendering the nation as 'a utopian symbol removed from lived reality and projected into some far away future'.[11] Interestingly, in 2011, as the Republic of Ireland faced severe economic challenges, Fintan O'Toole said the era in which viewers live impacts on how they make sense of the series.

> Even if you look again at those well-known *Irelantis* images, they are not at all the same as they were a decade ago. Back then, their humour was the most obvious thing about them. They seemed to make some kind of sense of a postmodern, hyper-globalised Ireland in which space and time were jumbled up together. Their wit and invention made this condition seem like something we could live with. What you see now in the *Irelantis* images, however, is above all the approach of the apocalypse. The montages are full of explosions, inundations, precipices, whirlpools, lightning storms and earthquakes ... Fabulous inventions they may be, but Hillen's creations now seem weirdly prescient and ruefully realistic.[12]

O'Toole hints at the importance of considering the ways *Irelantis* relates to reality. Consequently, *Irelantis* serves my project by highlighting historical reality through retrospection. That is to say, *Irelantis* captures a manner of perceiving and making sense of the photographic images of central Dublin published a half-century earlier. Moreover, in *Irelantis*, juxtapositions of content that we may, at first glance, consider to be contradictory, in actuality are interrelated discursively. In addition to looking backwards, also, they alert us to the trajectory of certain themes spanning the mid- to late twentieth century. Therefore, following the next section I

10   See, for example, Colin Graham, *Deconstructing Ireland: Identity, Theory, Culture* (Edinburgh: Edinburgh University Press, 2001) and Rosita Boland, 'Hillen's Hindesight', *The Irish Times*, 9 October 1999, 43.

11   Richard Kearney, 'Utopia and Reality', *The Irish Times*, 1 December 2001, 51.

12   Fintan O'Toole, 'The darker side of "Irelantis" was lost on us a decade ago', *The Irish Times*, 19 February 2011.

discuss how Hillen's *The Oracle of O'Connell Street Bridge, Irelantis*, 1995
(Figure 11.3) and *Boating on the Liffey, Irelantis*, 1996 (Figure 11.4) reify
situations familiar to that earlier era. In the conclusion, I return to these
scenes in order to touch on questions of heritage they seem to have posed
for late twentieth-century viewers.

Modernity and Political History on the '[N]ation's Main Street' During the 1950s

> Metaphorically speaking, Dublin is in the middle of Ireland and, in a sense, O'Connell Street is the nation's Main Street.[13]

As government officials, intellectuals and the press in Ireland and the
United States recommended that 'Ireland's immediate, biggest and No. 1
dollar earner must be her tourist industry,'[14] the present and future nation
they desired resonated in photographic images that transposed the area of
O'Connell Bridge and Street into a sign of modernity for viewers in Ireland
and abroad. Early examples appeared in The Irish Tourist Association's
Introducing Ireland, 1951, a 'book [that] is intended to portray in pictures
some of the many facets of the scenery, life and industry of Ireland' largely
for 'American business and tourists', and *Portrait of Ireland*, 1951, published
in London yet 'Dedicated to Irish Men and Women All Over the World.'
Irish Illustrated shared this orientation. Beginning in 1956, the 'monthly
news-photo magazine, printed and published in Ireland' promoted 'Irish
interests in tourism, industry, trade and politics' in 'pictorial news and
essays of Irish (and subsequently Irish-American) affairs' that 'serve as a
link between the Irish at home and the Irish in all other areas of the world'.
Consequently, some authors fostered the link by transposing features of

13   Stephen Rynne, *All Ireland* (London: B. T. Batsford, 1956), 15.
14   H. G. Smith, 'Ireland Entering a Prosperous Era', *New York Times*, 4 January 1950,
      60.

Ireland into characteristics of place familiar to American readers. By asserting that 'O'Connell Street is the nation's Main Street',[15] Rynne, author of
All Ireland, 1956, not only conflated the bridge and street area with the
Republic. Additionally, he implied that the site contains what popular culture treated as a mainstay of American cities and towns – a clearly demar-
cated geographic, commercial and civic core. Writing in *Holiday*, Seamus
Kelly explained, 'flying over central Dublin, you will see below you the
familiar pattern of an American town – rectangular streets and squares as
regular as graph paper'.[16]

As they iterated central Dublin as a sign of Ireland's aspirations for
modernity, photographs of the bridge and street also conveyed something
about its 'place in the world'.[17] Primarily, they achieved this by touching
on Ireland's history of being ruled by Britain and concomitant efforts
to achieve political sovereignty. To this point, they employed a heritage
approach, a 'selective use of the past for contemporary purposes ... heritage
can be seen as an aggregation of myths, values and inheritances determined
and defined by the needs of societies in the present'.[18] For the Republic of
Ireland, those needs included cultivating tourism as an economic mainstay.
Correspondingly, images depicting what was being heralded as the heart
of the commercial sector of its capital city, or 'Main Street', also referenced
specific monuments, buildings and streets as 'icons of identity and spatiali-
zations of [their] history',[19] meaning, in the words of *Irish Illustrated*, for
the benefit of an extended nation – both 'the Irish at home and the Irish
in all other areas of the world', such as Irish of the diasporas, the émigrés
and their progeny.

15   Rynne, *All Ireland*, 15.
16   Seamus Kelly, 'Dublin', *Holiday* 19.1 (January 1956), 38.
17   Fox, 'Ireland Harnesses Industry to Marshall Plan Economy: Champion Jersey Heifer',
     The Christian Science Monitor (11 April 1950), 6.
18   Sara McDowell, 'Heritage, Memory and Identity', in Brian Graham and Peter Howard
     (eds), *The Ashgate Research Companion to Heritage and Identity* (Aldershot: Ashgate,
     2008), 37.
19   McDowell, 'Heritage, Memory and Identity', 40.

Publications facilitated this work by hinting at a united nation. In *All Ireland*, Rynne described Ireland as having thirty-two counties in total, which means he considered the number of counties in the Republic of Ireland and in Northern Ireland to constitute Éire as a single entity. Rynne also used the geographic unity of an island to transcend the politics of partition: 'This book commenced with pictures of the Irish coast; it is fitting then that the last picture should again remind you that Ireland is an island.' The theme of Éire as one nation resonated in commentary about the O'Connell Bridge and Street. In the first issue of *Irish Illustrated*, the article 'Dublin Re-Visited', which reproduced a large photograph of 'O'Connell Street', asserted, 'When you arrive in Dublin you are in the centre of all things Irish', as if to mean, you are in the centre of an inclusive totality of what is Irish. When Rynne proclaimed, 'Dublin is in the middle of Ireland and, in a sense, O'Connell Street is the nation's Main Street',[20] he invited readers at home as well as those located throughout the world to appreciate Ireland as one nation, north combined with south, for which Dublin serves as the privileged core. This tendency surfaced in captions too. In *Introducing Ireland*, the photograph for the caption, '66. O'Connell Street, Dublin' does not show any government buildings. Nevertheless, the caption describes the location of the photograph as the 'centre of the capital city of Ireland ...'.[21] (Figure 11.1).

In other ways, captions and commentary about photographic images of O'Connell Bridge and Street interjected the politics of Ireland's history into the site. Whelan reminds us that colonialism and nationalism equally motivated the semiotics of Dublin's public places during the nineteenth century.[22] Narratives of national identity resonated during the 1950s, too. 'As every Irishman remembers, O'Connell Street was the scene of some of the bitterest fighting during the Easter Rising of 1916. The General Post Office ... stands halfway along it ...',[23] James Laver extolled in 'Strolling

---

20   McDowell, 'Heritage, Memory and Identity', 15.
21   *Introducing Ireland* (Dublin, 1951).
22   Whelan, *Reinventing Modern Dublin*, 228.
23   James Laver, 'Strolling down O'Connell Street', *Ireland of the Welcomes* 1.1 (1952), 16.

down O'Connell Street.' On the other hand, some links between the site and Ireland's long quest for political autonomy were visualised but not verbalised. The prime example involves the namesake of the bridge and street. Although proposed in 1884,[24] then occurring in usage,[25] Sackville Street, named for 'a former Lord Lieutenant, Lionel Cranfield Sackville, the first Duke of Dorset',[26] became O'Connell Street in 1924.[27] Thus, in addition to the O'Connell Monument, the name of the bridge and street evokes the history of Ireland as shaped by the man who achieved Catholic Emancipation and went on to crusade for the repeal of the Act of Union. There is also the possibility that mention of the name O'Connell in the title or description of photographs elicited an awareness 'of the metropolitan history that is narrated and of those other histories against which (and together with which) the dominating discourse acts',[28] such as expatriates' hopes for a united Ireland free of connections to Britain in the north, or their consciousness of strife separating Ireland into two political states.

Some authors disparaged signs that modernity was taking precedence over historical commemoration. In light of 'the fact that O'Connell Street has been the site of great political history', Rynne thought Ireland was superficial in its modern tourist industry epitomised by a 'large modern hotel (with tourists sitting out in the portico) and the numerous cafeterias with their juke boxes, iced drinks and peanut stands.'[29] Yet, insofar as many structures in the area of the bridge and street referenced Irish history, their appearance in widely circulated photographs could be said to have promoted a 'selective use of the past for contemporary purposes', such as compelling potential American and British tourists to reflect on Ireland's 'great political history'. The visual treatment of Nelson's Pillar is a case in

---

24   Whelan, *Reinventing Modern Dublin*, 107.
25   Whelan, *Reinventing Modern Dublin*, 103.
26   Whelan, *Reinventing Modern Dublin*, 101.
27   Whelan, *Reinventing Modern Dublin*, 58–9.
28   Edward Said, *Culture and Imperialism* (New York: Alfred A. Knopf, 1993), 51.
29   Rynne, *All Ireland*, 16.

point. Whelan explains that between its unveiling in 1909[30] and before it was blown up in 1966,[31] it 'acted as a focus for the divergent views of Dubliners through a period of radical political and social change. While for some the Pillar had become a jarring symbol of colonial rule, for others it constituted an obstruction to the flow of traffic through an ever-expanding city'. During the 1950s, Nelson's Pillar marked the northern horizon in many widely circulated photographic images of the bridge. What is more, sometimes it appeared in close proximity to other monuments, and the juxtapositions allowed viewers to consider how together, they narrated Ireland's past. For example, Hinde, in his postcard, used light grey to pick out the facade of the General Post Office from among a block of adjacent buildings in shadows (Figure 11.5). Perhaps to indicate that the site has great spatial presence and feels all encompassing, Hinde widened the scene while compressing its distance, including between built structures. One result is that the O'Connell Monument, which in actuality is nearer to the bridge than the GPO or adjacent Nelson's Pillar, nevertheless visually appears horizontally clustered with the two monuments in the middle ground centre of the composition and together, the GPO, O'Connell Monument and Nelson's Pillar evoke many historical situations and events ranging from Ireland's colonial history and efforts at sovereignty, the Easter Rising, the Proclamation of the Irish Republic and later repair of the GPO by the Irish Free State, and imperial Britain's military dominance, including Irish sailors who served Nelson in breaking the Napoleonic blockade by France and Spain.[32] To similar effect, the photograph Sheridan published in 'Looking at Dublin', hones in on the profile of a female allegorical figure at the base of the O'Connell Monument. She appears to hold the facade of the General Post Office and Nelson's Pillar equally in her gaze, as if compelling readers to inquire about the relationship of the historical events and individuals they memorialise.

30   Whelan, *Reinventing Modern Dublin*, 201.
31   Whelan, *Reinventing Modern Dublin*, 206.
32   Whelan, *Reinventing Modern Dublin*, 203.

IRELAND

OF THE WELCOMES

VOL. 9   NO. 1   PRICE 1/6   MAY-JUNE 1960

Figure 11.2: 'O'Connell Street, Dublin', cover of *Ireland of the Welcomes*
(9.1, May–June 1960).

From the visual treatment of monuments along O'Connell Street, viewers may have gleaned a message about the nation's ability to remember its

history within its flourishing modernity. To be sure, in 'Strolling down O'Connell Street', Laver alleged that Nelson's Pillar and, perhaps by inference, the famous British officer who is its subject, appear to carry greater significance than the monument and person of Ireland's Liberator, wrapped in his 'repeal cloak, and standing upon a great bronze drum, around which are grouped such oddly assorted personifications as Patriotism and the People, Eloquence and the Arts, Commerce and Courage, and Erin breaking her chains':[33] '[t]here is a much higher monument than O'Connell's in the very centre of O'Connell Street, a tall column, one of the highest in these islands, surmounted by the figure of – Nelson.'[34] On the other hand, what intrigued Rynne was Ireland's ability to accommodate evidence of a powerful Britain who once ruled over her. 'The Republic of Ireland can easily digest all such symbols of foreign domination,'[35] including Nelson's Pillar. 'Truth to tell, Ireland meant nothing to Nelson, or Nelson to Ireland, but the Pillar is pleasing to the eye.'[36] Rynne anticipated what film scholar Harvey O'Brien observes about the 'depoliticized political history' espoused by the historical documentary films that Gael-Linn began sponsoring during the 1950s:[37] 'in presenting the facts as incontestable documentary images of the period, the internal contradictions and meta-narratives of the history itself are ignored, and the only conflicts presented are those between Ireland and England (with the further notable absence of detailed discussion of the status and role of Northern Ireland in the Civil War)'.[38] To this point, the period's ubiquitous photographs of the O'Connell Bridge and Street omitted references that could have verged on polemics, such as contemporary debates about removing Nelson's Pillar or an attempt to destroy it that involved posting of a picture

33 Whelan, *Reinventing Modern Dublin*, 63.
34 Laver, 'Strolling down O'Connell Street', 15.
35 Rynne, *All Ireland*, 16.
36 Rynne, *All Ireland*, 16.
37 Harvey O'Brien, 'Projecting the past: historical documentary in Ireland', *Historical Journal of Film, Radio and Television* 20.3 (August 2000), 335.
38 O'Brien, 'Projecting the past', 343.

of Republican martyr Kevin Barry.[39] Instead, what Rynne's remark about
the Republic of Ireland 'easily digest[ing] all such symbols of foreign
domination'[40] indicates is the possibility that photographs of O'Connell
Bridge and Street publicised Dublin as a place where one could engage
civilly, even pleasurably, with 'the history of the state within memorable,
non-complex (non-party-political) terms without reference to the intri-
cacies of economic or social policy'.[41]

As Benjamin Porter explains, '[w]hen combined, heritage and tourism
result in a particular type of travel aimed not at exploring the unknown
or exotic, but at learning, celebrating, and displaying one's relationship
with the past'.[42] Representations of O'Connell Bridge and Street mediated
people's varying relationships with Ireland's past by permitting 'language,
practice, and objects that are concrete and publicly accessible' to connote
various 'subjective meanings' of history[43] as if part of the everyday flow
of activity in the city. There, as the photographs indicate, memorials in a
space named for an Irish patriot permitted viewers to 'learn, celebrate and
display' their relationship with Ireland not in terms of political activism.
Instead, as Laver concludes, '[t]he casual visitor might walk or drive along
O'Connell Street nowadays without noticing anything amiss. The damage
has been repaired, the wounds healed'.[44] Crucially, the sublimation of what
could have fostered contention about colonial and civic conflicts in Ireland's
history, in combination with optimistic views of the nation's capital as a
centre of transport and commerce, served Ireland's nascent tourism industry
by alluding to its ability to balance modernity with heritage. By the same
token, the photographs met the nation's economic need to show foreign
finance, trade, and industry that it could remember and even convey its

39   Seán O'Mealoid, producer and director, *Scannal: Nelson's Pillar*, RTÉ One (air date
     January 2010).
40   O'Mealoid.
41   O'Brien, 'Projecting the past', 341.
42   Benjamin Porter, 'Heritage Tourism: Conflicting Identities in the Modern World',
     in Graham and Howard, *The Ashgate Research Companion to Heritage and Identity*,
     268.
43   Porter, 'Heritage Tourism'.
44   Laver, 'Strolling down O'Connell Street', 16.

past with equanimity even as it progressed in 'building a modern state with a bold enterprise and common sense'.[45]

However, what are we to make of photographs and commentary that avoid referencing the site's markers of Ireland's history? In *Ireland of the Welcomes*, Arnold Haskell described O'Connell Street as 'one of the "grand boulevards" of Dublin'.[46] His caption leveraged Dublin's street into an international lineage of cosmopolitan places. Like so many other photographers, in stationing viewers above the city to look down on O'Connell Street spreading north, Hinde, in his postcard (Figure 11.5), illustrated the scene John Sheridan described in 'Looking at Dublin':

> One of the delights of Dublin is that you can see it – literally – at a glance, that with a little briefing you can look down at the whole spatter and spread of it. The close-ups come later, for Dublin is rich in so places and can beguile you for a day or a fortnight, but you must get your perspective right first and not miss the wood for the trees.[47]

From this vantage point the nation's capital proved especially pleasing. Spread across one or more pages in a magazine or stretched across a postcard, it was consumable, too. In addition, it leavened politics into modernity.

This stemmed from a 'cartographic impulse' that Edward Said explained as 'a third nature, not pristine and pre-historical ... but deriving from the deprivations of the present'.[48] 'Deprivations' include Ireland in its historical status as beholden and peripheral to Britain. As Said states, 'One of the first tasks of the culture of resistance was to reclaim, rename, and reinhabit the land. And with that came a whole set of further assertions, recoveries, and identifications, all of them quite literally grounded on this poetically projected base.'[49] During the mid-twentieth century, the

45   J. M. Mead, 'Erin Goes Boom but no Complacent', *The Washington Post*, 14 March 1954.

46   Arnold Haskell, 'Dublin – A Hurried Impression', *Ireland of the Welcomes* 1.6 (March–April 1953), 5.

47   John Sheridan, 'Looking at Dublin', *Ireland of the Welcomes* 6.6 (March–April 1958), 28.

48   Said, *Culture and Imperialism*, 226.

49   Said, *Culture and Imperialism*, 51.

'cartographic impulse' characterised Ireland using its land to foster its economic independence. Photographs of O'Connell Bridge and Street served as the project's social imaginary by fostering a 'common understanding that makes possible common practices and a widely shared sense of legitimacy'[50] for the Irish at home and between Ireland and the world it wanted to engage in advancing its interests.

Belonging to Ireland through Place

The postcard and magazine images that Hillen combined to make *Irelantis* evoke incongruities in a nation shaped by its past yet registering breakneck change. In this respect, from the late twentieth century they picture some realities the Republic of Ireland experienced during the mid-twentieth century.

That Hillen features the O'Connell Bridge and Street in two scenes indicates its importance for this end of the century, when rapid social and cultural changes fuelled popular and academic reflection on the nation's identity along with its historical patrimony. Authors often treated these topics as points of departure for inquiring about the state of Irishness and contemporary Irish culture at home and abroad; several featured scenes from *Irelantis*. For example, *The Oracle of O'Connell Street Bridge, Irelantis* (Figure 11.3) appears on the cover of *Nouvelles d'Irlande*.[51]

In this context, *Irelantis* affirms O'Connell Bridge and Street Lower as part of the visual iconography of the nation's 'aggregation of myths, values and inheritances'.[52] Forty years earlier, photographs of the site conveyed urbanity, commerce and transport as constitutive of a modern Dublin, thus implicitly affiliating it with an international corpus of modern capital

50   Charles Taylor, *Modern Social Imaginaries* (Durham: Duke University Press, 2004), 23.
51   Michael Cronin, *Nouvelles d'Irlande* (Québec City: L'Instant Même, 1997).
52   McDowell, 'Heritage, Memory and Identity', 37.

Figure 11.3: Sean Hillen, *The Oracle of O'Connell Street Bridge, Irelantis*, 1995.

cities. What is more, they cast this part of Dublin not simply as its centre but also as the site from where the nation reached out to foreign business and tourists including to an 'Irish Diaspora [that] is accepted as part and parcel of the Irish nation.'[53] Within this context, photographs imaged the site as progress stippled with memorials to heroic events in national history, which downplayed the theme of loss so often associated with Ireland.[54]

In recognition of 'the needs of [Irish] societies in the present', meaning the late twentieth century, Ireland's symbolic 'Main Street' spreads across the core of *The Oracle of O'Connell Street Bridge, Irelantis* (Figure 11.3), providing key linkage between the Old World signified by the ancient Greek Delphic Oracle in the lower left foreground, and the new, indexed by the Bonaventure Hotel of Los Angeles rising, in the background, against the orange and purple sky as a majestic spectre of postmodernism. In this pivotal position, Ireland's 'Main Street' alludes to mid-century Irish governments' aspirations for their nation's involvement in a world consisting of potential tourists and trade as well as Irish citizens who formerly emigrated to Europe or the United States or chose to pursue transnational lives. Interestingly, Hillen's iteration of 'Main Street' lacks Nelson's Pillar. Either the postcard Hillen worked with post-dated the Pillar's destruction in 1966, or Hillen removed it from this scene in *Irelantis*. In either case, Hillen maintains the ubiquitous image of Dublin from the 1950s, minus an obvious sign of British imperial power.

Boating on the Liffey (Figure 11.4) likewise contends with an Ireland that is neither 'pristine' nor 'pre-historical'.[55] However, in contrast to *The Oracle of O'Connell Street Bridge, Irelantis*, it re-envisions Dublin as seen from below the bridge, favouring the east side as a bucolic site made outrageous by a pair of rowers who seem unaware that towering above them are the gigantic raised, dripping flukes of a whale diving into river. Other features of the scene are confusing. In its hazy dawn – or is it twilight? – where do the blocks of buildings begin and end? What serves as the site's geographic boundaries? Along with a line indicating where Hillen joined postcards or magazine pictures, the imagery points to the invented quality

53   Philippe Cauvet, 'Irish Nationalist Discourses on Nation and Territory before and after the Good Friday Agreement', *GeoJournal* 76 (2011), 86.
54   Timothy O'Grady, 'Memory, Photography, Ireland', *Irish Studies Review* 14.2 (2006), 257.
55   Said, *Culture and Imperialism*, 226.

of the image. Yet, its combination of a pastoral river passage and urban setting accurately index the mid-twentieth-century identity of Dublin as a 'three-way relationship between the countryside, modernisation and national identity'.[56]

'[T]he [N]ation's Main Street' and Pastoralism

In his postcards Hinde depicted figures boating or fishing in the Irish countryside. In Hillen's collage (Figure 11.4), the man and woman boating on the river resemble them. Moreover, the quietude of this passage in Hillen's collage disassociates the couple from the commerce signified by the buildings above and behind them, or does it? Gibbons explains that 'rural ideology' may consist of 'idealizations of rural existence, the longing for community and primitive simplicity' not simply as 'a genuine expression of country life' but as 'the product of an urban sensibility' providing 'cultural fictions imposed on the lives of those they purport to represent'.[57] Correspondingly, Hillen's insertion of a bucolic river scene in the vicinity of Ireland's 'Main Street' was neither anomalous nor contradictory because during the mid-twentieth century, pastoralism interrelated with 'Main Street'.

In 1949, Minister for Industry and Commerce Daniel Morrissey expressed a need to circulate representations of Ireland in 'those countries from which it is most likely that tourists can be attracted to this country'.[58] Members of Dáil Éireann estimated that tourists would hail from Britain and the United States. 'The tourists for whom we should cater are those whose ancestors left our shores in generations gone by and who are now

---

56   Jeremy Burchardt, 'Editorial: Rurality, Modernity and National Identity between the Wars', *Rural History* 21.2 (2010), 144.

57   Luke Gibbons, *Transformations in Irish Culture* (Notre Dame: University of Notre Dame Press, 1996), 208.

58   Daniel Morrissey, 'Committee on Finance', *Dáil Éireann* 115 (25 May 1949) <http://historical-debates.oireachtas.ie/D/0115/D.0115.194905250030.html>.

Figure 11.4: Sean Hillen, *Boating on the Liffey, Irelantis*, 1996.

coming back to the land of their forebears', Patrick Giles remarked.[59] A
colleague clarified, 'They are people who perhaps emigrated from this
country ten, 15 or 20 years ago and, through hard work, they succeeded
in saving, over a long period of years, sufficient money to enable them to
take a holiday in their native land for a short term ... these people supply
the bulk of our tourist traffic.'[60] William Norton said American tourists

59   Patrick Giles, Tourist Traffic Bill, *Dáil Éireann* 129 (28 February 1952; 1951 – Second Stage
     (Resumed)) <http://historical-debates.oireachtas.ie/D/0129/D.0129.195202280072.
     html>.
60   Thomas O'Hara, Tourist Traffic Bill, *Dáil Éireann* 129 (6 March 1952; 1951 – Second Stage
     (Resumed)) <http://historical-debates.oireachtas.ie/D/0129/D.0129.195203060048.
     html>.

consisted of two types, 'the natural-born American who decides that he is going to leave the American Continent and see what is happening in other parts of the world' and 'the Irish-American who made good ... he wants to come back and see his homeland ... [h]e feels an urge to see how things are in the old land'.[61]

Formed in 1949, the Cultural Relations Committee advised the Minister for Foreign Affairs on how 'to carry out or give financial support to Irish culture projects of a high artistic standard, with a view to the enhancement of Ireland's image and reputation abroad'.[62] Also, it planned a 'general survey of present-day Ireland' intended for 'the principal Irish centres in the US' along with photography exhibitions for circulation abroad.[63] In 1952, the Office of the Minister for Industry and Commerce began publishing Ireland of the Welcomes to demonstrate to 'readers overseas' that Ireland had 'all the ingredients of a thoroughly enjoyable holiday'[64] to 'the old land'.[65]

At the same time, in The Bell, Anthony Cronin criticised the Cultural Relations Committee as 'an advertising agency for Irish Culture'[66] that 'seems in any case to have very little to do with anything that might be described as culture' and instead, emphasises 'the running of photographic exhibitions' including in an American department store.[67] He accused the government of promoting a type of nationalism he considered repressive

61   William Norton, Tourist Traffic Bill, Dáil Éireann 129 (6 March 1952; 1951 – Second Stage (Resumed)) <http://historical-debates.oireachtas.ie/D/0129/D.0129.195203060048. html>.

62   Department of Foreign Affairs, Challenges and Opportunities Abroad, White Paper on Foreign Policy (Dublin: Stationery Office, 1996), 313.

63   Frank Aiken, 'Ceisteanna – Questions. Oral Answers. – Cultural Relations Committee', Dáil Éireann 127 (21 November 1951) <http://historical-debates. oireachtas.ie/D/ 0127/D.0127.195111210038.html>.

64   Ireland of the Welcomes 1.1 (May–June 1952).

65   Norton <http://historical-debates.oireachtas.ie/D/0129/D.0129.195203060048. html>.

66   Anthony Cronin, 'The Cultural Relations Committee', The Bell 17.8 (November 1951), 7.

67   Cronin, 'The Cultural Relations Committee', 6.

and retrogressive.[68] Given this framework, Cronin may have perceived photographs emphasising rural Ireland as contributing to this provincialism. He ejected, 'The Tourist Board pretends to the rest of the world that if it comes there for the fishing it will find a never-never land of unspoilt simplicity and a people racy of the soil.'[69]

Nelson's Pillar, O'Connell Street, and Bridge, Dublin, Ireland.   Colour Photo by John Hinde, F.R.P.S.

Figure 11.5: John Hinde, *Nelson's Pillar, O'Connell Street, and Bridge,*
Dublin, Ireland, c. 1958.

Cronin's jabs notwithstanding, in Ireland, England and the United States, books, magazines and newspapers used several techniques to integrate 'the old land'[70] into the 'urban sensibility' of 'Main Street'.[71] One

68   Cronin, 'The Cultural Relations Committee', 13.
69   Cronin, 'The Cultural Relations Committee', 15.
70   Norton <http://historical-debates.oireachtas.ie/D/0129/D.0129.19520306 0048.
      html>.
71   Rynne, *All Ireland,* 15

combined a photograph of a rural scene with text or a caption about the Irish economy, industrialisation, manufacturing or the tourism industry. In *The Washington Post*, for example, a caption for a photograph showing a man walking down a long stretch of rural road read, 'Despite industrial growth, modern Éire still offers pastoral scenes such as this road in Tipperary.'[72] Another technique involved publishing mostly photographs of rural scenes, save for O'Connell Bridge and Street, as in Morath's *Portrait of Ireland*, 1951. *Ireland in Colour*, 1957, and *The Emerald Isle*, 1952, both reproduced a photograph by Allan Cash depicting O'Connell Bridge low, from the east side, as a glassy still expanse bordered by blocks of buildings. In the former book, Rodgers said the river scene manifests modernity in its 'enormous contemporaneousness' that pulls together references to its past: 'Time and space are joined in one flesh round the ever-and-nevering nerve of the Liffey, and the feeling of piety and porter is never far from it.'[73] In contrast, in *The Emerald Isle*, Taylor removed Ireland from historical time.

> Ireland is unique among European nations in having no history. We have a natural history, indeed, at which we ourselves sometimes throw a wondering glance, and which is a frequent delight to foreigners. And we have a supernatural history. Beyond that, for what is in most of Western Christendom, the main historical period, we have, instead of history without prefix, only an enormous contemporaneousness – an ageless era from Henry the Second of England to the Heroic Defence of the Post Office, during which Time is without structure, lacking those customary long-receding vistas, familiar temporal perspectives.[74]

A third technique conflated the bridge and street scene with pastoralism. 'Strolling down O'Connell Street', the title of Laver's article, summoned a flâneur-inspired meandering that situates Ireland's 'Main Street' in the era of Baudelaire. Yet, Laver also distinguished Dublin from other Western cities. For instance, whereas in Paris 'one might fancy that the city was the world, forgetting altogether the country that lies beyond', in Dublin, '[o]ne is almost conscious that underneath its pavements lies the immemorial

---

72 Mead, 'Erin Goes Boom'.

73 William Robert Rodgers, *Ireland in Colour* (London, 1957), 44.

74 Geoffrey Taylor, *The Emerald Isle* (London: Evans Brothers, 1952), 13.

black earth of which all Ireland is made, and one feels that in this leaf-mould are history and pre-history ....'[75] Furthermore, 'Dublin retains, in spite of its efficient bus service and up-to-date hotels, something incredibly, primitive and remote'.[76] Along these lines, in 'Looking at Dublin', Sheridan concluded,

> And here we have the secret of Dublin – which is that it is not cut off from the rest of the country but a living, breathing part of it. It is Kerry and Monaghan, Mayo and Donegal, and nine out of every ten Dubliners are permanent immigrants who are only a generation or so away from the title-deeds of a farm.[77]

Similarly, in *Introducing Ireland*, Finn observed,

> No one could mistake Dublin for anything but a capital city; an aspect she shares with Edinburgh and which is sadly lacking in many a town of greater size. But while, when within it, one is conscious of being in a metropolitan and increasingly industrialised area, one is equally conscious that the countryside is only just over the back doorstep, and that in Ireland the country is still more important than the town.[78]

In iterating Dublin's modernity, the authors reassured their readers that city and nation shared an innate rural foundation if not also a nationalistic history. The issue of *Ireland of the Welcomes* that featured a colour photograph of O'Connell Bridge and Street on the cover allowed for the site's modernity, too; yet, the related article emphasised the past (Figure 11.2):

> O'Connell Street, Dublin. Visitors to Dublin find a capital that is agreeably different. Whilst it has some of the hustle and bustle associated with all great modern cities, it is best remembered for the spaciousness and graciousness of its broad streets and elegant eighteenth century squares which breathe an atmosphere of quiet dignity. And it's so easy to explore ...[79]

75   Laver, 'Strolling down O'Connell Street', 16.
76   Laver, 'Strolling down O'Connell Street'.
77   Sheridan, 'Looking at Dublin', 31.
78   Rex Welldon Finn, *Introducing Ireland* (London: Museum Press, 1955), 161.
79   *Ireland of the Welcomes* 9.1 (May–June 1960), 5.

In addition to the monuments, references to rural Ireland imbued the nation's site of modernity with heritage, 'a view from the present, either backward to a past or forward to a future'.[80]

Conclusion

Irelantis looks both ways, too. It does so by repurposing previously published photographs into scenes affording reflection on how the visual culture of Dublin engaged with narratives about national identity and the nation's status in the world. By the late twentieth century the themes filtered many Irish citizens' sense of self. Some even considered the collective Irish self in jeopardy, not least because '[s]ince 1991 there has been a profound shift in Ireland's migration profile: from 'emigrant nursery' to immigrant destination'.[81]

Something else compelled reflection on the trajectory of Ireland's identity from past to present and future. Based on the Good Friday Agreement, in order for reunification to occur the Republic of Ireland and Northern Ireland, north and south, must agree on the issues and their resolution. This prompted Philippe Cauvet to wonder if the prerequisite to peace deterritorialised Ireland by reducing it from the inclusive Éire corresponding with the nation as an island, to two political entities that must be recognised as existing separately in order for discussion about any resolution to advance.[82] What relevance does this have for the modernity that photographs of O'Connell Bridge and Street promoted during the mid-twentieth century? It puts into question whether and if so how, then and thereafter, the Republic of Ireland held fast to pastoralism and

---

80   Brian Graham, Greg Ashworth and John Tunbridge, *A Geography of Heritage: Power, Culture and Economy* (New York: Oxford University Press, 2000), 2.

81   Mary Gilmartin and Allen White, 'Revisiting contemporary Irish migration: new geographies of mobility and belonging', *Irish Geography* 41.2 (July 2008), 144.

82   Cauvet, 'Irish Nationalist Discourses', 78.

geography (that is to say, Ireland the nation is the island and vice versa) as its historical if not also essential character. In turn, this raises questions about Ireland's modernity – whether, for example, it was or is a superficial gloss on an essential Ireland that is always 'pre-modern, the archaic and the maladapted; [associated] with all those things whose inevitable fate it was to be vanquished by modernity',[83] which, consequently, places Ireland at the 'periphery to the European mainstream, [as] a place that was out of the world, beyond the world, an alternative to the world' having tradition as opposed to progress'.[84]

On the other hand, the mid-century photographs, along with Hillen's *Boating on the Liffey, Irelantis*, 1996, trouble the notion that modernity 'connote[s] an epochal rupture with the "pre-modern" or the "non-modern"'.[85] They manage to engage with Ireland's ambitions for political and economic sovereignty as well as history and pastoralism, hinting at the agency of a nation that self-reflexively constructs its identity for the world. In *Boating on the Liffey, Irelantis* (Figure 11.4) the combination of passages from various postcards and magazines remind us about the role that agency plays in the artist selecting and integrating representations to best suit his interests and needs. Correspondingly, by reconstructing the 'old picture' of Ireland, Hillen, like the photographers of Dublin active during the 1950s and 1960s, revived that picture and its discourses involving national identity in international contexts, to explore what Ireland meant as 'a view from the present, either backward to a past or forward to a future'.[86] As Terry Eagleton advises about history: 'The point, then, is to be neither incarcerated by the past (afflicted with memories) nor to disavow it in a frenetic hunt for self-invention, but to find a way of using it which will get you beyond it'[87] – to its next iteration.

83   Cauvet, 'Irish Nationalist Discourses', 3.
84   Cauvet, 'Irish Nationalist Discourses', 10.
85   Cauvet, 'Irish Nationalist Discourses', 2.
86   Graham et al., *A Geography of Heritage*, 2.
87   Terence Eagleton, 'History, Remembrance and Oblivion', in Liam Harte, Yvonne Whelan and Patrick Crotty (eds), *Ireland: Space, Text, Time* (Dublin: The Liffey Press, 2005), 13

12   Clearing the Air: Irish Women Poets and Environmental Change

For Irish women poets writing since the 1960s, feminism has been perhaps the most significant critical intervention shaping the terms in which their poetry is read. Whether or not an individual poet directly embraces feminist principles, these underpin the acts of reading work by Irish women, especially in the 1970s and 1980s. The role of feminism within the national tradition is, of course, a contested one. While an awareness that the concept of national identity has significant repercussions for the understanding and representation of Irish women's roles has long been acknowledged, there are still difficulties in assimilating the two areas productively.

For some critics, the relationship is a particularly vexed one: Moynagh Sullivan[1] argues that the field of Irish studies, as currently constituted, is inhospitable to the work of women due to the deeply held – but not critically problematised – judgement that to be fully expressive of female experience, women's writing must be antithetical to the national ideal. In the past decade, the impact of globalisation and environmental change has begun to shape critical thinking in important ways. My argument in this chapter is not that an ecocritical sensibility has replaced a feminist one, but rather that the representation of nature – always a significant dimension of poetry by women – now partakes of some of the complex debates that mark contemporary ecocritical thinking. In exploring a range of work by contemporary Irish women poets I have chosen to focus on collections published since 2000, in order to consider the most current responses to

---

1   Moynagh Sullivan, 'Feminism, Postmodernism and the Subject of Irish and Women's Studies', in P. J. Mathews (ed.), *New Voices in Irish Criticism* (Dublin: Four Courts Press, 2000), 243–51.

ecological debate. In their involvement with these issues, these poets signal a willingness to view questions of identity and power in a larger context, and to contemplate the new light shed on acts of representation by this particular dynamic.

The role of feminism in the development of women's poetry and in its critical profile is indicative of the strong connections between this work and the cultural and social circumstances that prevail for women writing and publishing in the second half of the twentieth century. The ways in which writing by women has been critically received is formative of both current and retrospective assessments of their creative work, and of the kinds of opportunities available to women seeking an audience for their writing. That women's poetry is a neglected area is a critical commonplace; that work by women, when read, is often used to bolster perceptions of the work as 'private' or 'self-absorbed' is equally clear. The importance of radical feminism, especially in America, and its influence on feminist thinking in Ireland can indicate a complex relationship between politics and poetics. Indeed, the importance of Irish studies to an international community of scholars means that the production of new readings of Irish literature, history and culture are being performed both inside and outside the Irish community. The role of the environment has particular significance in this regard since the importance of ecological debates both within the American academy and in culture at large there, necessarily adds new layers to the study of Irish writing. From this dynamic emerges the question of how global issues can be negotiated within a national literature and how cultural determinants may shape the role of ecology within a given context. In this respect poetry offers particular insight into the current evolution of ecological thinking in Ireland. While both the concentration of poetic language and its ability to express complex interior states makes it highly suited to investigations of identity politics, the lyric emphasis on the individual perspective engages with core issues of ecological debate in both subtle and intense ways.

The evolution of feminism and ecofeminism has occurred at different historical moments so that each is necessarily related to the critical times in which it exists. In order to remain open to the fullest range of debate, ecofeminism constructs a space where 'a variety of positioned subjects with different viewpoints can unite on the basis of shared politics and ethics, rather than a unified restrictive ideological or epistemological position'.[2] Yet in spite of this inclusive impulse, it continues to have strong links to socialist politics, which has rarely been a prominent part of Irish culture or of its creative processes. While the direct impact of academic ecofeminism on contemporary Irish women poets is slight, ecofeminism nonetheless has a role to play in the reconceptualising of feminism, as Karen Warren argues, and it is this oblique influence I wish to explore here.[3]

The extent to which changing material conditions demand constant re-evaluation of issues is pertinent both to the evolution of ecological debates and to the emergence of poetry by women in a new globalised Ireland. Warren also emphasises the importance of personal narrative as a vehicle of theory-building, seeing it as an effective means of expressing forms of relationship and of asserting the power of the voice.[4] Both of these elements are at the core of the lyric mode, which also boasts subtlety of interpretation and enduring interest for readers among its attractions. The importance of feeling is of pivotal significant in the relationship between poetry and ecology, since the acknowledgement of feeling is crucial to both areas. The emphasis on the experiential that is the inevitable result of this ethical position has caused problems for some ecocritics, however, especially for those adopting the perspective of deep ecology. They argue that the role of the private or the subjective is problematic because it can be judged to be itself the cause of greed and exploitation.[5] There are other critics for whom the self is already relational, though, so that self-realisation is both rooted in the particular and shaped by responsibility to the universe.[6] The

---

2   Elizabeth Carlassare, 'Socialist and Cultural Ecofeminism: Allies in Resistance', *Ethics and the Environment* 5.1 (1999), 101.

3   Karen J. Warren, 'The Power and the Promise of Ecological Feminism', *Ecological Feminist Philosophies*, ed. Karen J. Warren (Bloomington and Indianapolis: Indiana University Press, 1996), 19.

4   Warren, 'The Power and the Promise of Ecological Feminism', 26.

5   Warwick Fox, *Toward a Transpersonal Ecology: Developing New Foundations for Environmentalism* (Albany, NY: SUNY Press, 1995), 462.

6   Arne Naess has moved towards a position where the acceptance of ecological responsibility does not exclude acknowledgement of selfhood. In his essay on Naess, Christian

tension between the desire to validate the individual human experience and to move beyond it to a deeper philosophy of connected and collaborative living is an important journey for the woman poet, and one which many of the younger generation are trying to enact.

A significant re-evaluation of women's relationship to the past and to their particular environment is an important aspect of feminist and postfeminist debates. This act of re-evaluation itself is one that exists on many levels and in different spaces, and it is essential that it should do so. For Eavan Boland, blending poetry, personal anecdote and critical reflection has proved central to her creative process, as her book *Object Lessons*, and its relation to her poetic career, has highlighted.[7] This connectedness of different creative forms foregrounds the relationship between objective and subjective positions and acknowledges the vexed role of memory in creative process: 'Memory is treacherous. It confers meanings which are not apparent at the time.'[8] Here time and space are jointly implicated in woman's struggle to understand her relationship to the world, so environment cannot be separated from history: it must be seen not merely as the setting for events but as an important determinant in their outcome. Eavan Boland's preoccupation with the relationship of women and Irish nationalism has involved the repeated telling of the life-stories of women from the past, chiefly through the medium of poetry. This circularity possesses a talismanic property, with repetition imbuing the story with lasting meaning and significance for the reader. Its reliance on an historic landscape that is at once recognisable to the reader yet needs to be affirmed each time – in order that the full force of the message be transmitted – is an important part of its power. The metaphorical con-nections between territory and womanhood are not new but even this potentially dominated state is far

---

Diehm explores the implications of Naess's view of self-realisation. See Diehm, 'Arne Naess, Val Plumwood, and Deep Ecological Subjectivity', *Ethics and the Environment* 7.1 (2002), 25–8.

7   Eavan Boland, *Object Lessons: The Life of the Woman and the Poet in Our Time* (Manchester: Carcanet, 1995).

8   Eavan Boland, *A Kind of Scar: The Woman Poet in a National Tradition* (Dublin: Attic Press, 1988), 74.

from simple. While woman as 'Other' may seem to be an easily definable category, the boundaries are far more fluid in the case of the colonised nation. Here 'Otherness' is necessarily impure, because the 'Other' includes elements of the self. This is also true of nature, of course, in that the human may simultaneously be perceived as an antagonist of nature and as part of the web of life, behaving according to his or her own needs.

Significantly, some of Boland's recent poems have contemplated the landscape of history directly, bringing what was once the backdrop to human activity into focus. 'In Our Own Country', from her 2007 collection *Domestic Violence*, comments on the transformation of the landscape of Ireland by the construction industry. For Boland, this act of transformation is not only of ecological concern, it also fundamentally changes the nature of Irishness itself:

> They are making a new Ireland
> at the end of our road,
> under our very eyes,
> under the arc lamps they aim and beam
>
> into distances where we once lived
> into vistas we will never recognize[9]

The first casualty of this extraordinary change is the subject position in this poem. The contested categories of 'we' and 'they' are never clearly revealed, so that they might simply reflect opposing sets of values, or frames of mind, or they might partake of the most familiar opposition in Boland's work – that between collective female experience and male hierarchical structures. This interpretation is a useful starting point here, given the masculine world of engineering and the female associations of home and garden, but it is oblique enough to allow the binary to move beyond gendered structures and towards larger ethical considerations.

The immediacy of the change is a striking dimension of this poem, especially for a poet whose treatment of the past can be at once particular and imprecise. Here, events occur 'under our very eyes' both describing the

---

9   Eavan Boland, *Domestic Violence* (Manchester: Carcanet, 2007), 20.

act of witness and testifying to its essential importance – a conviction that has emerged through Boland's work over the past twenty years. The prospect of creating a 'new Ireland' should suggest a positive transformation – even a liberation – in Boland's terms, yet any possibility of optimism unravels in the course of the poem. That the changing of the landscape is also the changing of history has particular significance for this poet's representation: now the distances, both temporal and spatial, through which the past could be understood are rendered unrecognisable. Europe is no longer a historical and cultural force, but a mechanised invasion that destroys both the meaningful past and any hope of natural regeneration.

The ambiguous subject position in this poem marks a movement away from what some critics have seen as Boland's tendency to slip into a mythic conception of female subjectivity.[10] Charges of essentialism in Boland's portrayal of both national and gendered identities may in turn reflect certain critical assumptions concerning poetry written by women. This dynamic can be linked to its counterpart within ecocriticism – the claim that women are biologically 'closer' to the natural world than men, as exemplified in the use of the term 'Mother Nature'.[11] Such metaphorical allusions need to be treated with care as they risk a kind of simplification that Eavan Boland alludes to when she writes: 'Womanhood and Irishness are metaphors for one another. There are resonances of humiliation, oppression and silence in both of them.'[12] It is easy to see how the ideas of 'Otherness' that shape this

10   Gerardine Meaney makes this argument in 'Myth, History, and the Politics of Subjectivity: Eavan Boland and Irish Women's Writing', *Women: A Cultural Review* 4.3 (1992), 136–53. Andrew J. Auge cites Meaney and contends that while certain poems support this view, the trajectory of Boland's work presents a more complex and 'fissured' awareness of the issues of gender, nation and history. See Auge, 'Fracture and Wound: Eavan Boland's Poetry of Nationality', *New Hibernia Review/Iris Éireannach Nua* 8.2 (2004), 122. The implications of this trajectory for Boland's most recent work is of concern to me here.

11   Catherine Roach argues that by viewing the earth as mother we see it as endlessly providing for our needs and removing our waste, an undeniably one-sided view of this significant relationship. Roach, 'Loving Your Mother: On the Woman-Nature Relation', in Warren, *Ecological Feminist Philosophies*, 55.

12   Rebecca Wilson, 'Interview with Eavan Boland', *Sleeping with Monsters: Interviews with Irish and Scottish Women Poets* (Dublin: Wolfhound Press, 1990), 84.

assertion could apply to nature and to its subjugation by human pursuit of control. Many ecofeminists argue that the hierarchical conceptualisation that links women and nature in this way is the cause of social injustice in both gender and ecological terms; certainly resistance to such domination is at the core of both feminist and ecological movements.

For a less overtly political poet such as Kerry Hardie, nature is opposed not by a visible act of human destruction but by a much less definable threat. Hardie's territory is the evocation of delicate emotional states that are expressed through minute attention to the external world, and as such her work is particularly attentive to nature and to its influence on human consciousness. 'Derrynane '05' (2006) renders the almost hypnotic power of landscape, revealing how attentiveness to language is itself a kind of spiritual act. To turn away from the natural world, then, is to reject the possibilities for transcendence that it offers, especially in times of trouble. Interestingly, in Hardie's work, such transcendence is reached through patient and observant communion with nature, not through the transition from fear to elation that the encounter with the sublime generates. In this poem, the cormorant that surfaces and dives could be a figure for the poet herself, in her mediation between the worlds of observation and of feeling. The solitary position of the humans in the poem is both constitutive of its meditative aspect and an interesting reflection of a world teeming with natural life. Yet in spite of the vividness of this world, its ephemeral quality is what is at the heart of this poem:

> We stayed on – the pale sand, the evening,
> the islands all turning
> smoke-blue and floating away –
> stayed as we'd done so often before,
> but might not again,
> the times being frailer.[13]

That even the most peaceful retreat is under threat from forces outside its own control is a common feature of ecological concern. That such concern

---

13 Kerry Hardie, *The Silence Came Close* (Loughcrew, Co. Meath: Gallery Press, 2006), 71.

is indicative of a larger spiritual malaise is the particular and telling conviction of this poet.

The reflective connection between human and natural worlds emerges in the work of younger poets, too. Of these, Caitríona O'Reilly (b. 1973) presents the most sustained engagement with the natural world, in some subtle and finely made poems. One example is a sequence called 'Six Landscapes' from her second collection *The Sea Cabinet* (2006), which contemplates some very different environments and their attendant emotional states. The first poem in the sequence is 'The River' and from its opening line matter itself seems tenuous. Here the natural world is on the brink of dissolution and change: the 'coming night' is redolent of autumn and its wood-smoke; 'the black river pauses / between two tides'.[14] This hesitation between states of being is enhanced by the evocation of memory and by the irregular ebb and flow of the lines – each stanza begins with two long opening lines, followed by two short lines, before a slight expansion and final contraction completes the rhythm. The river as metaphor for Heraclitus' conceptual flux is taken up in this poem:

> It is never changing, never the same –
> the ancient trees of the rookery in silent commune
>   with the river's
>   different darkness
> when we pass ...[15]

The continuity in nature is important to the meaning in this poem, and to the connections between the six poems that the sequence encompasses. Yet the particularity inherent in phrases such as 'this time', and the comparative grammar of 'once ... now', suggests that ongoing engagement with nature does not preclude acute connection in the present.[16] Neither the river itself nor the identity of future watchers can be predicted, and in this O'Reilly draws attention not only to the flux of nature but to the changing dynamics of human involvement in it. In doing so, she enters complex philosophical territory concerning the idea of observation itself

14   Caitríona O'Reilly, *The Sea Cabinet* (Newcastle: Bloodaxe Books, 2006), 30.
15   O'Reilly, *The Sea Cabinet*, 30.
16   O'Reilly, *The Sea Cabinet*, 30.

as constitutive of meaning, a question that links the processes of science and those of creativity in fundamental ways.

Similarly, though in a very different form, 'The Pines' (2005), a poem by Colette Bryce (b. 1970) obliquely considers the act of witnessing through another aphoristic channel:

All around,
the tapering pines
teeter, teeter,
jittery,
and with good cause
on a ground crossed
and counter-crossed
with the fallen,
that seem to sink
are slowly lost
to a lush mess
of grasses, mosses.

Each is born
to bow and die.[17]

Here the tree that falls in the forest is not only heard, but is itself imputed with a kind of human self-recognition. This is not, however, an act of appropriation, but rather one that asserts the relational dimension of all living things and explores the issue of selfhood in new ways. At first the teetering pines seem to reflect the inevitability of their own downfall, the cyclical process of their collapse and regeneration. The form of the poem mimics both the tall tapering trees and the precariousness of their position. Significantly Bryce places us among the trees – they are 'all around' and we are implicated in their fate. Yet, like so many of Bryce's poems, it is the singular or the unusual that catches her imagination. In this case it is the one tree that tilts 'awkwardly / to another's arms'.[18] Ultimately it is the auditory imagination that the poet appeals to here, the tension that

17   Colette Bryce, *The Full Indian Rope Trick* (London: Picador, 2005), 34.
18   Bryce, *The Full Indian Rope Trick*, 34.

'seeks out / its release in sound'.[19] If this is a poem about transgressive love, about the 'one/speared soul / under a fearful, / startling moonlight' and the reverberations – the 'low glissando' – that can be heard by the 'keepers / of the secret hours', it is also a poem in which the observation of nature draws us towards a deeper understanding of the human condition.[20] Just as Boland's poem calls on us to bear witness, Bryce's bids us listen to the unspoken language of a world beyond human limitation.

Kerry Hardie's 'The Dregs of the Year' (2006) is dedicated to Colette Bryce and it reveals nature at the very end of its resources: birds 'squeez[ed] ... down to the bone', 'the last shrivelled hands / on the chestnut trees'.[21] This is a familiar process though – one that Hardie calls 'ceremonial' – and the enumeration of creatures and of aspects of the landscape reinforces this ritual quality through the manipulation of poetic form. Here language is stripped back and phrases economise energy by becoming single words:

> There's the wedge of a daylight moon with a bleeding edge
> [...]
>
> Water. The world. Sodden.
>
> The ash is a rag-tree of crows.[22]

That the boundaries here are not clear, though, is both what makes this world disturbing and what offers hope of transformation. In Caitríona O'Reilly's 'The Avenues' – the fourth poem in the 'Six Landscapes' sequence – it is the ambiguities of nature that prove vital to its representation. Again O'Reilly's treatment of apparent contradictions is nuanced and the approach of winter is changed by the perspective from which it is viewed. What might be seen, then, as universal, is in fact highly particularised by human expectation, sometimes whimsically so: 'Strange that in a place /

19   Bryce, *The Full Indian Rope Trick*, 34.
20   Bryce, *The Full Indian Rope Trick*, 35.
21   Hardie, *The Silence Came Close*, 40.
22   Hardie, *The Silence Came Close*, 40.

of so much sky there is just one view, / but it is England ...'[23] Later in the
poem it is the contradiction between the presence of ice on the pond and
the appearance of crocuses that blurs the boundaries between seasons and
hints at the impossibility of coherent, separate realms. Human agency also
alters this landscape: from the tannery chimney to the sounds of children's
voices, the human is both differentiated and merges with its environment.
Though the speaker keeps her 'side of the bargain, tamping / down the
tulip bulbs', she simultaneously evokes a world in which human actions
count and one in which they are dwarfed by the complex evolution of
nature though time.[24]

Eavan Boland's poem 'And Soul' (2007) evokes the breakdown of such
boundaries in similar ways, but with very different intent. Like so much
of Boland's work it is bound to return to the past before it can realise the
future: fittingly its title alone seems to conclude a phrase, though its missing precursor offers multiple possibilities, such as 'body', 'life' or 'heart'.[25]
All three are applicable to a deeply personal poem about the death of the
poet's mother; all three illuminate the ambiguities of environment with
which Boland is lately much concerned. The rain, which fills the poem,
moves beyond pathetic fallacy and its inevitable associations of grief to the
more fundamental connection between humans and their environment –
both the body and the city are 'almost all / water' and 'every single day the
elements begin / a journey towards each other that will never, / ... fail'.[26] For
Boland the city is of enduring imaginative importance, both as a marker
of her own growth as a poet and as a repository of history with which she
endlessly engages. Early in her career, in such poems as 'Anna Liffey', the
differentiation of space is of vital importance to her consideration of the
intersection of gender and history. Here, she takes the relational aspect
of space, on which much of her earlier contextualisation of women's lives
depended, to new extremes of environmental observation:

23   O'Reilly, *The Sea Cabinet*, 34.
24   O'Reilly, *The Sea Cabinet*, 34.
25   Boland, *Domestic Violence*, 25.
26   Boland, *Domestic Violence*, 25.

the ocean visible in the edges cut by it,
cloud colour reaching into air,
the Liffey storing one and summoning the other,
salt greeting the lack of it at the North Wall ...
                    ... all of it
ending up almost every evening
inside our speech
coast canal ocean river stream and now
mother[27]

Again the proximity of the most significant human emotions and the processes of the natural world are of notable importance to Boland. Through the merging of the manifestations of water in nature, she is better able to understand the fate of the body in death, but what of the free-floating soul of the title? And where, within this merging of matter, is the particularity of human experience on which Boland is usually so insistent? It marks a significant development of her art that these questions remain open here.

Some of the complex relationship between nature and the process of writing itself is foregrounded in Moya Cannon's work. It raises one of the key issues concerning ecological writing – that the act of representation itself radically intervenes in the human relationship to nature. In privileging the act of observation, the power of the human over the natural world is affirmed. This dynamic has obvious resonance for women poets in highlighting the dynamics of power and objectification in the act of representation itself. For these poets, not only are issues of power of vital importance but attention to the formal control involved in the process of composition takes on a particular political slant. In 'Timbre' (2007), Cannon is fundamentally concerned with the evolution of language, with the ways in which language can be 'pressed into a different service' through the processes of usage.[28] This service, as in so many of Cannon's poems, is the representation of nature; and further, a consideration of the relationship between nature and art. Wordplay exposes this idea in the title, where the tone of voice and the substance of the tree are conjoined in a single word,

27   Boland, *Domestic Violence*, 25.
28   Moya Cannon, *Carrying the Songs* (Manchester: Carcanet, 2007), 15.

before being teased out through the course of the poem. The ways in which language is formed to accommodate new realities has particular bearing on the ecological turn in poetry by women. What we expect, then, is for new forms and styles to emerge from these pressures of representation. The interconnectedness of all things – the web of nature that for some ecologists removes the ascendancy of the human – applies to language itself, as the first line of 'Timbre' makes clear, '[a] word does not head out alone'.[29] The interiorisation of meaning is significant here: like the tree, the human may also keep the 'record / of the temper of years / well hidden'.[30] It is significant that this disclosure is folded into the centre of the poem, for just as language itself serves to release experience, so the process of writing the poem creates the voice in which 'pain and joy' can be unlocked.

Another poem, also from *Carrying the Songs* (2007), draws attention to the close relationship between the poetic impulse and engagement with nature. In 'First Poetry', by likening poems to migrating birds, Cannon contemplates the dichotomy of belonging and estrangement, of being both of the community and 'Other' to it. The imagination, she suggests, needs these tensions for its own progression:

> They needed, for no obvious reason, two worlds
> in which to feed and breed,
> so they needed a capacity for sustained flight,
> a fine orientation,
> an ability to sleep on the wing
> an instinct for form and its rhythms.[31]

There is a resistance to an entirely rational approach here – neither nature nor creativity can be subjected to explanation, even though their qualities are vivid and particular. Ironically, this particularity applies equally to the flight of birds and to the creative process, seeming to support the view that a connection to larger schemes of understanding is implicit in significant acts of self-realisation, such as those prompted by the closest creative engagement.

29   Cannon, *Carrying the Songs*, 15.
30   Cannon, *Carrying the Songs*, 15.
31   Cannon, *Carrying the Songs*, 17.

Of all the poets considered in this chapter, Paula Meehan exhibits the most sustained engagement with environmental politics, often in connection with her Dublin childhood and the subsequent fate of the city's public spaces. Ecofeminism itself increasingly offers a flexible engagement with power relations, which has implications not just for women's relationship to nature but for that of other marginalised identities.[32] As a poet with strongly held convictions concerning issues of both class and gender, Meehan's consideration of the environment shows a prescient attention to this vital contemporary debate. Her work also demonstrates some of the key tensions within ecocriticism concerning the role of the personal, since her poems often represent individual experience while mapping a dynamic and interconnected world.

One such poem, 'Elder', captures the delicate balance between these approaches in ways that interrogate the complex role of humanity in nature. From the opening of the poem the pervasive aspect of the natural world, and its way of entering the domestic space, is pre-eminent. Yet it is the independence of the tree, its 'left alone / self designing wildness' that attracts the speaker.[33] The tree also possesses a strangely sexualised identity here in the reek of its 'tomcat pungency' throughout the room. The perspective that the speaker occupies in relation to the tree is not at first apparent, but when revealed offers an interesting twist to the relationship. The tree is viewed from the window of a flat and thus is not, in any sense, 'possessed' by the speaker: 'I content / myself with window-boxes and the tops of wardrobes. / I feel like a cliff dweller, three floors up.'[34] Yet, positioned as it is in the slippage from one stanza to the next, it seems that this contentment is reluctantly acknowledged. The speaker turns into a Circean figure, concocting sleeping draughts for her partner even as she herself is bewitched by the elder tree, a tree that is imaginatively transformed into a 'night tyger' that finally enters the space of greatest human intimacy – the bed.

---

32   Richard T. Twine, 'Ma(r)king Essence – Ecofeminism and Embodiment', *Ethics and the Environment* 6.2 (2001), 33.

33   Paula Meehan, *Dharmakaya* (Manchester: Carcanet, 2000), 41.

34   Meehan, *Dharmakaya*, 41.

This movement between the created spaces of the human and those of the natural world finds echo in a poem from Rosita Boland's latest collection, *Dissecting the Heart* (2003). 'The Last House on the Island' is arranged in couplets, with the repetition of '[t]hey lost' opening five of the nine pairs.[35] Formally then, this poem mimics the incursion of the elements, with which it is thematically concerned, so that the tidal 'turn' at the close can be incorporated into the endless cycle of nature. Even in its title, this poem speaks of a frail boundary between human and natural orders: here human habitation is on the edge, both spatially and temporally, so that its erosion reflects not just its situation but also the passage of time itself. Evocative of Elizabeth Bishop's famous sestina 'One Art' (1976) in its progressive treatment of loss (from the insignificant to the life-changing), this poem shows the elements first responsible for the loss of inconsequential objects but finally for one of the most significant of tragedies: 'They lost their bairn to a rogue wave / and then their reason shortly after.'[36] Ultimately, though, the poem projects the washing away of the house itself, an event suggestive of liberation rather than destruction as human habitation ceases resistance and instead yields to the forces of nature: 'its twin gables will be taut sails / trimmed for a voyage, shining white'.[37]

A dynamic and sometimes uneasy relationship between inner and outer is also a hallmark of Vona Groarke's representation of the house in her work. It was such a predominant trope in her first collection *Shale*, that her second, *Other People's Houses*, used it as a unifying device. Her approach has both flexibility and range, though, and moves easily from childhood memories, through historical reflections, to consider ideas of subjectivity and relation to others. These last issues are prominent in her poem 'Glaze', from the 2006 collection, *Juniper Street*. Groarke is known for the condensed complexity of her poetry; though she often chooses either domestic or local settings for her work, these frequently open out

35   Rosita Boland, *Dissecting the Heart* (Loughcrew, Co. Meath: Gallery Press, 2003), 19.
36   Boland, *Dissecting the Heart*, 19.
37   Boland, *Dissecting the Heart*, 19.

into reflective philosophical material. In common with many of Groarke's poems (and with Boland's 'In Our Own Country') the 'you' and 'I' that appear here are problematically positioned. The poem opens with a frozen river 'after a night of rain'.[38] The tension between forms of matter here is significant, since it disturbs our sense of a landscape in which the rules of nature holds true. The solitary bird that appears in this scene is 'sleek as my breastbone', offering an intimate perspective on this scene.[39] The 'you' whom the speaker addresses seems to be the bird itself, and the knowledge that the creature has yet to acquire is of its own environment: 'the cold on your wingtip, / the ice on your tongue'.[40] Yet the presence of the tongue is a disturbing one – an intimately human aspect expressive not just of sensory appreciation but of the function of language itself. The mesmerising link between the speaker and the bird is captured in the final line and a half: 'With your eye setting / on where I still you, I all but turn away.'[41] That the act of looking has an effect on the observed object inflects the very language here, where the verbs read like nouns slipped from place. The title too has multiple associations: the film of ice, the protective surface, the unseeing eye.

One of the distinctive features of contemporary Irish women poets is aptly demonstrated here – their unwillingness to represent fixed positions or to be assimilated into groups or movements within the poetic tradition. Few aesthetic patterns emerge; indeed, these women challenge the existence of such patterns not only through their relentless individuality but also through the many metamorphoses that their work has undergone. Even poets who can be more distinctively located in terms of class or sexual politics can never be seen as simply representative, but rather as individuals working within the compass of their own experience to explore more far-reaching territories. For the younger Irish poets – those beginning to write in the 1990s and beyond – the impact of feminism has arguably been

---

38   Vona Groarke, *Juniper Street* (Loughcrew, Co. Meath: Gallery Press, 2006), 54.
39   Groarke, *Juniper Street*, 54.
40   Groarke, *Juniper Street*, 54.
41   Groarke, *Juniper Street*, 54.

an indirect one. Their work possesses an independent and often highly individualised dimension which tends to defy the perception of these writers as any kind of group. These poets are certainly less likely to engage directly with feminist principles or to adopt the kind of concerted address on questions of gender representation that Eavan Boland initiated in the 1970s and has been developing ever since.

13   Nomadic Artists, Smooth Spaces and Lines of Flight: Reading Colum McCann through Joyce, and Deleuze and Guattari

From his first collection of short stories, *Fishing the Sloe-Black River* in 1994, up to *Zoli*, released in 2007, the foci of Colum McCann's writings have been emigration, nomadism, the diasporic condition, the crossing of frontiers and the blending of cultures and languages. If the fictional Stephen Dedalus did manage to create a new conscience for his race by evoking the irresistible attraction of flight and exile, it is perhaps indeed in such a re-imagining of the relation between art and nationality as exemplified by McCann's books that the continuing influence of that conscience is to be felt. An Irishman living in New York for many years, who has lately made himself famous for writing about a Russian dancer or a Gypsy poetess, McCann's work embodies the type of dialectic between Irishness and cosmopolitanism that Joyce's work pioneered. Simply they display at once an acute awareness of historical determinism and the most earnest desire to transmute these binding forces of history into the liberating power of the imagination. We find in McCann's fictions the substance of Joycean ethics and aesthetics: the figure of the wanderer whose fate overcomes the limits of individuality, the transformation through the creativity of language of the most down-to-earth reality into poetic material, the recourse to myth, whether Irish or otherwise, to transcend and escape the entrapments of history and, most of all, the substitution of time – the traditional provider of causality and meaning in narrative – by space, an opening onto an infinite multiplicity of stories.

    Because of the legacy of the long Irish history of eviction, displacement and forced emigration, McCann is especially alert to the predicament of exile, to the pains of dispossession and to the effects of nostalgia. But as

bearer of this national memory, he also finds himself in a suitable position to deliver the most convincing indictment of the limitations of such
Dedalian 'nets' as family, nationality, or religion. It is no coincidence in
this regard that his only book exclusively located within Ireland is his collection of short stories, *Everything in This Country Must*, which deals with
the Northern Ireland 'Troubles'. Like Joyce before him, McCann seeks to
translate reality and the human experience through a store of images and
a language in which space and geography, both literally and figuratively,
tend to replace time and history. In chapter one of *A Portrait of the Artist
as a Young Man*, young Stephen stares at his own writing on the flyleaf of
his geography book. There, after writing down his name, he added: 'Class
of Elements, Clongowes Wood College, Sallins, County Kildare, Ireland,
Europe, The World, The Universe,'[1] thus inscribing his existence in a continuum through space, as opposed to time, and picturing himself in a limitless expanse regardless of such hurdles or constraints as frontiers or borders.
This statement of one's identity is immediately contradicted, in Joyce's deft
handling of oppositions, which underlie the whole novel, by his fellow student Fleming, who writes on the opposite page: 'Stephen Dedalus is my
name, Ireland is my nation. Clongowes is my dwelling place and Heaven my
expectation.'[2] In Fleming's limerick, Ireland is not merely a spot on the map
but a nation, that is to say a cultural construct based, as Benedict Anderson
has shown,[3] on univocal interpretations of history. In Fleming's worldview,
the universe is not a wide, limitless expanse surrounding the individual,
available to the traveller's and the explorer's appetite for discovery: it is
defined as 'Heaven', the transcendental pillar on which religion, especially
Christianity, is built. In other words, while Stephen, whose name evokes
the inventor of a flying machine, dreams only of travelling through open,
unexplored space, and braces himself to face the dangers this adventure

---

1   James Joyce, *A Portrait of the Artist as a Young Man* (Ware, Herfordshire: Wordsworth
     Editions Limited, 2004), 10.
2   Joyce, *Portrait*, 10.
3   Benedict Anderson, *Imagined Communities: Reflections on the Origin and Spread of
     Nationalism* (London and New York: Verso Press, 1983).

may expose him to, the majority of his fellow-citizens are content to think in terms of rootedness, sedentary living and genealogy.

Space in that context is subsumed by the famous sense of place ('Clongowes is my dwelling-*place*') reputedly inseparable from Irishness, as propounded by Seamus Heaney and exemplified by his poetry; the future is not envisaged as an unknowable, endless range of possibilities open to the creative energies of individual will, but as a well-traced itinerary which must inevitably aspire to the same transcendental goal, 'heaven'. Individuals are assigned a name which is not meant to be connected to the unlimited store of myth, as is Stephen's strange name ('What kind of a name is that?'),[4] but to circumscribe their existence to the linear, hierarchical pattern of genealogy that links them to their fathers and forefathers. Stephen, who rejects his biological father in favour of a mythical one, also turns his back on the notion of genealogy, most often materialised by the image of the family tree. Now Joyce's critique of the privileging of 'dwelling' over 'flying', of 'being' instead of 'becoming', of the sacralisation of history, all of which stir his hero to rebellion and give rise to his vocation as nomadic artist, finds echoes in contemporary preoccupations with such notions as de-centering, de-constructing, or in Deleuzian terms, de-territorialisation.

The image of the tree for example is precisely what Gilles Deleuze and Félix Guattari set out to challenge when they invented the concept of 'rhizome'. Western thinking, they argued, has always been characterised by the cult of the origin, the search for roots or ancestors, the emphasis on early childhood as the key to one's development: 'It is odd how the tree has dominated Western reality and all of Western thought, from botany to biology and anatomy, but also gnosiology, theology, ontology, all of philosophy ... the root-foundation, *Grund, racine, fondement*'.[5] Rhizome is only one element in Deleuze's store of imaginative concepts, the expression of which is inspired by an experience of space rather than time, to

---

4   Joyce, *Portrait*, 4.
5   Gilles Deleuze and Félix Guattari, *A Thousand Plateaus, Capitalism and Schizophrenia*, trans. Brian Massouri (Minneapolis: University of Minnesota Press, 1987), 20.

the point that he and Guattari came to call their work a 'geophilosophy',[6] central to which are such notions as 'territory', 'deterritorialisation', 'lines of flight', 'nomadic, or war machines', and also the 'geology of morals'.[7] Deterritorialisation in Deleuze and Guattari's lexicon can be mental, physical or spiritual; they use and discuss the concept in different theoretical contexts, such as science, art, music, literature, philosophy and politics. It describes a movement, producing change, whereby objects, animals, instruments, places, signs, gestures, etc, are liberated from their habitual, conventional 'codes', or usage, to be immediately overcoded again, in a subsequent phase of 'territorialisation' into other meanings, other values, other usages or other lives. Deterritorialisation is a creative process, it is 'a coming undone'.[8] It is also associated with the advent of capitalism, which seeks to deterritorialise objects, people, habits, cultures in order to make them enter a flux of values which is the basis of the market economy.

During the early phases of industrialisation, when capitalism was gaining momentum, a system of deterritorialising flows prevailed: markets were expanding, social activities were undergoing radical changes, and populations moved from rural to urban environments. But capitalism also imposed a law of general equivalence in the form of monetary value. To that destructive movement organised by the 'state apparatus', Deleuze and Guattari oppose what they call the 'war machines', which can be conceived in a 'nomadic space', as opposed to 'sedentary space'. In *A Thousand Plateaus* they also contrast 'smooth spaces' with 'striated spaces'. Smooth is the equivalent of what Deleuze and Guattari call 'a body without organs', that is to say 'a non-organised, non-stratified body', free for instance from such determinisms as family, religion or nationality, and which can move through space without encountering any obstacles or inhibitions; striated space, or land (*terre* in French, which means both earth and soil), means a

6   Gilles Deleuze and Félix Guattari, *What is Philosophy?*, trans. Hugh Tomlison and Graham Burchell (New York: Columbia University Press, 1994).

7   Deleuze and Guattari, *A Thousand Plateaus*, 20.

8   Gilles Deleuze and Félix Guattari, *Anti-oedipus. Capitalism and Schizophrenia*, vol.1, trans. Robert Hurley, Mark Seem and Helen R. Lane (Minneapolis: University of Minnesota Press, 1983), 322.

space which has been 'territorialised', that is to say was imprinted by codes, rules, laws, organisations, systems. The desert or the ice-floe are examples of smooth spaces that non-organised, stateless nomads can walk through, whereas cities and cultivated fields are striated spaces inhabited by sedentary people having organised themselves into states, or nation-states. The nomad is the person or thinker who, by moving from place to place, constantly creates spaces, through the trajectory of his passage from one territory to another or from one striated area to a smooth one. Deleuzian 'geological' concepts, as opposed to genealogical ones, are meant to avoid all reference to any kind of transcendence, and should enable us to think in terms of multiplicity, becoming and re-arrangements of elements, or of what Guattari calls 'assemblages'.

It seems that this recourse to geography, geology and more generally to the vocabulary of space, to express new concepts, which as we pointed out can also be found in Joyce's exploitation of the myth of Daedalus and of the nomadic artist, has echoes in the fiction of Colum McCann. His stories stage such stateless nomads as the restless Irish-born photographer and his Mexican wife in *Songdogs*, the multi-ethnic immigrants employed in the construction of the New York subway system in the 1920s and their homeless descendent Treefrog in *This Side of Brightness*, the emotionally damaged Russian dancer Rudi Nureyev in *Dancer*, or the Romish poetess marginalised even from her own people in *Zoli*. The constitution of new territories, or *nouvelles terres*, which would escape the divisions and demarcations assigned by history or ideology, the urge to choose a 'line of flight', nomadism in a literal and a figurative way, are indeed all features that McCann seeks to evoke through a language and a style of narrative that are also in flux, as is evidenced by the metaphoric quality of his writing. His characters seem to be carried away by a never ending, irresistible movement onward, a flow which carries many dangers with it but must never stop, for fear of entrapment, paralysis and ensuing death, as is beautifully suggested by the image of the crane frozen in the waters of the Hudson River in the opening chapter of *This Side of Brightness*.

The river itself belongs to McCann's recurrent imagery, already foregrounded in *Fishing the Sloe-Black River*, where individuals were shown to be no more than the flotsam and jetsam of the currents of life, to be compared to all the refuse that the paralytic Fergus in the story 'Along the Riverwall' strives to identify among the murky waters of the Liffey: old black kettles, pennies and prams, shovels and stovepipes, coins and whistles, horseshoes and footballs, and 'many an old bicycle.'[9] In that collection of stories, most of the various characters of emigrants or immigrants are driven away from home by such all-too-familiar features of Post-Famine, Pre-Celtic Tiger Ireland as economic poverty, cultural deprivation, and moral censorship. But with *Songdogs* McCann shifts the causes and meaning of exile and wandering to a less deterministic, more existential level. Economic migrancy becomes less the result of the hazards of history than of a self-assigned singular fate. As a matter of fact, there is no actual, material reason why Conor's father should have left Mayo in the first place. His decision to leave home seems as natural, as mysterious and as unavoidable as the flow of the river, 'bound to move things on,'[10] set into motion by an invisible, unnameable law which forbids stasis and a sedentary mode of living. His rootlessnness is emphasised by the broken lines of his genealogy, his birth the chance result of a single encounter between two individuals who should never have met, his education the work of two Protestant ladies marginalised by their religion and their probable homosexuality. As an adult he also withdraws from his role as father and bearer of the Law to his son Conor, just as he turned his back on his own ascendency, familial or national legacy. Conor's father, at the age of eleven, renames himself Michael Lyons, 'a name that was common among many of the locals, a name that could have belonged to his father'.[11] This gesture suggests that he acts as if to reinvent his origin, and it seems to follow one of those Deleuzian 'lines of flight' which prevent territories from becoming encoded by the weight of history. Even though his travels bring him to stumble upon the scene of some major historical events, such as the Spanish Civil War, he always remains an exterior witness, an onlooker, as is made obvious by his role as photographer, impervious to the lure of political involvement. Contrary to the migrants McCann previously pictured in *Fishing the Sloe-Black River*, Conor's father is free from the weight of memories, does not try to

9   Colum McCann, *Fishing the Sloe-Black River* (London: Phoenix, 1994), 147.
10   Colum McCann, *Songdogs* (London: Phoenix, 1995), 26.
11   McCann, *Songdogs*, 7.

find in the space he travels through any of the signs of recognition which would enable him to reconstruct a new world similar to the one he left behind. His crossing of deserts and undefined, loose territories reminds us of Wim Wenders' film *Paris, Texas* (1984), the opening scene of which shows Travis, the amnesiac character played by Harry Dean Stanton, walking through the desert, as it were emerging from a long, limitless peregrination the origin of which remains obscure, luggageless, nameless, heading towards an unknown destination.

In *A Thousand Plateaus*, Deleuze and Guattari mention another of Wenders' films, *Kings of the Road* (1976), in which two characters undertake two different kinds of journey, one, a 'Goethean, educational journey', which Deleuze calls 'striated', and the other, made of 'experimentation and amnesia', through a smooth space. Such seems to be the kind of journey favoured by McCann's character, who wanders through Mexico while the rest of the world is being blown apart by the horrors of the Second World War:

> He was treading the middle line between drifter and coward, I suppose. He could have gone to Europe to photograph or fight, but instead he continued his peregrinations, heading westward, away from the smell of the sea, wind in the vast emptiness, all the way through the mountains, across Coahuila, to the eastern side of the Chihuahan desert.[12]

His marriage to the Mexican Juanita seems at first an illustration of what nomadic love could be like: the union of two people with no roots in common, who refuse to 'territorialise' their love by settling down in one place in order to start a family. Juanita herself is a lover of winds: 'When she was eleven she had given the wind different colours.'[13] It is no coincidence that Conor's father and Juanita's wanderings should take them to San Francisco, where they encounter a couple of 'beatniks'. Here McCann pays tribute to the poets of the Beat Generation, among which Kerouac's *On the Road*, or Henry Miller's *Big Sur* stand out as essential references. In *A Thousand Plateaus*, Deleuze makes a distinction between the 'European

12   McCann, *Songdogs*, 35.
13   McCann, *Songdogs*, 38.

mode of travelling' and the 'American one', and suggests how much the beatniks owe to what he calls Miller's 'patchwork' representation of the city, even if beatniks made 'a new usage of space located outside the cities'. But as Deleuze warns us, there is no deterritorialisation without reterritorialisation, smooth space merges with striated one, and a line of flight can easily become no more than a line of destruction: 'A line of flight can become ineffectual, lead to regressive transformations, and even reconstruct highly rigid segments. It can become no more than a line of destruction.'[14]

In *Songdogs* the movement that caused Michael and Juanita to move onwards is arrested when they get stuck in the 'striated space' of New York; much later, Conor finds a photograph of his parents showing them 'in a Bronx tenement street, hermetically sealed at the end of the 1950s'.[15] Interestingly, Conor's parents' decision to finally settle down back in Mayo has to do with the father's passion for photography, defined in the text as 'place and motion caught together'.[16] Photography, in the sense that it arrests movement and freezes for eternity what was originally in flux. The photos that really bring about the couple's sad failure are intimate ones of Juanita, revealing Michael's attempt to imprison her into well-defined contours, and to appropriate both her body and her life. Worse, he tries to publish the photos in a book and to sell it: an example of the destructive deterritorialisation and reterritorialisation operated by capitalism when it changes people, things into a flow of monetary values. Back in Mayo, Juanita withers away like a wild flower in a vase or a bird locked up in a cage; years later, her son Conor retraces her itinerary and compares Ireland to Wyoming where his parents once lived: 'Curious how different the sense of space is here … But it's confined here, the land, the space.'[17] The West of Ireland – traditionally evoked as the seat of a native Irish identity, its soil being idealised as a repository of layers upon layers of the nation's rich history, and reminiscent of Deleuzian 'strata' – is in McCann's story presented in terms of insularity, confinement, immobility, and finally hopelessness

---

14   Deleuze and Guattari, *A Thousand Plateaus*, 229.
15   McCann, *Songdogs*, 135.
16   McCann, *Songdogs*, 211.
17   McCann, *Songdogs*, 94.

and death. Indeed, Conor finally discovers that his vanished mother, whom he still imagined to be wandering through endless expanses in fact 'walked her way into the river'[18] to rest for ever. The 'line of flight' thus gives way to the image of the circle that closes upon itself, and repetition sets in where there was a search for difference. Conor retraces his parents' steps, Michael spends his old age fishing for salmon, that migrant fish which is moved by a mysterious instinct to return to the river where he was born to reproduce and die, after swimming the wide expanses of the ocean for most of its life.

In *This Side of Brightness* the river that connects one generation to another, and also gathers various migrants and nomads, is first of all the Hudson River, under which a tunnel is dug to allow the New York subway to run. There are also the rivers and the swamps of Georgia where Nathan Walker originally came from. Contrary to that image of flux, the other principle that connects all the characters and underlies the pattern of the narrative is genealogy, the family tree, which stands for fixity, rigidity and oppression, as embodied by the tunnel, originally dug by the grandfather and which is years later used as a shelter by the homeless grandson. Indeed, what is at stake is the tragic fate of the Walker line, cursed from the start by the colour of their skin, as if fulfilling the Biblical prophecy according to which Cham, Noah's black son, and all his descendents, were cursed by the original patriarch for having seen him naked. More images borrowed from Genesis are connected to Nathan, such as his fight with a snake when he was a young boy in Georgia, or when he is comes out unscathed from a flood of the River Hudson ('No more spectacular resurrections and no more need of them – one life renewed, he knows, is enough').[19] McCann's novel thus highlights the centrality of the notion of origin in Western thinking, a notion which, as pointed out before, Deleuze challenged with the concept of the rhizome. Rhizome – an 'anti-genealogy' – questions the idea of an original, transcendent principle governing our whole mode of thinking, the principle of 'unity' from which derive all oppressive dichotomies between what Deleuze calls a 'major' and a 'minor': man–woman, white–black, child–adult, and human–animal. The world we live in offers

18   McCann, *Songdogs*, 208.
19   Colum McCann, *This Side of Brightness* (London: Phoenix, 1998), 45.

itself to us as a striated space which conditions our perceptions, our feel-ings, and our understanding. Man is a 'segmented animal'. Our lives are cut up into segments, whether they'd be binary, circular, and linear. To escape segmentation and the limitations of these 'territories' always already 'encoded', one can seek to become a 'nomadic thinker' and take a 'vanish-ing line' or 'line of flight'.

In *This Side of Brightness*, McCann plays with the literal and symbolic significance of different kinds of lines and gives examples of various forms of segmentation in American society: the colour line that separates Blacks from Whites; the horizontal railway line, which was built by a medley of immigrants; the Manhattan skyline cut out by the high-rise buildings, which Clarence Nathan Walker helps to build thanks to his inborn sense of balance; the vertical line separating the surface above, trodden by main-stream Americans, from the underground, inhabited by the homeless. The shape of the narrative mirrors this image of segmentation by fragmenting the time-line that separates the past from the present. Yet McCann's nar-rative, and the characters he has imagined, simultaneously experience the encoding of social and imaginary space, and defeat it by using their crea-tive energy to find other modes of writing and living, in other words take Deleuzian 'lines of flight'. For instance, Nathan's grandson takes on a new name once he has moved into the tunnel; not only is this a way for him of escaping determinism, the linear time-line, embodied by the heritage of oppression, slavery and segregation, handed down to him from one gen-eration to the next – he originally bears both the name of his father and his grandfather – but the name itself, Treefrog, is a way of transcending the ready-made binary mental categories on which society is built. The strange name alludes to hybridity, to the crossing of the line which alleg-edly separates the vegetal world from the animal one, and is reminiscent of Deleuze's discussion of what he calls the 'becoming-animal'.

It is important to bear in mind that Clarence Nathan has deliberately chosen to become homeless, and that his situation should not be interpreted as a mere denunciation of inequalities and social injustice in America. McCann depicts a nomadic character in the sense that he flees the 'terri-tory' that was assigned to him by society and custom: as the grandson of an Afro-American and an Irish immigrant, as well as his roles as married man, father, worker, citizen. Instead he finds refuge in a new territory which he completely re-invents, in the sense that Deleuze suggests that Beckett's characters make themselves a territory. First of all, he transforms the striated space of the city, with its network of streets and buildings in which each social role or function is assigned a specific location, into a smooth space, by using the underground as a kind of counter-city, where he and the other homeless people live an alternative existence, a sort of counter-life. Each nook and cranny of Treefrog's new 'home', which he thinks of as his 'nest', another signifier of hybridity and of the crossing of the line between human and animal, is deprived of the function it was originally assigned, in order to be reintegrated into a new, personal, re-imagined pattern. His home in the tunnel is also evocative of the rabbit hole which Deleuze refers to as 'an animal rhizome'.[20] Space inside the tunnel undergoes a complete erasure of previous 'strata' and offers itself to the writing of new prints, new codes, and new images. It is striking to note that McCann uses a Deleuzian analogy when describing the 'landscape' of Treefrog's habitat and actually resorts to the very image of the plateau: 'Here, the bedside table, rising up to a plateau. A long butte for his mattress. Circular mounds for the rise in the dirt floor. A cave for the Gulag'.[21] Treefrog also works hard on the drawing of a map of the tunnel, as if in response to Deleuze's definition of rhizome as 'a map, and not a tracing'.[22] 'The map is open and connectable in all of its dimensions, it is detachable, reversible, susceptible to constant modifications', the philosopher writes.[23] Likewise, drawing the map of the tunnel is for Treefrog a way of blowing up his environment into a larger dimension, to shape the contours of his cave into whatever open spaces he may imagine: 'he exaggerates the features to ten times their map size, so that, on the paper, the nest looks like a rumple of huge valleys and mountains and plains'.[24]

Living in the tunnel is therefore an act of creativity – as further evidenced by the presence there of Papa Love, a painter of murals – a reinvention of oneself and the world, such as they are denied by the reality above

20 Deleuze and Guattari, *A Thousand Plateaus*, 14.
21 McCann, *This Side of Brightness*, 61.
22 Deleuze and Guattari, *A Thousand Plateaus*, 13.
23 Deleuze and Guattari, *A Thousand Plateaus*, 14.
24 McCann, *This Side of Brightness*, 25.

ground. Indeed, at ground level, hybridity and racial mixing are punished by death and the weight of history keeps everyone a prisoner of fate. For example, the reason why Clarence splits from his wife is that she accuses him of touching his daughter when he was only trying to 'lift history out of her'.[25] Likewise, McCann revisits classical myths, Greek, Irish or Christian, and lifts their traditional meanings out of them. Thus, to the re-writings of Noah's story and the Flood already mentioned, we can add the allusions to Dante's *Inferno* or to the Greek Underworld as figured by the railway tunnel. Treefrog and his friends are renewed images of the damned, seeking oblivion in the waters of the Lethe/Hudson River. The ending of the novel plays with the Christian notions of redemption and resurrection, which McCann empties of their traditional meanings through the play on words, crossing the line between the sacred and the profane, as when Treefrog gets hold of used bottles and cans in order to get 'redemption money'.[26] Redemption and resurrection indeed seem a likely closure to the story of a line of characters being cursed from one generation to the next because of the colour of their skin, the original sin. But resurrection here means the ability to reinvent and to recreate oneself and one's identity. As Clarence Nathan repeats it twice: 'Our resurrections aren't what they used to be':[27] it does not necessarily mean being born again, but becoming, in the sense, as Deleuze puts it, that 'Becoming is an anti-memory'.[28] In the same way, Clarence Nathan has 'emptied himself of history'.[29]

In *This Side of Brightness*, a novel of becoming, one is struck by the numerous allusions to balance and the body, and in fact Clarence Nathan is described as having 'changed the structure of his body'[30] by the end of the novel. No wonder then that McCann should have been drawn for the subject of a new novel to the story of the famous dancer Nureyev. McCann confessed in interviews that he knew nothing about ballet and dancing

25   McCann, *This Side of Brightness*, 247.
26   McCann, *This Side of Brightness*, 241.
27   McCann, *This Side of Brightness*, 247.
28   Deleuze and Guattari, *A Thousand Plateaus*, 324.
29   McCann, *This Side of Brightness*, 240.
30   McCann, *This Side of Brightness*, 247.

before he decided to use Rudolf Nureyev's life-story; one may also wonder about the novelty for him of experimenting with such a genre as fiction-alised biography. Yet, it appears quite clearly that, whether it was based on facts or not, the character of Nureyev afforded McCann with yet one more splendid figure of a nomadic artist seeking to deterritorialise himself through the crossing and blurring of several kinds of lines. Like Clarence Nathan's, Rudi's destiny seems written out for him by the force of history. He was born at a most momentous time, when two totalitarian Empires, Stalinist USSR and Hitler's Reich, used all their might to try and destroy one another. The USSR was supposed to free humanity from the threat of fascism and to bring peace, freedom and prosperity to all its citizens. Yet the Soviet revolution is one example of a sort of deterritorialisation which very soon settled into a new, even more deeply and fully 'striated' territorialisation. Indeed, the new, victorious 'state apparatus' that ensnares Rudi and his family turns out to be one of the most oppressive political systems in the twentieth century, with its tight control over the citizens' lives, assigning each individual a specific place in society from which he/ she is not allowed to budge. One of the features of the Stalinist regime was the way whole peoples were uprooted, dispossessed of their native lands or customs and transported into new ones. Thus Anna, a former Kirov dancer, and her husband Sasha were banished from Leningrad, and exiled to Ufa, where she meets Rudik and gives him his first dancing lessons. Stalinist USSR was a country where people may only live where they were told to: Yulia, Anna's daughter, has to move to a new apartment assigned to her by the government.

The power of state over individual is thus symbolised by the setting up of striated spaces in all areas of life, as exemplified by the omnipresence of frontiers, enclosures, boundaries, multiple prohibitions, rampant censorship and the deployment of sophisticated surveillance systems. Thus the charac-ter of Nureyev enables McCann to narrate the story of a magnificent flight away from various kinds of 'nets', which take on the same heroic dimension as Stephen Dedalus' escape. But whereas Stephen meant to fly away on the metaphorical wings of literature, Rudi chooses dancing, another form of language, which uses space as a medium. Like Stephen, Rudi first escapes the nets of family, as epitomised by a relationship with his father which proves as complex and antagonistic as the one experienced by his literary predecessor. Rudi also substitutes Anna, who helps him to be born again as a dancer, in the place of his real mother, and, further, he runs away from a nation that tends to claim too much of his freedom and identity. What transpires in McCann's novel is that Nureyev was the proper material for a fictionalised biography because he was himself an artist who managed to create a new identity – changing his name from Rudik to Rudi – and to forge a new destiny for himself, evading and transcending all predictable patterns, through the sheer force of art and imagination.

The form of the novel, which juxtaposes various characters' points of view on Rudi, intersects with segments of Rudi's own interior monologue or extracts from his fictional diary, provides a kaleidoscopic image of his personality, which as a consequence remains elusive and erases the fixed contours of a stable definition. In this way, the reader finds it difficult to categorise Rudi's behaviour according to the limiting traditional dichotomy between good and evil, as for instance the protagonist consistently betrays those who offer him their love and support, starting with his own family. Rudi's decision to defect to the West is as morally ambiguous as Stephen Dedalus' departure to Paris, and the famous dancer suffers the same kind of subsequent remorse at having let down his mother, seeing her again only on her death-bed, exactly in the same way as Stephen does: going into exile is a rebellious gesture, which marks the artist's rejection of all constraints and his utter dedication to art, but the price to pay for it is high. Indeed there is also something Wildean in Rudi's indulgence in his outrageous and self-destructive use and abuse of drugs and sex, as if self-destruction were the counterpart of a dangerous pact granting him the possibility of changing his destiny from peasant-boy to internationally acclaimed artist. Like Dorian Gray, Rudi's dazzling beauty on the stage fills the world with wonder, while people remain ignorant of the debauchery he indulges in back-stage, or between the acts; they also remain blind to the agony of suffering that lurks behind the mask of the dandy. Rudi's dedication to art and dancing is a challenge he mounts to such 'territorialised' notions as family, motherland, morality, the state-apparatus, and the world–order in general, as he defies all kinds of frontiers: between states – as when he crosses the Iron Curtain, and hops from one big city to another – between sexes, between social classes, as he, the former peasant boy from Ufa, mixes with the planet's rich and famous. The 'weapon' that he uses to fly by those nets is not in his case 'silence, cunning and exile' – although exile is certainly part of the experience – but dancing, a language which itself challenges such founding principles of Western civilisation as territoriality, segmentarisation, sedentarity, gravity. Through dancing, Rudi seeks to transcend the laws of physics, especially the law of gravity.

In *A Thousand Plateaus*, Deleuze establishes a difference between two sorts of science, royal science and nomadic science. For royal science, 'Gravity in this regard will be the law of all laws, in so far as it regulates the bi-univocal correspondence between two bodies.'[31] Gravity is another way of distinguishing a striated space from a smooth one:

> Grave would be the laminary movement which striates space and which goes from one point to another; but swiftness, celerity, would apply only to a movement which diverges only slightly, and from then on takes on a whirling speed while occupying a smooth space, and tracing the smooth space itself.[32]

No doubt it is this search for celerity instead of gravity, and the creation of a smooth space by the drawing of lines 'that do not go from one point to another' but 'that trace the smooth space itself' which McCann hints at when he depicts Nureyev dancing: '... And he is in the air now, forcing the legs up beyond muscular memory, one last press of the thighs, an elongation of form, a loosening of human contour, he goes higher and is skyheld.'[33] Again we are reminded of Deleuze's image of 'becoming-animal' in that description of Rudy's attempt to overcome the limits of the human body, to reach a state of inbetweenness where nothing is decided and everything remains possible: '... as if all the doors are open everywhere leading to all other open doors nothing but open doors forever no hinges no frames no jambs no edges no shadows this is my soul in flight born weightless born timeless ...'.[34] Rudy's art of dancing is about searching for 'the quiet point

---

31   Deleuze and Guattari, *A Thousand Plateaus*, 408.

32   Deleuze and Guattari, *A Thousand Plateaus*, 409.

33   Colum McCann, *Dancer* (London: Weidenfeld and Nicolson, 2003), 168.

34   McCann, *Dancer*, 168.

the still point where there is no time no space only pureness moving'.[35] Or, in Deleuze's words about abstract art,

> ... a line which does not delineate anything, which no longer outlines any contour, which no longer goes from one point to another, but passes through the points, which does not cease to decline from the horizontal and the vertical, while ceaselessly changing direction, that line mutating without an outside or an inside, without form or content, without beginning or end, as alive as an on-going variation.[36]

But no human body can actually remain in mid-air for very long and one has to conform at one stage or another with the laws of gravity. Balance can seldom be achieved and it cannot be sustained for long. That is why McCann's dancer is always on the brink of collapsing into all sorts of trappings, such as vanity, ridicule, egotism, but also pain, both physical and moral, especially in the shape of guilt and nostalgia. Rudi's memories of his homeland, of his mother and of his friends lurk, blocking his movement towards 'becoming', bringing him back to his initial 'territorialised' state; despite the dancer's efforts to live through space only, instead of time – as is further evidenced by the way Rudi continues to dance after his prime is long past – history returns to taunt him with such notions as origin, genealogy, territory, state. Thus, when he meets Venezuelan Victor, they 'spent the hours talking, not about the world around them but the worlds they had come from, Ufa and Caracas'.[37] McCann's imagining of the scene where Rudi is finally reunited with his mother, already on her deathbed, hints at the pathos of the dancer's life, straining towards an ideal that is possibly out of reach, in contradiction with the liberating, revolutionary aspect of nomadic art such as described by Deleuze. Yet again we cannot but be struck by the Deleuzian accents of Rudi's statement when he writes to his sister: 'I go from country to country. I am a non-person where I became a person. I am stateless where I exist. So it is [...] Goethe says: Such a price the gods exact for song, to become what we sing.[38]

35   McCann, *Dancer*, 169.
36   Deleuze and Guattari, *A Thousand Plateaus*, 556.
37   McCann, *Dancer*, 206.
38   McCann, *Dancer*, 140.

This tension between the drive to live in a permanent state of becoming as opposed to the need to belong to a well-defined territory, whether geographic, intellectual, political or cultural, is brought to an even higher level of pathos in McCann's next novel *Zoli*. Zoli's story could be summarised as the tragedy of a nomad who re-territorialises herself and thereby deprives herself of the possibility of a becoming. The creation of the character of a Gypsy poetess can be interpreted as the fulfilment and the logical outcome of McCann's pursuit of the image of the nomadic artist throughout his oeuvre; yet the life-pattern he assigns to that character proves much less heroic, exhilarating or liberating than that of Michael in *Songdogs*, of Clarence Nathan in *This Side of Brightness*, or of Rudi in *Dancer*. Zoli's predicament seems to spell out the contradictions and the tensions at work behind the attraction of flying and nomadism. On the one hand, her people's way of life does exemplify Deleuze's description of *nomos* and nomadism as opposed to sedentarity: 'Sedentary space is striated, by walls, boundaries and paths between boundaries, whereas nomadic space is smooth and only marked by 'strokes' which are erased and displaced as the trajectory unfolds.'[39] In this regard, Zoli's people are indeed at war with the state-apparatus, embodied in this novel as in *Dancer* by two totalitarian regimes, Fascism and Stalinism. Both systems seek to destroy the nomads, through murder or forced sedentarisation.

But the Gypsies, this Deterritorialised par excellence',[40] have also their own, unwritten laws, which tend to assign each individual his/her place in the group: this particularly applies to women, who are given a husband at a very early age, and are not supposed to stray from their assigned role and function by any means. Yet Zoli is not punished for adultery, even if she is guilty of that crime too; but for breaching one of the founding laws of her people, which concerns writing, especially in print, when her poems are published by her lover Stephen. As Stephen puts it in his segment of the narration,

> There's only ever been a few Gypsy writers scattered across Europe and Russia before, and never any who were part of the establishment. It was an oral culture, they

39   Deleuze and Guattari, *A Thousand Plateaus*, 416.
40   Deleuze and Guattari, *A Thousand Plateaus*, 418.

had no books or written-down stories to speak of, they distrusted the unchange-
able word.[41]

Whereas Deleuze, in his introduction to A *Thousand Plateaus*, argues that
'In a book, as in all things, there are lines of articulation and segmentarity,
strata and territories; but also lines of flight, movements of deterritorialisation and destratification',[42] McCann makes Zoli the defeated victim of the
tensions at play in that definition. While Deleuze suggests flux and movement in the dialectic between segmentarity and deterritorialisation, Zoli
finds herself arrested in her creative flux, and punished by the very means
she was using to escape, namely poetry, itself a nomadic art. Instead of
being used as a weapon to fight the Dedalian nets, poetry and writing here
become the trap that ensnares and imprisons the artist. Sentenced to silence,
when Stephen wished to use silence as a weapon; banished from her own
people, as opposed to voluntary exile, Zoli, like Orpheus, the fabulous poet
and musician, is doomed to roam the earth, not at all in the constructive,
liberating way of the nomads, but like a wanderer, always threatened to be
ripped apart and killed by the people she comes across, like Orpheus being
finally ripped apart by the mad women of Thrace. Zoli's tragic fate – even
if she is rescued at the end, and becomes a sedentary wife and mother, in
a most traditional fashion – echoes Juanita's death and Michael's solitude
at the end of *Songdogs*, Treefrog's infernal sojourn in the subway tunnels in
This Side of Brightness and Rudi's loneliness in *Dancer*. Thus, it appears that
McCann's attraction for nomadic art and lines of flight is counterbalanced
by a sense of the threats and dangers of such endeavours: as if he found
it difficult to see exile only as a supreme form of freedom and creativity:
as if he were too aware of the sufferings and the sense of loss involved in
the heroic performance of deterritorialising at once oneself, the word and
the world. As if he found the challenge of freeing oneself of the weight
of history, of the verticality of genealogy, the territoriality of the city, the
segmentation of life, and the running away from striated spaces, perhaps
only just another myth that we can live by.

41   Colum McCann, *Zoli* (London: Weidenfeld and Nicolson, 2006), 62.
42   Deleuze and Guattari, *A Thousand Plateaus*, 15.

CARMEN ZAMORANO LLENA

14 Multiculturalism and the Dark Underbelly of the Celtic Tiger: Redefinitions of Irishness in Contemporary Ireland

> Oh my body, make me always a man who questions!
> — FRANTZ FANON, *Black Skins, White Masks*[1]

In their book *Writing Ireland: Colonialism, Nationalism and Culture* (1988), David Cairns and Shaun Richards open the first chapter entitled 'What ish my Nation?' by defining the departure point of their study and of the Irish nationalist project. Noting how Edward Said has commented on how '[b]eginnings have to be made for each project in such a way as to *enable* what follows from them,'[2] Cairns and Richards argue that 'our beginning lies with the reality of the historic relationship of Ireland with England; a relationship of the colonized and the colonizer.'[3] This colonial relationship was the background against which Irish nationalist ideology constructed a sense of the Irish nation at the end of the nineteenth century, and which has shaped the Northern Irish conflict well into the twenty-first century.

The sense of Irishness defined by the nationalist discourse was based on the binary opposition 'them/us'. After centuries in which colonial ideology defined the Irish as the inferior 'other', Ireland needed to begin its

1   Frantz Fanon, *Black Skins, White Masks* (London: Pluto, 1991), 232.
2   Edward Said, *Orientalism* (Harmondsworth: Penguin, 1985), 16.
3   David Cairns and Shaun Richards, *Writing Ireland: Colonialism, Nationalism and Culture* (Manchester: Manchester University Press, 1988), 1.

nation-building project by constructing an idealised, unified, and homogeneous image of Irishness with which to oppose the disputable centre. With
this aim, a number of organisations and institutions, such as the Catholic
Church, republican parties, and the Gaelic Athletic Association (GAA),
were supported and founded at the turn of the twentieth century, which
contributed to defining 'the markers of national "authenticity"'.[4] However,
as suggested by Homi K. Bhabha in *Nation and Narration* (1990), one of
the crucial elements in any nation-building project is the literary language
which will provide the necessary imagery to construct the symbol of the
nation. According to Bhabha:

> Nations, like narratives, lose their origins in the myths of time and only fully realize
> their horizons in the mind's eye. Such an image of the nation – or narration – might
> seem impossibly romantic and excessively metaphorical, but it is from those tradi-
> tions of political thought and literary language that the nation emerges as a powerful
> historical idea in the west.[5]

Bhabha argues that although nationalist projects aim to construct unified and permanent images of the nation, the fact is that 'the idea of the
nation as a continuous narrative of national progress'[6] is in itself a myth.
As Benedict Anderson claimed in his seminal work on the nation as an
imagined community, the nation is a construct and, as such, it is not immutable, but subject to the variations in the historical context and the 'cultural
systems ... out of which – as well as against which – it came into being'.[7]
The concept of the nation is thus under continuous reconstruction and
the national narratives both contribute to and reflect the redefinition of
this concept. The Irish case is no exception to this mutability, and the main
aim of this chapter will be to focus on the current process of redefinition
of the idea of the Irish nation as reflected and promoted by Roddy Doyle's

---

4   Carmen Kuhling and Kieran Keohane, *Cosmopolitan Ireland: Globalisation and
     Quality of Life* (London: Pluto Press, 2007), 67.
5   Homi Bhabha, *Nation and Narration* (London: Routledge, 1990), 1.
6   Bhabha, *Nation and Narration*, 1.
7   Benedict Anderson, *Imagined Communities: Reflections on the Origin and Spread of
     Nationalism* (London: Verso and New Left Books, 1983), 19.

The Deportees and Other Stories[8] and Cauvery Madhavan's first novel *Paddy Indian*.[9] To this end, I will first focus on an analysis of multiculturalism and its relationship to definitions of Irishness. I will then proceed to analyse these two literary works from a Bhabhian perspective as contributing to the contemporary reconstruction of the symbol of the nation and of what it is to be Irish.

In his study on the 'Definitions of Irishness in Modern Irish Literature', Maurice Harmon points out the way in which the historical upheavals experienced by Ireland and its people between 1916 and 1922 required a redefinition of the nation and, consequently, of its national literature:

> The new Ireland required new attitudes and values. The romantic, subjective literature of the Literary Revival, with its freedom to express the heroic and the mythic, was not suitable in the changed mood of the country. Modern Ireland was being born and the writers, somewhat bewildered by the speed and the immensity of the changes taking place, were compelled to be realists.[10]

At the end of the twentieth century not only writers, but also socio-economic analysts, commentators and the general public were, once again, 'somewhat bewildered by the speed and the immensity of the changes taking place', and discussions about the emergence of a new Ireland began to be publicly debated.[11] The Celtic Tiger economy was the main motor behind these changes and caused radical socio-economic and cultural transformations in the Republic. One of the main features of this new Ireland, which is especially relevant for the purpose of this chapter, is the increasing number of immigrants, be it as Irish returnees, migrant workers, asylum-seekers or refugees, that the country has received, especially since 1996.

In just over a decade, the composition of the Irish population has noticeably changed. The year 1996 marked the second time since the Famine

8   Roddy Doyle, *The Deportees and Other Stories* (London: Jonathan Cape, 2007).
9   Cauvery Madhavan, *Paddy Indian* (London: BlackAmber Books, 2001).
10   Maurice Harmon, 'Definitions of Irishness in Modern Irish Literature', in The Princess Grace Irish Library (ed.), *Irishness in a Changing Society* (Gerrards Cross: Colin Smythe, 1988), 45.
11   Harmon, 'Definitions of Irishness', 45.

that Ireland had experienced net inward migration (Immigrant Council of Ireland). In 2006 Ireland's population exceeded 4 million for the first time since 1871, with an increase of 8.2 per cent in four years (2002–6). About 10 per cent of the Irish population has been born outside Ireland (Central Statistics Office, CSO, 2007), and according to a study by the National University of Ireland (NUI) there are over 167 languages spoken by 160 different nationalities in the Republic of Ireland.[12] The speed and intensity of these changes have led some analysts to claim that 'Ireland, north and south, has had a crash course in cultural diversity'.[13] However, by the end of the 1990s what was initially welcomed as the new cosmopolitanism of Irish society had begun to raise questions about the country's capacity to face what was often perceived by society and in journalistic circles as a novel situation of multiculturalism in a mostly ethnically homogeneous nation.[14]

As Fintan O'Toole, the key commentator of this new Ireland, foresaw in his 1999 article entitled 'Redefining Irishness within a Mixed-Race Society': 'Slowly and inevitably, Ireland will, over the coming years, begin to develop as a multiracial and multicultural society. Yet already there are

12   Carl O'Brien, 'From Acholi to Zulu, Ireland a Land of over 167 Languages', *The Irish Times*, 25 March 2006 <http://www.ireland.com>, accessed 2 May 2008.

13   Robert Wilson, 'Time to Take an Integrated Approach to Cultural Diversity', *The Irish Times*, 9 May 2008 <http://www.ireland.com> accessed 9 May 2008.

14   As defined by Douwe W. Fokkema, cosmopolitanism emerged in the Enlightenment and was replaced in the nineteenth century by the predominance of nationalism and romantic emphasis on the value of historical ties to a national community. According to Fokkema, 'if cosmopolitanism fitted a period preceding the rise of the nation-state, it is likely to return after its decline' (1998: 12). However, he also argues for the need to redefine it within the contemporary context of globalisation in which it has re-emerged. For an analysis of this new cosmopolitanism in relationship with globalisation and current redefinitions of nationalism see, for example, Pascal Zachary's *The Global Me: New Cosmopolitans and the Competitive Edge* (New York: PublicAffairs, 2000), Philip Leonard's *Nationality between Poststructuralism and Postcolonial Theory: A New Cosmopolitanism* (Basingstoke: Palgrave Macmillan, 2005), and Kwame Anthony Appiah's *Cosmopolitanism: Ethics in a World of Strangers* (New York: Norton, 2006).

ominous signs of xenophobia and intolerance.'[15] As if on cue, the Irish media have since then reported on the increasing levels of racism visible in society and in specific institutions, and an abundance of studies has already been produced in the last decade on racism and multiculturalism in Ireland. Many of the main specialists[16] in this field coincide in believing that the current definition of multiculturalism in Ireland is impaired by the fallacy of its novelty in Irish history, as often depicted in media and political debates. Contemporary racist reactions are often explained by arguing that they are 'a response of a homogenous society to the unknown'.[17] However, as specialists argue, this traditionally monocultural representation of Irish society is itself a social construct that has its roots in the nineteenth-century nation-building project, which was largely dependent on 'falsely homogenising Irish culture and [on] excising cultural forms deemed to be Other'.[18] As Ronit Lentin and Mary Hickman have contended in their respective studies, an Irish multiculturalism that fails to pay attention to the reality of these past fallacies is doomed to failure. If Irish multiculturalism is to be possible and prove more successful than its assimilationist (French) and integrationist (British) variants, a double course of action is required. On the one hand, it is necessary to expose its present weaknesses. On the other, it is necessary to revisit the Irish past and to foreground the ethnic minorities (such as black Africans, Asians, Jews, Protestants and Travellers) that predated the Celtic Tiger and whose presence was made invisible by the Irish nationalist project based on the coloniser/colonised, English/Irish, them/us binaries.

---

15 Fintan O'Toole, 'Redefining Irishness within a Mixed-Race Society', *The Irish Times*, 23 July 1999 <http://www.ireland.com> accessed 5 May 2008.

16 See, for example, Bryan Fanning's *Racism and Social Change in the Republic of Ireland* (Manchester: Manchester University Press, 2002), Ronit Lentin and Robbie McVeigh's 'Irishness and Racism – Towards an E-Reader', in *Translocations: The Irish Migration, Race and Social Transformation Review* 1.1 (2006), and Mary J. Hickman's 'Immigration and Monocultural (Re)Imaginings in Ireland and Britain', in *Translocations: The Irish Migration, Race and Social Transformation Review* 2.1 (2007).

17 Fanning, *Racism and Social Change*, 18.

18 Kuhling and Keohane, *Cosmopolitan Ireland*, 67.

As Ronit Lentin argues, 'instead of a "politics of recognition"' of new
ethnic minorities, integrating them to an unquestioned existing Irish society,
'a "politics of interrogation" of the Irish "we"' is required.[19] Consequently,
the current moment in Ireland requires a redefinition of what it is to be
Irish with the aim of producing a more inclusive symbol of the nation. In
this sense, Homi Bhabha's model of 'the Janus-faced discourse of the nation'
which 'investigates the nation-space in the process of the articulation of
elements' through narrative is highly useful in analysing the contribution
of Roddy Doyle's *The Deportees and Other Stories* and Cauvery Madhavan's
Paddy Indian to the questioning of the nation-space and, simultaneously,
to the articulation of new narratives of the nation.[20] As shown in this essay,
these two texts offer 'counter-narratives of the nation that continually evoke
and erase its totalizing boundaries – both actual and conceptual – [and]
disturb those ideological manoeuvres through which "imagined communities" are given essentialist identities.'[21]

The stories collected in *The Deportees* were first published on a monthly
basis in *Metro Éireann*, an electronic multicultural newspaper founded in
April 2000 by Abel Ugba and Chinedu Onyejelem, two Nigerian journalists living in Dublin. In his previous fiction, Roddy Doyle had emerged
as a Dublin chronicler of urban stories whose protagonists had restricted
access to the mainstream nationalist images of Ireland. With works such
as *The Commitments*[22] and *The Woman Who Walked into Doors*,[23] Doyle
contributed to bringing centre stage an urban reality which had been rarely
encountered in Irish fiction. With this work Doyle had already started to
re-think and re-figure inherited images of Ireland and of Irish identity by
giving voice to the marginalised Irish. *The Deportees* can be viewed as a
continuation of this project.

19   Ronit Lentin, 'Responding to the Racialisation of Irishness: Disavowed
     Multiculturalism and Its Discontents', *Sociological Research Online* 5.4 (28 February
     2001), n.p. <http://www.socresonline.org.uk/5/4/lentin.html> accessed 8 May 2008.
20   Bhabha, *Nation and Narration*, 3.
21   Bhabha, *Nation and Narration*, 300.
22   Roddy Doyle, *The Commitments* (Dublin: King Farouk, 1987).
23   Roddy Doyle, *The Woman Who Walked into Doors* (London: Jonathan Cape, 1996).

As Doyle suggests in the foreword to this collection of short stories, his offer to collaborate with *Metro Éireann* was prompted by his need to counter the urban legends that started to circulate about the new migrants and that depicted them as 'the spongers, the freeloaders, the people screwing the system', in the words of Fianna Fáil's Noel O'Flynn, TD for the Cork North Central constituency.[24] As Doyle notes, 'I heard those [stories] from taxi drivers. I thought I'd like to make up a few of my own'.[25]

The stories were first published in electronic format with an 800–word limit and written to a deadline. As Doyle notes, 'the stories have never been carefully planned' and they were not rewritten when printed in book form.[26] Consequently, the collection may at points suffer from a loose structure, where 'questions are asked and, sometimes, not quite answered',[27] as well as from unbalanced achievement. However, these stories are crucial in their role to 'generat[e] other sites of meaning'[28] within the Irish narrative of the nation.

One of the elements to which Doyle casts his critical eye is the constructedness of the definition of Irishness as exemplified in contemporary academic, political and legal discourses. In the short story '57% Irish' Doyle displays his sagacious use of satire to expose the constructed nature of

24   'Fianna Fail Cork TD Attacks "Freeloader" Asylum-Seekers', *The Irish Times*, 29 January 2002 <http://www.ireland.com> accessed 9 May 2008.

25   Doyle, *The Deportees*, xii. As suggested by various reports in Irish newspapers, cross-cultural conflicts and issues of racism are noticeable in the taxi industry. *Metro Éireann*, for example, reports on an urban legend that circulated around Dublin in 2008, according to which 'non-Irish persons, specifically men of African origin, are driving around Dublin city centre and looking to pick up female passengers with the intention of harming or even raping them' (Posudnevsky 2008). *The Irish Examiner* also reports on the allegations of racism against the Cork Taximen's Association that were made in March 2009. Derry Coughlan, president of the association, has stated that the 'association's constitution does not allow non-national members at the moment'. However, Coughlan also admitted that, although the association has non-Irish members, 'none of its members is black' ('Taxi Driver Denies Accusations of Racism' 2009).

26   Doyle, *Deportees*, xiii.

27   Doyle, *Deportees*, xiii.

28   Bhabha, *Nation and Narration*, 4.

national identity and to criticise institutionalised racism. The central character in this story is Ray Brady, a young researcher who obtains funding to write his doctoral thesis entitled 'Olé Olé Olé – Football and the Road to Irishness', on designing 'techniques that would let him measure love of country via football'.[29] He supports his analysis by field research and subjects his respondents to the test of watching Robbie Keane's goal against Germany in the 2002 World Cup, while their emotional responses are registered by sensors attached to their heart and their genitalia. However, after three years of inconclusive results, and having left his pregnant Russian girlfriend, Brady is dispirited with the project. In the middle of his disenchantment he is employed by the new Minister for the Arts and Ethnicity, who considers that the arts are 'grand, but a lot of it is bolloxology' and who regards his new responsibilities for ethnicity in Ireland as a 'new yoke'[30] forced upon him by the shift to the left in 'fuckin' Europe'[31] and the attempt to do away with the politically incorrect tag of 'Fortress Europe'. As a reaction to Brussels's more liberal policies, the Minister sets this new responsibility to Ray: 'We want you to make it harder to be Irish, [but] you have to make it look easier.'[32]

Reflecting on how to fulfil this goal, Ray considers the idea of setting an exam on what he considers to be the defining components of Irishness – History, Geography, Religion, Food and Football. This citizenship test, which is a satirical reference to the test that has been suggested or introduced in reality by countries such as Germany, Britain, Canada, Australia, the United States, and the Netherlands,[33] is dismissed by Ray because

29   Doyle, *Deportees*, 101.
30   Doyle, *Deportees*, 104.
31   Doyle, *Deportees*, 105.
32   Doyle, *Deportees*, 106.
33   In 2006 Germany went through a public debate about establishing a citizenship test by which would-be citizens would have to pass a German language and culture test, including questions that, according to a majority in Germany, 'many German university students would have trouble passing' (Richard Bernstein, *New York Times*, 2006). For a further analysis of the tests designed in other countries, see Edward Rothstein's 'Refining the Tests That Confer Citizenship' (*New York Times*, 2006), and Rob Taylor's 'Australia Rethinks Migrant Citizenship Test' (*Reuters* UK, 2008).

'answers could be learned'.[34] He eventually designs a 'Fáilte Score', whose name evokes the positive image of Ireland as the country of the thousand welcomes, a popular phrase originating in the expression *céad mille fáilte*, or hundred thousand welcomes, which has medieval origins, and has profitably been exploited by the tourist industry developed in recent years.[35] The irony of the name given to a test designed to curtail immigrants' access to Ireland is highly noticeable. The test consists in measuring respondents' emotional responses to viewing a video with images of what, according to Ray, characterises the current shared imagery of Ireland in popular culture, namely Riverdance, 'and the Celtic Tenors, and the Donegal Tenors, and *Faith of Our Fathers* and that GAA centenary tape, and the *Best of Eurovision*, and the Pope's mass in Galway, ... and *The Commitments*', as well as images of 'the Irish porn industry [which] was thriving by 2005'.[36] Ray's brother fails the test and the Minister scores a poor 57 per cent. The story finishes with a final manipulation of the test so as to adapt it, not to the government's conservative interests, but to Ray's own private advantage and ideals. Ray's manipulation of the test defining who is to be Irish is only found out when he is middle-aged and, in the meantime, this has opened up the doors of citizenship to 'over 800,000 Africans and East Europeans'.[37]

In '57% Irish' Doyle resorts to Swiftian sarcasm in his pursuit of sociopolitical criticism, by focusing especially on the malleability of the construct of Irishness and different forms of institutionalised discrimination against immigrants – including an implicit reference to the 2004 Irish Citizenship Referendum and the subsequent Nationality and Citizenship Act of the same year.[38] A similar criticism against institutionalised racism is also made

---

34   Doyle, *Deportees*, 107.
35   *Fáilte* is the Gaelic word meaning *welcome* used in the last lines of the medieval poem 'Eibhlin a Ruin' written by the Irish bard Cearbhall O'Dalaigh. The word *Fáilte* has more recently been used by the National Tourism Development Authority of the Republic of Ireland in the name of Fáilte Ireland and its predecessor Board Fáilte, governmental departments in charge of promoting the tourist industry in Ireland.
36   Doyle, *Deportees*, 110.
37   Doyle, *Deportees*, 128.
38   For a critical analysis of the discriminatory implications of both the Referendum and the subsequent passing of the Reform law, see Silvia Brandi's 'Unveiling the Ideological

in 'Black Hoodie'. In this short story, three adolescents in their Transition Year Programme set up a very peculiar company as a school project. The narrator, a white Irish-born boy, his Nigerian girlfriend and another friend, set up a consultancy company whose aim is to prove the failure of shops' security systems due to their 'stereotyping of young people' and the security guards' ingrained racism.[39] They visit various shops in Dublin and, while the narrator and his Nigerian girlfriend wearing hooded sports jackets go around the shop and are followed by the security staff because of their suspicious appearance, their friend, pretending to be handicapped in his brother's wheelchair, shoplifts small articles freely. After completing their activity, the group gathers and shows the shop-owners the failures in their system. Their enterprise works until they are eventually caught by the Garda who, during interrogation, address the Nigerian girl using racist language. The criticism in the story against racism in the Irish national police echoes accusations of racial discrimination by the Gardaí published in the Irish media,[40] and subsequently dealt with by the government through different measures, such as favouring the recruitment of 'Irish residents from differ-ent ethnic backgrounds' for the Irish national police.[41]

Most of the stories in the collection cast a critical eye upon various manifestations of racist or xenophobic views in contemporary Ireland, with special attention paid to Dublin. However, two of the eight stories – 'Home to Harlem' and 'The Deportees' – are significant for including references to a pre-existing multicultural society, which had its differences silenced by the nationalist discourse. In this sense, a significant scene is included in 'The Deportees', the title story and sequel to *The Commitments* which Doyle had always been highly reluctant to write. In this story Jimmy

---

Construction of the 2004 Citizenship Referendum: A Critical Discourse Analytical Approach', *Translocations: The Irish Migration, Race and Social Transformation Review* 2.1 (2007).

39   Doyle, *Deportees*, 135.

40   Mary Carolan, 'Survey Says Gardaí among Those Guilty of Racism', *The Irish Times*, 7 September 2001 <http://www.ireland.com> accessed on 9 May 2008.

41   National Action Plan Against Racism, 'Garda Recruitment Initiative', 2006 <http:// host2.equinox.ie/diversity/procontent/Home/Home_Page/index.html> accessed on 9 May 2008.

Rabbitte, married with three children and his wife expecting their fourth child, decides to start a new band whose defining trait is going to be its multicultural composition. Rabbitte starts the selection process of the band members bringing the principle of positive discrimination to extremes; it is apparent that their skin colour often prevails over their musical talent. Despite his initial doubts about including white Irish – he had even thought of including the sentence 'white Irish need not apply' in the job advertisement he sent to the Irish music magazine *Hot Press* – Rabbitte eventually lets two in because 'a couple of old-fashioned Irish rockers would look good onstage with the rest'.[42] With all the different nationalities and ethnic groups in the band there is no suggestion of ethnic antagonism between its members. It is only with the addition of the new singer Paddy Ward, a member of the Traveller community, that the first and only hint of a clash appears, and that only by the Irish guitarist from Roscommon:

> Kenny had objected to Paddy when he'd turned up a few nights before.
>   – Is he what I think he is? said Kenny.
> Jimmy was ready.
>   – He's a traveller, yeah. Have you a problem, Ken?
>   – Eh –
>   – Cos we'll be sorry to lose you.
>   – No, no, fuck no. It's just, it's unusual though. A, a traveller, like. In a band.
>   – Look around you, Kenny, said Jimmy. – It's an unusual band. That's the whole fuckin' idea. Are you with us?
>   – God, yeah. Yeah. Thanks.[43]

As suggested here, Kenny's racism against the Traveller is not unexpected, but the representation of a new form of multiculturalism in the band contributes to defuse past conflicts between Irish traditionalist views and the marginalised elements of pre-Celtic Tiger Ireland.

In 'Home to Harlem' Declan is an Irish university student whose black origins are due to his maternal grandmother's affair with an American soldier during the Second World War. Doyle reverses the customary journey

---

42   Doyle, *Deportees*, 36.
43   Doyle, *Deportees*, 58.

to Ireland of the protagonists of the Irish Diaspora in search of origins performed by so many Americans by sending Declan 'home to Harlem', 'the land of his ancestors'.[44] The subversion of traditional images is continued by Declan's intention to do research on the influence of the Harlem Renaissance poets on Irish literature and his determination to 'prove that Harlem had kick-started Ireland's best writing of the twentieth century'.[45] The topic of his research is initially motivated by his antagonism to a country whose sense of Irish identity did not include his ethnic reality. Consequently, Declan longs to identify with a marginalised otherness that succeeded in subverting stereotypical and alienating representations of the liminal Black other by the American nationalist ethos. Throughout Declan's stay in New York, he matures and realises the performative nature of identity: 'That's what being Irish is a lot of the time, passing for something else – the Paddy, the European, the peasant, the rocker, the leprechaun. It's sometimes funny; it's sometimes dangerous and damaging. And then there's being black and Irish'.[46] Recognising the constructedness of national identity allows Declan to gain the necessary distance so as to realise that the time is ripe for him and for post-Celtic Tiger Ireland to question the inherited 'we' from the advantageous liminality with which his hybrid identity provides him.

Cauvery Madhavan's *Paddy Indian* links in with Doyle's 'Home to Harlem' in that its main aim is to focus on identity issues, especially those resulting from a transnational context favoured by globalisation. Cauvery Madhavan, born in India, is one of the first 'non-national' Irish writers to be published within the contemporary Ireland of 'new multiculturalism'. Her first novel signals the arrival of the new minorities to the Irish literary scene. Significantly, the experience of the migrant is now not only mediated through Irish national writers; Cauvery Madhavan offers her own perspectives on ethnic relationships in contemporary Ireland.

The novel opens with Padhman, a young Indian doctor, arriving in Dublin in 1989 to become a fully qualified gynaecologist, thus following

44   Doyle, *Deportees*, 180.
45   Doyle, *Deportees*, 181.
46   Doyle, *Deportees*, 201.

the family tradition. Published in 2001, the action of the novel is, however, set in 1989, between Ireland and India. Setting the action in pre-Celtic Tiger Ireland interestingly situates the novel at a crossroads; on the one hand, setting the action in 1989 spares Madhavan the pressure of having to write about the various forms of institutionalised ethnic discrimination – including those against doctors and nurses in Irish hospitals – that had populated the Irish media, especially since the early 2000s, but which had been in existence before then.[47] On the other hand, the publication of the novel in 2001 sets the reading of this work against the background of the new Ireland, which makes Madhavan's treatment of identity issues highly relevant. Padhman's experience of split identity and of being a 'foreign doctor' in Ireland exposes people's racial prejudices. However, the book is most interesting in that it does not aim to condemn Irish prejudices against non-Irish in Ireland. By revealing Padhman's parents' prejudices against the West, Madhavan underscores the similarities between Irish and non-Irish cultures.

Padhman's parents are the symbol of the wealthy bourgeois Indian family with Western customs and Eastern beliefs, and a symbol of the contradictory identity that emerges out of what Homi Bhabha refers to as 'colonial mimicry', that is, the process by which 'the colonial discourse encourages the colonized subject to "mimic" the colonizer, by adopting the colonizer's cultural habits, assumptions, institutions and values',[48] and producing a subject which is 'almost the same, but not quite'.[49] However, Bhabha also notes the subversive power of the 'mimic man', for the imitation of Western ways can at times imply a satirical criticism of the imperial power. At a more practical level, Padhman's traditional family embodies the subversive contradictions and ambiguities of Indian national identity: it has combined the hierarchy of the Indian caste-system and an admiration

---

47   See, for example, Aoife O'Reilly's 'Health Sector to Address Ethnic Diversity', 2001; Nuala Haughey's 'Living in Harmony', 2002; Marese McDonagh's 'Abused Immigrant Doctors Keeping Our Hospitals Open', 2002; and Barry Roche's 'Integrating Foreign Nurses "a serious issue"', 2007.

48   Bill Ashcroft, *Key Concepts in Post-Colonial Studies* (London: Routledge, 1998), 139.

49   Homi K. Bhabha, *The Location of Culture* (London: Routledge, 1994), 86.

for the West – it is in the West where Indian doctors go to become fully qualified – with understandably anti-colonialist views and a prejudiced perception of Westerners. Westerners are seen by Indians as very liberal in their sexual life – as Padhman's Amma would express it: 'respect for women is what he [Padhman] has been taught all his life, but the problem is the women there [in the West] have no respect for themselves'; and they show no understanding of or interest in Indian culture.[50] As Padhman's friend Sunil notes, 'it would be the rare Irish person who would know of the Congress *Party*. They all knew it for the one week after *Gandhi* was released in the cinemas. Then we went back to being the country that Mother Theresa lives in.'[51]

When Padhman first arrives in Ireland, he often surprises himself by seeing the Irish from his mother's perspective and expecting them to be racist against him. However, as the novel progresses and Padhman's experience of Irish reality and his circle of Irish friends widens – including Aoife, his Irish girlfriend – he realises that the Irish can be as prejudiced or accepting of Indians as Indians can be of Westerners. This is best exemplified in the novel by the similarities in Padhman's and Aoife's respective mothers to this cross-cultural relationship. As Padhman notes after meeting Aoife's mother for the first time: 'She had been cordial and polite – too polite, he thought. It was an antagonistic reflex in reverse that he recognized straight away. Amma [Padhman's mother] had often been like that with girlfriends that she reckoned or hoped would not last.'[52]

The implicit irony in the book is that both Irish and Indians, formerly colonised by the British, show an ingrained xenophobic attitude that mimics the British colonialist's marginalisation of the colonised 'other'. Padhman becomes aware of his ingrained prejudices and colonial mentality through contact with this new culture, and the implicit solution for his mother's disapproval of Aoife is that she meets her in person. As suggested in this novel, it is through personal cross-cultural encounters that cultural and ethnic prejudice, often kept in the abstract, are minimised. As noted

50   Madhavan, *Paddy Indian*, 188.
51   Madhavan, *Paddy Indian*, 36.
52   Madhavan, *Paddy Indian*, 133.

by Peter O'Mahony, the 2005 *Sunday Tribune*/Millward Brown IMS poll suggests that 'those who have more direct contact with immigrants are less likely to feel threatened by or opposed to immigration'.[53]

To conclude, it can be argued that these texts succeed in suggesting a more complete view of multiculturalism in Ireland, which exposes the weaknesses of the present and the fallacies of the past. According to Bhabha, 'the construction of nationness as a form of social and textual affiliation'[54] required a process of homogenisation of national identity by which minorities were marginalised and made to constitute 'the boundaries of society, and the margins of the text'.[55] The contemporary redefinition of national identity depends on turning 'the scraps, patches, and rags of daily life … into the signs of a national culture, while the very act of the narrative performance interpellates a growing circle of national subjects'.[56] Following Bhabha's formula, the contemporary redefinition of Irish national identity is dependent on a process of 'dissemi-nation', that is, of exposing the fallacy of a homogeneous national identity through a narrative performance that incorporates a multicultural vision of Irishness past and present. In this process, a 'cultural liminality – *within the nation*'[57] contributes to redefining the nation through the articulation of new narratives of difference and diversity. Consequently, 'once the liminality of the nation-space is established, and its "difference" is turned from the boundary "outside" to its finitude "within", the threat of cultural difference is no longer a problem of "other" people. It becomes a question of the otherness of the people-as-one'.[58] Hopefully, the new country born out of this process will be one in which every member of this new Ireland may identify it as 'my country'.

53   Peter O'Mahony, 'The Challenge Now Is to Deal with the Fears Some People Have towards Immigration', Irish Refugee Council, 1 May 2005, n.p. <http://www.irishrefugeecouncil.ie/ pub05/fears.html> accessed on 10 May 2008.
54   Bhabha, *Nation and Narration*, 292.
55   Bhabha, *Nation and Narration*, 296.
56   Bhabha, *Nation and Narration*, 297.
57   Bhabha, *Nation and Narration*, 299.
58   Bhabha, *Nation and Narration*, 301.

15   Inside Out: Time and Place in Global Ireland

The piper, it is said, calls the tune but in Ireland he is often expected, in addition, to explain it. The great piper and folklore collector Séamus Ennis was no exception and he frequently prefaced his tunes with an account of their origin. One such tune was *Cornphíopa na Sióg* or the Fairies Hornpipe and Ennis's story went as follows. A man returning home from a wedding loses his way and 'if that happens to any of you, you have but to take off your coat and turn it inside-out and put it on again and you'll find your way home alright'.[1] The wedding reveller does this and he ends up three fields away from his own house. At the bottom of the long field in which he finds himself there is a fairy host dancing to music played by a piper. Listening to the music he falls asleep and when he awakes next morning and goes home to tell people what he saw, no one believes him. It was only when they hear him play the tune he picked up from the fairies on the pipes that they decide he was not making it up. Thus, ever afterwards the tune is known as the 'Fairies Hornpipe'.

In a twinkling, the wedding guest is transported to the vicinity of his house. The vignette from Irish folklore anticipates the phenomenon of space-time compression in modernity where successive generations find getting people and information from one point to another takes progressively less time. In Ennis's story, losing your way is also about finding your way but finding your way involves change, transformation, inversion ('you have but to take off your coat and turn it inside-out'). The coordinates in the musical parable are space and time. What happens when trying to find out where you are might involve turning your world upside down before the sceptical welcome of homecoming. In this chapter, we will explore the

1   Séamus Ennis, *Ceol, Scéalta, Amhráin* (Baile Átha Cliath, 2006).

consequences for contemporary Ireland of changes in perceptions and experiences of place and time as they are experienced in late modern Ireland. The Czech novelist Milan Kundera in his first French-language novel *La Lenteur* (1995), published in English as *Slowness* (1996), notes that when people try to remember, they slow down and when they want to forget, they accelerate. He describes a man walking down the street:

> At a certain moment, he tries to recall something, but the recollection escapes him. Automatically he slows down. Meanwhile, a person who wants to forget a disagreeable incident he has just lived through starts unconsciously to speed up his pace, as if he were trying to distance himself from a thing too close to him in time.[2]

For Kundera, place is bound up with pace. The more you seek to get away from a place, the faster you go. Conversely, the slower you go, the more you become aware of place, and more particularly, the more you become aware of the place of memory. Mnemosyne for the writer is the deity of deceleration. It is not surprising then that when we go to look at narratives from contemporary Ireland, an exploration of place is going to involve the manipulation of time.

Muintir

In order to provide a properly stereoscopic view of a place at a particular moment the chapter will begin with two prose narratives, one in English and one in Irish, both published in 2007 and both dealing with the lives and characters of suburban Dubliners. The novels are *The Gathering* by Booker Prize winner Anne Enright and *Cnoc na Lobhar* by Lorcán S. Ó Treasaigh. In Enright's novel the death in England of a family member, Liam, brings the family together for his funeral, a story narrated principally by his sister Veronica who is responsible for the repatriation of his body.

---

2   Milan Kundera, *Slowness*, trans. Linda Asher (London: Faber, 1996), 34.

The protagonist of Ó Treasaigh's work, Labhrás, is in an old folks' home awaiting in bitter recrimination the inevitable end stop of death. Death and old age bring with them their own rhythms. Both works, then, are studies in the effects of a change in tempo, memories bustling in as a fast-paced globalised Ireland is bracketed by grief and loss.

A common preoccupation for both Labhrás and Veronica is how to prevent a gathering in from becoming a falling out. That is to say, as they find time to think about the place in which they live and have lived, they are forced to think about the people who have shared that place with them, whether it be in the present or in the past. Labhrás, an old school national-ist, who has remained all his life deeply committed to the cause of the Irish language, sees his ideal of a shared place initially in expansive, communi-tarian terms. The Ireland that he has dreamed of is a collective enterprise:

> Roinn siad saol is teanga, brón is áthas, gliondar is briseadh croí, sheas siad le chéile ag baisteadh is pósadh, thóg ualach a chéile idir chliabhán is chónra agus bí cinnte má bhain an saol tuisle asat ar an mbóthar go mbeadh lámh do chomharsan faoi do chloigeann sula mbuailfeá le talamh é.[3]

> [They shared life and language, sadness and happiness, joy and heartbreak, they stood side by side at baptisms and weddings, they supported each other from the cradle to the grave and you can be sure that if life did you a bad turn there would always be a helping hand to stop your fall. (My translation)]

'Muintir' is the term that is used by Labhrás to describe this cooperative community of equals who were united at an undetermined moment in the past by their common condition of being inhabitants of a particular place and remaining committed to the language of their forebears. As the story of Labhrás's life unfolds, however, the semantic range of the term contracts and Labhrás, up late drinking in the silence of his fractured household, contemplates his present with contempt:

> Seo é an teach agam, seo iad mo mhuintir agus seo é mo shaol, a bhí mé ag ceapadh sular thit mo chodladh orm sa tolg agus mé ag brionglóidí ar a bheith in áit éigin eile ar thaobh eile an domhain seachas a bheith i m'aonar i ngarraí leathscoite i mo

3   Lorcán Ó Treasaigh, *Cnoc na Lobhar* (Baile Átha Cliath: Cois Life, 2007), 68.

shaoránach i measc na saoránach leathscoite ag casadh na cré ar mhaithe lena casadh
go dté mé lá éigin inti, cré dhubh mo mhéine, cré fhuar na cille.[4]

[This is my house, this is my family and this is my life, I was thinking before I
fell asleep on the couch and I dreaming of being somewhere else on the other side
of the world instead of being on my own in my semi-detached garden, a citizen
among the other semi-detached citizens, turning the earth for the sake of turning it
until the day when I will descend into it, the black earth of my desire, the cold earth
of the graveyard. (My translation)]

'Muintir' is no longer the extended family of an imagined past but the
biological family of his living present. What is apparent in the narrative is
that the space he has shared with members of his own family has become
a place of intolerable strife as his ideological certainties inure him to a
world that is changing and to personalities and values which are evolving.
As time slackens, Labhrás begins in effect to take stock of the collapse of
this imagined community of place and of the fallout of casting his own
'muintir' in the image of an Ireland that was not to be.

Anne Enright's heroine Veronica is similarly troubled by how families fail to live up to their own promise. Not only does she feel temporarily
estranged from her own husband and children, but the experience of making
the arrangements for Liam's burial makes her realise the extent to which
her own experience of family growing up has always been deeply conflicted.
Her own memories of relationships between parents and children in late
modern Ireland on the eve of the economic boom are avowedly unromantic:

Back in Belfield, my best friend Deirdre Moloney had just been thrown out by her
mother for nothing at all: a very low-key sort of girl, she only ever had sex twice.
Children were being chucked out all over Dublin. All our parents were mad, in
those days. There was something about just the smell of us growing up that drove
them completely insane.[5]

More damaging evidence of dsyfunctionality in families in both novels
comes from hidden tales of abuse by close members of a family circle.
One could argue that the unhappy Irish family is such a staple of late

4   Ó Treasaigh, *Cnoc na Lobhar*, 142.
5   Anne Enright, *The Gathering* (London: Jonathan Cape, 2007), 96.

twentieth-century Irish fiction and memoir that its repeated appearance is more wearisome than illuminating. However, it is worth considering the collapse of a certain idea of muintir or family, not as yet another tired sally in the battle against Mother Church or Mother Ireland, but as relating to a very real crisis in how wider communities are to function in an Ireland deeply implicated in global socio-economic relations.

Progeneration

To see how this might be the case it is worth examining briefly the distinction the social anthropologist Tim Ingold makes between 'genealogy' and 'relation'. In the genealogical model, individuals are seen as entering the lifeworld with a set of ready-made attributes which they have received from their predecessors. The essential parts which go to make up a person, his or her 'culture', are handed on, more or less fully formed. The popular image for this conception of personhood and community is that someone has something in their 'blood' or, more recently, 'in their genes'. The metaphor indeed became commonplace in the last general elections in Ireland where certain independent TDs were described by media pundits as being in the Fianna Fáil 'gene pool'. The relational model, on the other hand, relates to the concept of 'progeneration' which Ingold defines as the, 'continual unfolding of an entire field of relationships within which different beings emerge with their particular forms, capacities and dispositions'.[6] That is to say, whereas the genealogical model is concerned with past histories of relationship, the unfolding development of a bundle of preset attributes in a given space, the progenerative model is primarily concerned with current sets and fields of relationships for persons in a given lifeworld.

The genealogical model has obvious affinities with the notion of 'family' or indeed, muintir, in both a narrow nuclear and wider kinship

6   Tim Ingold, *The Perception of the Environment: Essays in Livelihood, Dwelling and Skill* (London: Routledge, 2000), 142.

definition of the notion. It is the model which clearly informed the 2004 Citizenship Referendum that introduced the notion of bloodline into definitions of Irish citizenship. It is also a model which is implicit in the blueprint for future economic development promoted by the social commentator David McWilliams. In his work *The Generation Game*, based on a TV series of the same name, he argues that Ireland's hopes lie with its diaspora, who are seen to have a more viable emotional and cultural commitment to the island's future than recent non-diasporic migrants to Ireland.[7] In the genealogical model the descent line is separate from the life line and life and growth become the realisation of potentials that are already in place. So being Irish is to be a member of family which through immediate (domestic) or extended (diasporic) bloodline is endowed with a culture that is determined by essence rather than context. One consequence of the model is that cultural difference in Ireland is almost invariably construed as 'diversity'. That is to say, the notion of diversity, which is becoming something of a mantra of official pronouncements on multicultural Ireland, supposes that different groups possessed of different sets of ready-made attributes are juxtaposed in the shop window of contemporary Ireland and each group acting out their pre-defined cultural script contribute to the effervescent display of cultural diversity. So the invocation of diversity which is often seen as a way of countering nativist genealogical exclusiveness in fact tends to partake of the same logic but simply multiplies the examples of genealogical inheritances rather than challenges the basic logic.

In the narratives of Enright and Ó Treasaigh, the logic is questioned, albeit in less than explicit ways. Labhrás finds sympathy and self-understanding of a kind through his conversations with Darach, a refugee in time from the ravages of the Black Death in fourteenth-century Ireland. Darach comes not only from a different age but he is outside Labhrás's family circle. He is an antecedent not an ancestor. Similarly, Veronica's movement beyond the emotional stalemate of her life is not through the fraught communion with her immediate family but by way of the encounters she has with relative strangers in Ireland and in England. Stephen Dedalus's befriending of

---

7   David McWilliams, *The Generation Game* (Dublin: Gill and Macmillan, 2008).

Leopold Bloom or Marcel's coming of age in the company of the *invertis* in *La Recherche* are earlier paradigms of a way of viewing personhood and community which is progenerative rather than genealogical. In other words, it is the sets of relationships which individuals and communities enter into at a given moment which engender change and the emergence of new forms, forms which are not obsessively pre-scripted by birthright. From this perspective, it is more appropriate to speak of positionality rather than diversity. Positionality, in effect, is to do with the sets of relationships obtaining at any moment between and within groups, relationships that are subject to an endless process of change, change which is the very stuff of the human life-line and which crucially includes the dimension of power. But even if the writers are suggesting that relationships need to be construed differently and that the cultural homeliness of the genealogical is no longer viable, where are these relationships going to take place and how will place itself affect them in a globalised world? How is the shared place that is the island of Ireland going to affect the forms that positionality will take as the society evolves through time?

Altericide

It is something of a philosophical and sociological truism (which does not make it any the less true) that our identity is defined through others. Just as difference is inconceivable without distinctness, so too identity is unimaginable without someone or something against which that identity is contrasted.[8] Ireland as a country, for example, has notably defined itself through its relationship to Faith (religion), Fatherland (nationalism) and Fataí (land). An intense sensitivity to the view and perceptions of others is a notable feature of Irish public life and the lavish domestic coverage of the then Taoiseach Bertie Ahern's address to the United States Congress,

---

8   François Julien, *De l'universel, de l'uniforme, du commun et du dialogue entre les cultures* (Paris: Fayard, 2008), 34.

as opposed to the general indifference of the United States media, showed how the good opinion of powerful others is an intrinsic component of Irish self-identity. Part of the difficulty in late modern Ireland is that the Others which defined the country, ethnic conflict (nationalism), a confessional state (religion) and an agricultural economy (land) are no longer dominant as ways of defining emerging Irish identities given that political, social and economic developments in the 1990s and 2000s spelled an end to Irish exceptionalism.[9] One of the more stable elements of Irish intellectual life for three decades was the anchor of conflict so that where anyone stood on the National Question was an infallible guide to whether the Other should be eulogised or excoriated in print. The structural cues of attrition are no longer there and their absence makes, among other things, the future of Irish studies deeply problematic. But the changing status of otherness needs to be situated in a wider context to get a keener sense of the dilemmas faced by populations trying to make sense of where they stand in the present global moment.

Dominique Quessada has argued in *Court traité d'altéricide* that the most striking feature of the contemporary age is the prevalence of what he calls 'altéricide' which he defines as the 'liquidation systématique des modalités d'existence de la figure de l'Autre'[10] ['systematic liquidation of the modes of existence of the figure of the Other'; (my translation)]. Quessada traces a history for altericide which begins, he argues, with the Christian Incarnation. When a deity takes on a human form, there is a diminution in the radical otherness of the divinity. As Yahweh, the radically unknowable Other, becomes Christ, the mortal human, the gods not only mingle with mortals, God becomes mortal. Jesus as man becomes the subject of readily identifiable human narratives in the gospels. Following through to the present, Quessada sees the collapse of Soviet communism and the worldwide embrace of the market economy as a further evidence of the demise of the Other, as the alternative economic and geopolitical order of the Soviet bloc gives way to the hegemony of commodity capitalism.

9   Michael Cronin, 'Minding Ourselves: A New Face for Irish Studies', in *The Field Day Review* 4 (2008), 175–85.
10   Dominique Quessada, *Court traité d'altéricide* (Paris: Gallimard, 2007), 40.

The very concept of globalisation itself with its notion of the 'global' as all-inclusive is symptomatic of the absence of an exteriority, of an outflanking of critique by larger categories of co-option. The death of the Other does not mean, however, that there are no longer any differences. On the contrary, there have never been so many. As Quessada intimates:

> Si les différences peuvent proliférer, c'est parce que l'Autre n'est plus là pour leur faire barrage globalement: le concept métaphysique de l'Autre est ce qui contenait (au double sens d'englober et de retenir-empêcher-freiner) les différences, puisqu'il représentait la différence absolue face à laquelle les différences et microdifférences qui coexistent aujourd'hui n'avaient pas le moindre sens en elles-mêmes.[11]

> [If differences can proliferate, it is because the Other is no longer there as an overall obstacle. The metaphysical concept of the Other is what contained (in the dual sense of encompassing and holding back-preventing-restraining) differences because it represented the absolute difference compared to which the differences and micro-differences which co-exist today did not have the slightest bit of meaning. (My translation)]

A direct consequence of the destruction of alterity is the multiplication of differences. It is not because the Other disappears that we are all condemned to sameness. It is possible to find the summary analysis of Quessada too glib and to point to American Special Forces in Iraq and Afghanistan as very much believing in a radical other that they have every intention of exterminating along with the persistence and deepening of global inequality as a reminder of the countless human Others who will not go away. However, it is nonetheless striking that the collapse of the public sphere in Ireland over the last decade is partly attributable to a native form of altericide. All the potential sources of political opposition in the form of unions, community groups and NGOs were brought into partnership arrangements with government and social partnership signaled the end of any serious opposition to official policy in the wider society. Similarly, the support of all four of the major parties for a Yes vote in the Lisbon referendum or the broad political front backing guarantees for the banking sector in October 2008 showed that any sense of radical otherness had succumbed to the

11   Quessada, *Court traité d'altéricide*, 63.

managerial consensualism of a professionalised political class. That this phenomenon does not somehow announce the end of difference is borne out by the hugely successful pop sociology of Brendan McWilliams whose *Pope's Children* is replete with the endless differentiation of the pollster and marketeer: 'Yummy Mummies'; 'GI Janes'; 'Hibernian Cosmopolitans' and so on.[12] The differences can be parsed endlessly because they no longer make any difference.

How then does altericide affect contemporary Irish perception of place and more specifically, how does globalisation inflect this perception in particular ways? A classic trope of Hegelian thinking is the master–slave dialectic, a recurrent figure in Hegelian descriptions of human interactions. Quessada evokes in the late modern world the existential figure of the *Esclavemaître*, 'un esclave qui est maître en même temps, tout en restant esclave, figure où maître et esclave sont littéralement indistincts, sans pour autant être confondus' ['a slave who is at the same time a master while remaining a slave, a figure in whom the distinctions of master and slave become literally indistinguishable, without the two states ever really being confused with one another'; (my translation)].[13] This collapse of categories, the emergence of this seemingly contradictory, hybrid figure that is the 'Slavemaster' is deeply revealing of a profound uncertainty about Ireland as a place in the early twenty-first century. In 2007, Maureen Gaffney, the psychologist and media pundit, offered the Master's narrative in a warm encomium to the feel-good factor of Irish affluence:

> We seemed to have used our prosperity as an opportunity to enjoy stable family relationships, to develop our personal expressiveness and to show the world what we're good at. Given Ireland's economic, cultural and religious history – still in living memory – we have embraced prosperity, the good life and personal freedoms with unabashed relish, and we won't lightly let them go.[14]

The tone is not untypical of a slew of articles and public pronouncements in the boom years which presented Ireland as moving beyond the depressed

---

12   McWilliams, *The Pope's Children: Ireland's New Elite* (Dublin: Gill and Macmillan, 2005).

13   Quessada, *Court traité d'altéricide*, 126.

14   Maureen Gaffney, 'What's the Craic?', in *Irish Times Magazine*, 25 August 2007.

divisiveness of the eighties to the irenic utopia of the twenty-first century. In contrast to the discourse of the Irish as Masters and Mistresses of all they Surveyed was an equally explicit narrative of dystopian malcontent. In this view, Irish society was one where citizens were the slaves of a brutalising and alienating system that led to the abandonment of values that had previously sustained it. The most notable exponent was the Ombudsman and Information Commissioner Emily O'Reilly in an address to the Ceifin conference in County Clare:

> Many of us if we have any developed sensibility recoil at the vulgar festival that is much of modern Ireland, the rampant, unrestrained drunkenness, the brutal, random violence that infects the smallest of our townlands and villages, the incontinent use of foul language with no thought to place or company, the obscene parading of obscene wealth, the debasement of our civic life, the growing disdain of the wealthy towards the poor, the fracturing of our community life, the God like status given to celebrities all too often replaced somewhere down the line with a venomous desire to attack and destroy those who were on pedestals the week before, the creation of 'reality' TV, more destructive in its cynical filleting of the worth and wonder of the human soul than anything George Orwell could have imagined.[15]

O'Reilly and Gaffney co-exist in the same society and both would presumably see themselves as describing the same country. What is less important than adjudicating the respective merits of the Master and Slave narratives here is to suggest that public receptivity to both of these radically different interpretations of a particular time and place is in part to do with the presence of the Slavemaster as a dominant paradigm in a liberal-democratic market economy. On the one hand, the citizen is consumer, the supreme master of choice, the active agent of destiny, the flattered subject of his or her multiplying desires. On the other, the citizen as producer is simply another object to be used, an eminently replaceable part of a process, a figure on a balance sheet, utterly subject to forces over which he or she has no control.[16] Hence, the repeated feeling that the citizen is both master and slave depending on which role he or she happens to occupy at any given moment. The overall emergent effect is that of the Slavemaster, the

---

15   Emily O'Reilly, 'What has happened to us?', in *The Irish Times*, 11 November 2004.
16   Christian Laval, *L'Homme économique: essai sur les racines du néolibéralisme* (Paris: Gallimard, 2007), 15.

shifting, uncertain inhabitant of contemporary Ireland whose view of the place is alternatively that of subject or object, in control or out of control, at home in the world or trying to cope with the world at home.

One factor that the citizen as Slavemaster has to contend with, and that we mentioned at the outset of this chapter, is the incidence of time and how the accelerated time-space compression of globalisation impacts on appropriations and reappropriations of place. Tim Robinson, in his work *Stones of Aran: Labyrinth*, speaks of the daughter of one of his native informants on Inismore: 'I imagine his daughter is one of the smart young women I see driving into Cill Rónáin as if they were on a freeway to a shopping mall, slamming themselves through the island's spaces; she runs a chilly, hygienic, tourist-board-approved B&B, and hardly tolerates her father in the back kitchen.'[17] The elderly man and the young daughter may inhabit the same geographical space but their time zones are markedly different. The daughter's car slams through spaces collapsed by the acceleration of time. What Robinson attempts to do in his work is to restore the infinite complexity of those spaces, partly through his own decelerated practice of walking the fields of Inismore but partly also through the memories of older inhabitants, his informants, whose physical slowing down becomes a creative act of remembering. In a sense, Robinson's move is linked to the rehabilitation of dwelling as a creative or enabling way of engaging with places subject to the peripheralising dismissal of velocity.

Dwelling

One of the most common icons of the global age is not surprisingly the globe itself. From the shots of the blue planet suspended over abyssal darkness courtesy of the Apollo space missions to the sketchy outline of earth on notices encouraging hotel customers to re-use their towels, the images of

---

17   Tim Robinson, *Stones of Aran: Labyrinth* (Dublin: Lilliput Press, 1995), 18.

the planet are increasingly common in the contemporary imaginary. Seeing things from a distance is as much a matter of subjection as observation. Occupying a superior vantage point from which one can look down on a subject people or a conquered land is a staple of colonial travel narratives.[18] There is a further dimension to the question of distance described by Tim Ingold where he draws a distinction between perceiving the environment as a 'sphere' or as a 'globe'. For centuries, the classic description of the heavens was of the earth as a sphere with lines running from the human observer to the cosmos above. As geocentric cosmology fell into discredit and helio-centric cosmology came into the ascendant, the image of the sphere gave way to that of the globe. If the sphere presupposed a world experienced and engaged with from within, the globe represented a world perceived from without. Thus, in Ingold's words, 'the movement from spherical to global imagery is also one in which "the world", as we are taught it exists, is drawn ever further from the matrix of our lived experience.'[19]

In the movement towards the modern, a practical sensory engagement with the world underpinned by the spherical paradigm is supplanted by a regimen of detachment and control. As the images of the globe proliferate, often ironically to mobilise ecological awareness, the danger is that these images themselves distort our relationship to our physical and cultural environment by continually situating us at a distance, by abstracting and subtracting us from our local attachments and responsibilities. However, it is precisely such an ability which is often construed as a basic requirement for both national and, more latterly, global citizenship. It is the capacity to look beyond the immediate interests of the clan or village or ethnic grouping which creates the conditions for broader definitions of belonging at a national or indeed global level. Szersynski and Urry argue, for exam-ple, that 'banal globalism', the almost unnoticed symbols of globality that crowd our daily lives, might, 'be helping to create a sensibility conducive to the cosmopolitan rights and duties of being a "global citizen" by generat-ing a greater sense of both global diversity and global interconnectedness

18   Mary Louise Pratt, *Imperial Eyes: Travel Writing and Transculturation* (London: Routledge, 1992), 216.
19   Ingold, *The Perception of the Environment*, 211.

and belonging.'[20] The promise of such citizenship is an almost axiomatic contemporary defence of why anyone should bother, for example, with translation. When Pascale Casanova in her survey of the World Republic of Letters tries to synthesise those elements which have conditioned eligibility for citizenship of this Republic, translation is very much to the fore:

> Dans l'univers littéraire, si l'espace des langues peut, lui aussi, être représenté selon une 'figuration florale', c'est-à-dire un système où les langues de la périphérie sont reliées au centre par les polyglottes et les traducteurs, alors on pourra mesurer la littérarité (la puissance, le prestige, le volume de capital linguistico-littéraire) d'une langue, non pas au nombre d'écrivains ou de lecteurs dans cette langue, mais au nombre de polyglottes littéraires (ou protagonistes de l'espace littéraire, éditeurs, intermédiaires cosmopolites, découvreurs cultivés ...) qui la pratiquent et au nombre de traducteurs littéraires – tant à l'exportation qu'à l'importation – qui font circuler les textes depuis ou vers cette langue littéraire.[21]

> [In the world of literature, if languages can also be represented using a 'floral figure', that is to say a system where languages on the periphery are linked to the centre by polyglots and translators then it is possible to measure the literariness (the power, prestige, the volume of linguistico-literary capital) of a language, not by the number of writers and readers in a language, but by the number of literary polyglots (or main players in the literary arena, publishers, cosmopolitan intermediaries, well-educated talent spotters ...) who know it and by the number of literary translators – for export as well as for import – who cause texts to be translated into or out of this literary language. (My translation)]

The global standing of a literature depends on the efforts of those language learners and translators who can stand outside their own language and learn the other language for the purposes of reading and/or translation. But Szersynski and Urry ask the following questions: 'Is this abstraction from the local and particular fully compatible with dwelling in a locality? Could it be that the development of a more cosmopolitan, citizenly

---

20 B. Szerszynski and J. Urry, 'Visuality, mobility and the cosmopolitan: Inhabiting the world from afar', in *The British Journal of Sociology* 57.1 (2006), 113–31: 122.

21 Pascale Casanova, *La République mondiale des lettres* (Paris: Seuil, 2007), 37.

perception of place is at the expense of other modes of appreciating and caring for local environments and contexts?'[22]

In opposition to the figure of the citizen we find the notion of the 'denizen' which has been propagated notably by the non-governmental organisation Common Ground where a denizen is deemed to be a person who dwells in a particular place and who can move through and knowingly inhabit that place. Therefore, Common Ground dedicates itself to encouraging the proliferation of vernacular, ideographic and connotative descriptions of local places which can take the form of place myths, stories, personal associations and celebrations of various kinds (<http://www.commonground.org.uk>). What Robinson's exploration of time and space on the Aran Islands points to is a form not so much of citizenship as of denizenship where 'caring for local places and contexts' is powerfully determined by an ability to shift time zones.

Implicit in the move is a relationship to land and place which is not wholly over-determined by an obsession with ownership. Finbarr Bradley and James Kennelly have noted that possession and care are not necessarily common bedfellows. They claim: 'In Ireland, ironically, a lack of concern with design and aesthetic quality tends to go hand in hand with a preoccupation with place. This affinity with place (it can hardly be called a sense of place) appears to have little to do with tending, cultivating or enhancing the material environment.'[23] In the light of Ireland's demonstrably poor environmental record,[24] a seeming allegiance to place, repeatedly articulated in advertising campaigns around GAA championship competitions, is accompanied by a manifest inability or unwillingness to care for them. The hold of property over the national psyche as evidenced by the almost neurotic rehearsal of anxieties and fears during the post-boom downturn stands in vivid contrast to the general lack of urgency and engagement in

22   Szerszynski and Urry, 'Visuality, mobility and the cosmopolitan', 123.
23   Finbarr Bradley and James Kennelly, *Capitalising on Culture, Competing on Difference* (Dublin: Blackhall Publishing, 2008), 49.
24   See, for example, Harry McGee and Tim O'Brien, 'Ireland far off emissions and waste targets, says EPA report', in *The Irish Times*, 9 October 2008.

addressing the systematic deterioration of place through climate change. In effect, what joins the concerns of Robinson to the ruminations of Enright's Veronica or Ó Treasaigh's Lahbrás is how to dwell properly in a place. How is it possible, for example, to dwell meaningfully in a country which has altered so dramatically in such a relatively short period of time?

Time

Quessada claims that one further consequence of the phenomenon of altericide is the triumph of the spatial over the temporal. That is to say that the preferred time of democracy is the present as both the past (different political regimes) and the future (everything from popular revolt to terrorism) both potentially threaten its legitimacy. He argues:

> L'absence de temps, spécifique de la marche de la démocratie vers son accomplissement, fait que, *pour être et avoir lieu, tout doit être et avoir lieu en même temps, c'est-à-dire dans le même espace.*[25]

> [The absence of time, specific to the movement of democracy towards its realisation, means that, *to be and to take place, everything must be and take place at the same time, that is to say, in the same space.* (My translation)]

Arguments take time. It takes time to put forward a thesis sequentially, a counter-thesis and eventually some form of synthesis. In the sound bite instantaneity of media-saturated democracies, the time of exposition is anathema. This is not to say that different viewpoints are not aired. They are, if only because there is a legislative obligation to do so. But to return to our earlier discussion of genealogy, what is offered is the spectacle of diversity rather than an engagement with positionality. In other words, different opinions on the budget are summarily aired, from the politicians to the trade unions to the employers' bodies. The opinions

25   Quessada, *Court traité d'altéricide*, 100 (his emphasis).

are simply juxtaposed as if they were all equally valid and everyone had the same ability to determine outcomes in the society which is patently not the case, as evidenced by strikingly uneven distributions of income in Irish society.[26] So there is much diversity of a kind but rather less understanding. The time needed to tease out strands of power and influence is denied in favour of the spatialised collage of clips, individuals and groups rehearsing the pre-scripts of the representational ('on behalf of my party I would like to say'). In a sense, space is what happens to place when time tends towards zero. The less time a person has to dwell on what it means to live in a particular place, the more the place they inhabit becomes filled with the spatialised ubiquity of commodity advertising, ratings-driven media product and context-less information bites. Place becomes the site of the multiple surfaces of consumption, a tantalisingly fragmented space, detached from any longer-term sense of what it means to dwell in and be responsible for a particular place and how the place might be positioned relative to others. In this context, there is nothing more conservative than the repeated exhortations to abandon the past (Tara) and move rapidly into the future (the kinetic utopia of the M3). The truly radical scenario is to abandon the obsessive-compulsive rigidities of the short term for the unsettling and innovative dwelling perspectives of the long term.

In the short term in Ireland, of course, there is nothing more difficult than planning for the long term. The acceleration of technological change, the short-horizon perspective of a market-driven economy, the next-election perspective of representative democracy and the frantic multi-tasking that has become the daily lot of so many living and working on the island mean that a potentially fatal short-sightedness becomes the norm.

It is often said that what a people strive for is the greatest happiness of the greatest number but it is worth bearing in mind that the greatest number have not yet been born. Therefore, when we speak about the greatest good, what we really mean is the longest good. There is not much we can do to improve the quality of life of those who are already dead on this

---

26   Brian Nolan and Bernard Maître, 'Economic Growth and Income Inequality: Setting the Context', in Tony Fahey, Helen Russell and Christopher Whelan (eds), *Best of Times: The Social Impact of the Celtic Tiger* (Dublin: IPA, 2007), 27–42.

island but immeasurable good can be done to improve the quality of lives of those who will be born or come to live on the island. In order to give force to this notion of the longest good, it would be necessary to make the taking of long-term responsibility the most important political issue of our time. How might we do this and what are the short-term implications of long-term thinking?

Writing in *The Irish Times*, Frank Convery argued that 'a sustainable climate change strategy for Ireland must focus on the long term'.[27] The Stern Report and the reports from the UN Intergovernmental Panel on Climate Change have clearly spelt out the consequences of global warming and unchecked carbon emissions for water availability, sea levels, species survival, agriculture, ocean acidification, coral reefs, weather patterns and human settlement. The repeated conclusion is that humanity must begin to act now if it is to avoid catastrophic consequences in the long term. So farming practices, the types of crops produced, the way cities are planned and transport systems are organised, the kinds of goods and services that are produced and how they might be produced must change in the short term if there is to be a viable long-term future for humans and many other species on the planet. However, in the era of the instant opinion poll, the relentless style barometers of 'What's Hot' and 'What's Cold' and the instantaneous e-mail message, how are citizens to escape the tyranny of the moment?

In the language of the Tewa Indians of the American Southwest there is an expression, 'pin peyeh obe', which translates as 'look to the mountain'. When the Tewa elders use the phrase they mean that if we look at things as if from the top of a mountain we get a broader view, we see what lies ahead.[28] We also, however, if we turn in another direction, see what lies behind. In other words, the long view is not only forwards but backwards. Just as our present was once someone's distant future, if we want to make sense of what might or ought to happen in the future we need to

27   Frank Convery, 'Climate Change must be factored into every aspect of our lives', in *The Irish Times*, 7 April 2007.

28   Stewart Brand, *The Clock of the Long Now: Time and Responsibility* (London: Phoenix, 2000), 144.

understand how we got here from our distant past. As our sense of time extends in both directions, being responsible for what might happen to future generations involves being equally responsible for learning appropriately from past generations. It is in this context that the downgrading of Old Irish as a full degree subject in the country's largest university and the threatened removal of the Chair of Old Irish had a significance which went far beyond the internal budgetary housekeeping of a particular educational institution. Ireland in comparative European terms was enormously fortunate at a very early period to have an extremely wide and varied body of writing in its vernacular language on a multitude of subjects from religion to jurisprudence.[29] The study, analysis and transmission of the language and the associated culture and society makes a powerful contribution to how we understand the development of Irish writing, culture and society over an extended period of time. To think that far back is to develop the reflex of the long view which is not the subsidised indulgence of the scholar but a core survival value of any culture that wants to exist into the future.

The stereoscopic stories of contemporary Ireland, the Irish- and English-language narratives of contemporary urban experience as they develop in the work of Enright and Ó Treasaigh point to the overwhelming need for the society to stand back, take stock and adopt the long view if the place that is Ireland is to have a sustainable future. What the novelists are suggesting and what this chapter has tried to articulate is that it is necessary to analyse how being turned 'inside out' by changing relationships of time and space affects in very profound ways the human capacity to dwell in any given place. But crises are famously moments of opportunity and it is perhaps time to call a different tune for the piper, a tune that is about place rather than property, about denizens rather than citizens and about the far-seeing rather than the short-sighted.

29   Dáibhí Ó Cróinín (ed.), *A New History of Ireland: Prehistoric and Early Ireland* (Oxford: Oxford University Press, 2008).

Notes on Contributors

LUCY COLLINS is Associate Professor of English at University College Dublin. Educated at Trinity College Dublin and Harvard University, where she spent a year as a Fulbright Scholar, she teaches and researches in the area of modern poetry and poetics. Recent books include *Poetry by Women in Ireland: A Critical Anthology 1870–1970* (2012) and a monograph, *Contemporary Irish Women Poets: Memory and Estrangement* (2015). She has published widely on contemporary poets from Ireland, Britain and America, and is co-founder of the Irish Poetry Reading Archive, a national digital repository.

MICHAEL CRONIN is 1776 Chair of French at Trinity College Dublin. He has published widely on questions of language, culture and identity. He is a member of the Royal Irish Academy and the Academia Europaea and an Officer in the *Ordre des Palmes Académiques*. His most recent work is *Eco-Translation: Translation and Ecology in the Age of the Anthropocene* (2017).

GERALD DAWE is Professor Emeritus of English and Fellow of Trinity College Dublin. He is the author of eight collections of poetry including *The Lundys Letter* (1985), awarded the Macaulay Fellowship in Literature, and, most recently, *Selected Poems* (2012) and *Mickey Finn's Air* (2014). His other publications include *The Proper Word: Collected Criticism* (2007) and *Of War and War's Alarms: Reflections on Modern Irish Writing* (2015). He has also edited several anthologies of Irish poetry and criticism, including *The Younger Irish Poets* (1982/1991) and *Earth Voices Whispering: Irish War Poetry 1914–1945* (2008). He is editor of *The Cambridge Companion to Irish Poets* (forthcoming). He was the John J. Burns Professor at Boston College, Charles Heimbold Professor in Irish Studies at Villanova University, Philadelphia, and Visiting Scholar at Pembroke College, Cambridge. An archive of his papers is held at Burns Library, Boston College.

LUKE GIBBONS is Emeritus Professor of Irish Literary and Cultural Studies at Maynooth University and the author of several books, the most recent of which is *Joyce's Ghosts: Ireland, Modernism and Memory* (2015).

JASON KING is Academic Coordinator of the Irish Heritage Trust. He has previously held positons as assistant professor, lecturer, postdoctoral researcher and visiting professor at NUI Galway, the University of Limerick, the Université de Montréal, Concordia University, University College Cork and Maynooth University. He has published extensively in the areas of immigration and Irish culture and literature, the Great Hunger and Irish migration, and Irish-American and Irish-Canadian culture and heritage. His recent publications include *Irish Famine Migration Narratives: Eyewitness Testimonies* (forthcoming), *Women and the Great Hunger* (with Christine Kinealy and Ciarán Reilly, 2017), *Irish Global Migration and Memory* (with Marguérite Corporaal, 2016), and a special issue (with Pilar Villar Argáiz) of *Irish Studies Review* 23.4 (2016) on 'Irish Multiculturalism in Crisis.'

DAVID LLOYD is Distinguished Professor of English at the University of California, Riverside, where he works primarily on Irish culture, settler colonialism, postcolonial and cultural theory and visual art. His most recent books are *Irish Times: Temporalities of Irish Modernity* (2008); *Irish Culture and Colonial Modernity: The Transformation of Oral Space* (2011); and *Beckett's Thing: Painting and Theatre* (2016). A collection of essays on aesthetics, representation and race, *Under Representation: the Racial Regime of Aesthetics*, will appear in 2018. *Arc & Sill: Poems 1979-2009* was published in 2012.

CAROLINE MAGENNIS is Lecturer in Twentieth- and Twenty-First-Century Literature at the University of Salford. She sits on the executive boards of the British Association for Irish Studies, the British Association for Contemporary Literary Studies and EFACIS, and the editorial board of the *Irish Studies Review*. She has published widely on theoretical approaches to contemporary Northern Irish literature and culture. Forthcoming work includes chapters in the *Cambridge History of Irish Women's Writing* and the *Oxford Handbook of Irish Fiction*.

EAMON MAHER is Director of the National Centre for Franco-Irish Studies in IT Tallaght, where he also lectures in humanities. He is the series editor of *Reimagining Ireland* and has edited and co-edited a number of books in the series. His most recent publications are *Tracing the Cultural Legacy of Irish Catholicism: From Galway to Cloyne and beyond*, co-edited with Eugene O'Brien (2017), and, with Derek Hand, *Assessing a Literary Legacy: John McGahern (1934–2006)*, which is forthcoming.

CATHERINE MAIGNANT is Professor of Irish Studies at the University of Lille. She was President of the French Society of Irish Studies (SOFEIR) and the European Federation of Associations and Centres of Irish Studies (EFACIS) for a number of years. After writing a PhD thesis on early medieval Irish Christianity, she now specialises in contemporary Irish religious history. Her research interests include the response of the Catholic Church to secularisation, interreligious dialogue, Celtic Christianity and the religious aspects of globalisation. She has published extensively in all these areas. In recent years she has developed an interest in the place of the Internet in contemporary religious developments.

VICTOR MERRIMAN is Professor of Critical Performance Studies at Edge Hill University. He is Director of the Performance and Civic Futures Research Group (2013–), and a founder member of One Hour Theatre Company (2016–). He publishes widely on Irish theatre, postcolonial criticism, public policy, pedagogy and cultural theory. His monograph *Because We Are Poor: Irish Theatre in the 1990s* was published in 2011. He has also edited special issues of the online journal *Kritika Kultura* (<http://journals.ateneo.edu/ojs/kk>; Issues 14/15 (2010); 21/22 (2013)). He was appointed a member of An Chomhairle Ealaíon/The Arts Council of Ireland by Michael D Higgins, then Minister of Arts, Culture and Gaeltacht. In that capacity he chaired the Review of Theatre in Ireland (1995–6). He is Treasurer and Membership Secretary of the British Association of Irish Studies.

SYLVIE MIKOWSKI is Professor of Irish and English Studies at the University of Reims-Champagne-Ardenne. She wrote her PhD thesis on 'Memory and Imagination in the Novels of John McGahern', and her *habilitation* on 'The Invention of a Tradition in the Irish Contemporary Novel.' Her main publications include *Le Roman irlandais contemporain* (2004), *The Book in Ireland* (2006), *Memory and History in France and Ireland* (2011), *Irish Women Writers* (2014), *Ireland and Popular Culture* (2014) and *Popular Culture Today* (2015). She has also published numerous book chapters and journal articles on contemporary Irish writers such as John McGahern, William Trevor, Colum McCann, Patrick McCabe, Roddy Doyle, Deirdre Madden and Sebastian Barry. She has been the literary editor of *Études Irlandaises* and is currently Vice-President of the SOFEIR, the French Society of Irish Studies.

NEIL O'BOYLE is Chair of the BA in Communication Studies Programme at Dublin City University. His work primarily examines the relationship between media, popular culture and collective identities, a topic he explored in his 2011 book *New Vocabularies, Old Ideas: Culture, Irishness, and the Advertising Industry*. His work has been published in a wide range of academic journals, including *Cultural Sociology, Social Identities, Journalism Practice, European Journal of Communication, Nationalism and Ethnic Politics, Sport and Society* and *Communication Education*.

EUGENE O'BRIEN is Senior Lecturer and Head of the Department of English Language and Literature at Mary Immaculate College, University of Limerick, and the director of the Mary Immaculate College Institute for Irish Studies. He is also the editor of the Oxford University Press Online Bibliography project in literary theory. His most recent publications include *Seamus Heaney as Aesthetic Thinker* (2016), *The Soul Exceeds its Circumstances: The Later Poetry of Seamus Heaney* (2016) and *Tracing the Cultural Legacy of Irish Catholicism: From Galway to Cloyne, and Beyond*, edited with Eamon Maher (2017).

TINA O'TOOLE is Senior Lecturer in English and Programme Director of the MA in English at the University of Limerick. Her scholarship focuses on Irish literature, gender and sexuality studies, and on migrant and transnational representations. Her books include *The Irish New Woman* (2013), *Documenting Irish Feminisms: The Second Wave* (2005; co-authored with Linda Connolly), and several edited collections including the recent *Women Writing War: Ireland 1880–1922* (2016; co-edited with Gillian McIntosh and Muireann O'Cinnéide). With Piaras Mac Éinrí, she co-edited a special issue of *Éire-Ireland: Journal of Irish Studies*, on Irish migrancies (2012). She has also published essays in *Modernism/Modernity*, *Irish University Review*, *New Hibernia Review*, *Études Irlandaises* and *Irish Studies Review*, among others.

JEAN-MICHEL RABATÉ is Professor of English and Comparative Literature at the University of Pennsylvania and is a co-editor of the *Journal of Modern Literature*. One of the founders of the Slought Foundation, where he curates exhibitions and conversations, he has been a fellow of the American Academy of Arts and Sciences since 2008. He has authored twenty-five books and edited fifteen collections of essays. Recent publications include *Crimes of the Future* (2014), *The Cambridge Introduction to Literature and Psychoanalysis* (2014), *The Pathos of Distance* (2016), *Think, Pig!* (2016) and *Les Guerres de Jacques Derrrida* (2016). Forthcoming are *Kafka L.O.L.* and *Rust*, as well as the collections *After Derrida* and *The New Beckett*.

JENNIFER WAY is Professor of Art History at the University of North Texas, where she specialises in the history, theory and methodology of art since 1900. She was awarded a Fulbright Senior Fellowship Award in the Department of Art History, Trinity College Dublin, and has also held a short-term Visiting Fellowship at the Clinton Institute for American Studies, University College Dublin.

CARMEN ZAMORANO LLENA is Associate Professor of English, and was previously lecturer in English, at the University of Lleida. She obtained her PhD in English from the University of Barcelona for a study that analysed postmodern feminist constructs of identity in the poetry of Fleur Adcock, Eavan Boland, Gillian Clarke and Carol Rumens. In 2006 she was granted a two-year Betriu de Pinós postdoctoral scholarship by the Catalan Agency for Research (AGAUR) for her project on postnationalist identity in contemporary Irish poetry, and has worked as a lecturer in English at

Dalarna University since 2008. She has published on contemporary Irish and British poetry and fiction and is co-editor of a number of collections of essays, including *The Aesthetics of Ageing: Critical Approaches to Literary Representations of the Ageing Process* (2002), *Transcultural Identities in Contemporary Literature* (2013) and *Authority and Wisdom in the New Ireland* (2016). She is also co-editor of the peer-reviewed journal *Nordic Irish Studies* and co-editor of Peter Lang's *Cultural Identity Studies* series. Her current research interests include representations of ageing in Irish and British literature, literature and globalisation, and the migrant experience in contemporary Irish and British literature.

Reimagining Ireland

Series Editor: Dr Eamon Maher, Institute of Technology, Tallaght

The concepts of Ireland and 'Irishness' are in constant flux in the wake of an ever-increasing reappraisal of the notion of cultural and national specificity in a world assailed from all angles by the forces of globalisation and uniformity. Reimagining Ireland interrogates Ireland's past and present and suggests possibilities for the future by looking at Ireland's literature, culture and history and subjecting them to the most up-to-date critical appraisals associated with sociology, literary theory, historiography, political science and theology.

Some of the pertinent issues include, but are not confined to, Irish writing in English and Irish, Nationalism, Unionism, the Northern 'Troubles', the Peace Process, economic development in Ireland, the impact and decline of the Celtic Tiger, Irish spirituality, the rise and fall of organised religion, the visual arts, popular cultures, sport, Irish music and dance, emigration and the Irish diaspora, immigration and multiculturalism, marginalisation, globalisation, modernity/postmodernity and postcolonialism. The series publishes monographs, comparative studies, interdisciplinary projects, conference proceedings and edited books.

Proposals should be sent either to Dr Eamon Maher at eamon.maher@it-tallaght.ie or to ireland@peterlang.com.

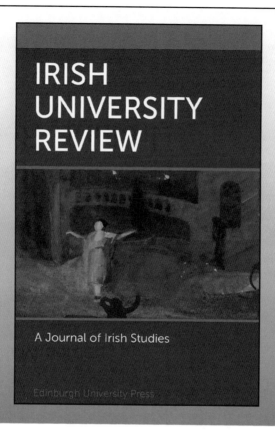